Introduction

He was christened Charles Barnet Harvey and remained Charles until an afternoon in 1921 when, as a young officer, he was supposed to be riding at ten stone in an Irish steeplechase at Punchestown.

However, when the scales showed he had failed to make it and would have to put up two pounds overweight, a senior officer jokingly remarked, 'You're a fat little pig. You're as bad as Roscoe Arbuckle!'

He was referring to Roscoe 'Fatty' Arbuckle, the obese and somewhat notorious star of those silent-film days. The name has stuck and I doubt if many of his countless friends and acquaintances even know his true christian names.

So, for us, he will be Roscoe from the very beginning of our story.

Roscoe – 'The Bright Shiner', Roscoe of the 'Shiny Tenth', the famous 10th Royal Hussars, to whom he has devoted so much of his life since he joined them sixty-seven years ago. The same gallant cavaliers, now amalgamated with their old friends, 'the Cherry- Pickers', the 11th Hussars (Prince Albert's Own), into The Royal Hussars, who have inspired and made possible this book, which I, as a Scots Grey, lifelong friend and admirer of both Regiments, am so proud and privileged to write.

I am particularly grateful to the Colonel of the Regiment, Colonel Sir Piers Bengough KCVO, OBE, for his assistance and to all members of his Regiment, who have helped me in divers ways to honour one of the finest cavalry officers and sportsmen of this or any other century.

vii

FOREWORD

by Sir Gordon Richards

The Brigadier and I – the General as I have always called
him – have been close friends for about sixty years, since
the days when he was a young Cavalry officer and I was a
young jockey. We had a lot of fun together before the war,
and afterwards when he was Stewards' Secretary, we
naturally saw a lot of each other!

He was such an outstanding horseman – he won on one
horse I couldn't win on – that I was glad he wasn't two
stone lighter, or I might have had a serious rival.
As the Senior Stipendiary Steward, his experience and
deep knowledge of racing and race-riding helped him to be
a scrupulously fair, understanding firm disciplinarian. He
is a real gentleman.

I was staying with the General when I broke one of my
records and we had to escape from the Press. We stepped
out of the back door of the weighing-room and just got to
his car in time. I never ran so fast in my life. Those Press
boys were right on our heels.

Whether racing, or a shooting party, after dinner or
anywhere, he is always the best, most amusing companion
in the world.

I will always maintain that the General is the greatest
man Racing has known in my lifetime.

GORDON RICHARDS
Kintbury, July 1986.

viii

Chapter One

Early Days

In 1900 Queen Victoria was still on the throne. It was a
year when the tide had turned in the Boer War. Early
defeats had turned to victories; jingoism was in fashion;
any excuse to wave the flag was enough and the
triumph of a Prince, who was soon to be King, not only
with Ambush in the Grand National but also with
Diamond Jubilee in the Triple Crown, touched off
celebrations such as Aintree and Epsom had never
seen.

It was the year when Roscoe was born in Sarawak,
where his father, a great friend of the White Rajah
Brooke, worked for the wealthy Borneo Company. He
was the youngest of three children. The eldest, John,
was eight when Roscoe was born. Then in between the
two boys was Patricia.

Although she was a Roman Catholic Cameron from
the Highlands of Scotland, Anne Harvey was a superb
horsewoman and, when her husband died soon after
the birth of her younger son, she could not wait to get
back to that lovely green land which could provide her
with the real love of her life, fox-hunting.

The England to which she returned with her children
in 1901 was very different from today. The population

1

of the British Isles was not much more than half its present size and was very differently distributed. There were about five times the present number of people living in rural areas. The country villages were much larger than they are today and the Squire and Parson ruled far more people. The big move to the manufacturing centres of the Industrial Revolution had virtually ceased by now and the population was relatively static. The only exception was emigration, particularly to Canada which up until 1914 was taking place at a remarkable rate. The Canadian National Railways offered free sections of land to immigrants from Britain at only a dollar an acre. So anybody willing to take the chance could buy himself a hefty stake in the land of new opportunity for very little money indeed.

In the towns the roads were reasonable, frequently made of wooden blocks or granite sets, but outside they usually petered out into heavily pot-holed tracks.

Motor cars were still scarce. Roscoe's earliest memory of family transport was the dog-cart, drawn by the little animal which became his first pony at the age of four. The country's railway network was already formidable and movement was governed to a large extent by the distance from home to the nearest railway station and the time which it took horse-drawn transport to cover that trip.

Although heavy industry had already seriously damaged some countryside and the suburban expansion of London, Bristol and Birmingham had made large inroads into Hertfordshire, Surrey, Gloucestershire and Warwickshire, fox-hunting was generally thriving. Anne Harvey, determined to enjoy her beloved sport to the utmost, settled with her family near Minchinhampton in the Beaufort country.

Roscoe says, 'My mother hunted like mad. She never missed a day if she could help it.'

Anne Harvey was already feeling the effects of arthritis and was determined to make the most of her time before the disease finally cut short her activities in the saddle.

She was one of a rapidly increasing number of women, who, riding side-saddle of course, were now gracing the hunting field, particularly with the Beaufort and the Leicestershire packs, although their presence was still deplored in many other parts of the country right up until 1914.

Perhaps what brought women out in the latter half of the nineteenth century was the practice of cutting and laying fences instead of leaving them as face-scratching, habit-tearing bullfinches. The Empress of Austria said, 'Remember, I don't mind the falls, but I will not scratch my face.'

Anthony Trollope had welcomed women riders: 'Women who ride, as a rule, ride better than men.' They had better hands naturally and they improved the atmosphere of the hunting field. However, some diehard provincial hunting men like 'Scrutator' disapproved because hunting was unfeminine. But their real complaint was that a gentleman had to stop and help the ladies when they fell. Nevertheless, although a young lady had to be extremely careful what she did and to whom she talked, never coming home in a coach unchaperoned, Trollope wrote, 'A middle-aged woman of fortune can do anything she likes without exciting the anxious sympathies of lookers-on, whether she is ducked in a brook or rides home in a fly tête-à-tête with a horse breaker.'

When Anne Harvey returned home, sheer numbers had already changed masculine attitudes with the Duke of Beaufort's hounds. Anne Harvey had chosen her last country dwelling wisely. She was able to instil in her younger son a life-long love of fox-hunting, the sport which she adored so much.

The Beaufort was wonderful country and the hounds were magnificent. The late 10th Duke, 'Master' as he was universally called, told me, 'It used to be a good scenting country, but now so much of it is ploughed up . . . It's a harder country to ride over than Leicestershire – all of these drop fences we have.'

Master, a couple of months older than Roscoe, had a wonderful memory right up to his death and painted many a picture of the time when both men were little boys on the occasion when I was privileged to share his last ever day's hunting, nine days before he died in January 1984.

On that auspicious morning in January 1984, hunting had been for some time in doubt because snow lay around, whipped by a bitter north-east wind, and there was still frost on the ground.

We left Badminton House at ten o'clock. Master, as upright as ever despite a recent fall that had gashed his hand, wore a cap in the regimental tweed of the Royal Horse Guards (Blues) of whom he was always so proud.

'When my father was alive, we had over a hundred horses in these stables here at Badminton,' he said.

Our picnic luncheon of sandwiches and a case of drink had been loaded into the Range Rover as we drove off with Master's old friend, Mrs Mary Hills, a former Master of the Mendip Farmers at the wheel.

We passed some children on the way to the Meet. 'I had several ponies as a boy,' Master said. 'The one I most remember was a white pony called Sinbad. I rode him a lot and grew up with him. In those days, before 1914, we used to have a local show and Sinbad and I won a number of jumping classes there.'

Roscoe laughs: 'I am afraid I never aspired to such heights,' he says. 'My little pony Meg never won jumping classes. A lot of her time was spent between the shafts of the dog-cart. But, while Master and his Sinbad were winning all those posh jumping competitions, Meg and I were cleaning up in the gymkhana classes. She was dynamite at Polo Bending, Apple and Bucket races, Musical Chairs, etc. And then of course there were the "Express Letter" races!'

The roped-off arenas of the West Country showgrounds made an ideal, if somewhat dangerous, racecourse for illegal pony racing or 'flapping' disguised as a gymkhana event. Giving each contestant an old envelope to stuff in the pocket of his breeches, they were able to get away with calling the events 'Express Letter' races. But they were just ordinary flat races, twice round, with bookmakers in attendance! Twenty years later they were still going on and, between the wars, I too learnt a lot about race riding. Some of the 'jockeys' were little gypsy children riding small thoroughbred weeds with six-ounce racing saddles.

Roscoe says, 'No quarter was asked or given. Twice round with the whips going and devil take the hindmost! It was a wonderful education. Most of them came from Wales!'

Many is the time that Meg took the family to the show in the dog-cart, competed in and won gymkhana events and then, harnessed up again, took her load back home. She thrived on it.

Although Roscoe and Master were of almost exactly the same vintage – 'He was probably about a term ahead of me at Sandhurst,' – and their paths crossed many times in later life, they were never the greatest of friends. But each respected the other for what he was and they got along well enough apart from one day's hunting with the Beaufort much later.

Nevertheless the Duke, who remembered that stage of his life particularly well, was able to put me in the picture of those days when Anne Harvey was still able

5

to hunt and her younger son, encouraged all the time by his mother, was learning about the horse and horse sports.

The Duke explained the name by which he always preferred to be called, 'Master'. He said 'I much prefer it, but it has nothing to do with being a Master of Fox Hounds. It has been my name since I was nine years old.

'For my ninth birthday I was given as a present the Crickhowell Harriers from Wales. They used to come up to Badminton for the Christmas holidays and we had a lot of fun with them. People used to come up and ask, "Where are you going to draw next, Master?" "Where are you meeting on Wednesday, Master?" and so on. It happened so often that we decided to change my name.

'The Harriers hunted hares alright, not foxes. Our own fox hounds had a six-day week in those days – out every day. Although there were plenty of foxes, there weren't too many and we had very long days too. We went on hunting six days a week right up to the start of the Second World War.'

Roscoe well remembers Master's father, the old Duke. 'He was enormous,' he says. 'A huge man.'

Master told me, 'My father hunted hounds right up until the First War, when he had two very bad accidents. First he broke his leg when riding and then, while trying to school four horses in a carriage, he turned the vehicle over and two of the wheels went over his leg, smashing it to smithereens.'

The Harvey family returned to England too late for the famous Great Wood Run which was to become legend not only in the Beaufort country but also in the entire hunting world.

Master pointed to a prominent wood. 'That is the Great Wood,' he said, 'where the famous run started. My father weighed about eighteen stone and, where other people had two horses a day, he would have three.

'On this occasion the fox went off from Great Wood up the steep hill away from it and my father followed, whereupon the fox turned around and came straight back again down the vale, over the Brinkworth Brook. Luckily Father saw it and avoided it.

'He was jolly lucky. His first horse was practically blown by then, having been up the hill, and he found his second horseman on the road so that he could change onto the fresh horse and gallop on.

'He went on into the V.W.H. country and right through it. He swam the Thames twice and in his green plush coat, soaked through to the skin, he must have weighed at least twenty-one stone.

'The second horse he was on could hardly keep going, but, as luck would have it, a farmer on a cob came along, saw the state of his horse and offered him the cob to finish off the hunt. He galloped on another two miles and ran the fox to ground under the road at a parsonage. The Parson came out of his house and told him off for hunting on Ash Wednesday! They were now in the Old Berks country near Swindon, a run of about twenty-three miles. Then Grandfather came up with about half a dozen other followers. They loaded the hounds into a train to take them back to Badminton.

'But Father remembered that he was Orderly Officer. So, still in his wet clothes, he boarded the train to London and caught a cab which took him to Regent's Park Barracks where the Regiment was based. Then he changed into his full dress and rode all the way to Horse Guards, which is quite a long ride, turned the Guard out as was his duty and rode back to Regent's Park.

'He never slept very much and was back in Badminton in time to go hunting the next day. At Badminton House we have some pictures of that wonderful run which were given to my Father.'

7

As Roscoe was soon to discover, foxhunting with those wonderful Gloucestershire packs, the Beaufort and the Berkeley, was a religion.

Master went to Sandhurst in 1918 and then joined the Blues, expecting to be sent out to France at any minute. But the Armistice came just at the beginning of the hunting season.

'Lord Tweedmouth commanded the Regiment when I joined,' he said . 'I had always been told he was a very frightening man. But he was most friendly when I went to him in fear and trepidation and asked whether, if I could arrange it with my brother officers, he would allow me to hunt my hounds two days a week. He agreed and I never missed a day.

'The local bus that went to Paddington called in at the Barracks in London evey week and I arranged with the chap who drove it to pick me up and take me to the station. (I gave him a fiver or something and he was quite happy to do it.) So I had no trouble. I would catch the six o'clock train which stopped in Badminton and was always at the Meet on time.'

Life was not so easy for the Harvey family, due first to the death of Roscoe's sister, Patricia, from appendicitis – 'Of course she would never have died today' – and then to Anne Harvey's arthritis, which finally prevented her from holding the reins and put an end to her foxhunting activities.

The Minchinhampton house was sold and she moved to Curzon Street in London with her small son. Brother John was already at Dartmouth en route for the Navy.

Roscoe reckons that he is the oldest client of Trumpers, the famous Curzon Street barbers.

London in 1908 was a far cry from the Beaufort country, but it was still full of horses. There were the Household Cavalry, the high-mettled hacks in Rotten Row, horses pulling vehicles of all kinds from smart private barouches and carriages down to the humble vans and carts. Predominant were the cab horses, pulling hansoms or the four-wheelers, 'growlers'.

It was a city where agile boys with brush and scoop used to dart about perilously under the busy traffic in order to keep the streets clean – a primitive method and one which was only partially effective. In very hot weather it was always possible to detect the smell of horse in the busier streets. As Roscoe says, 'That was for most a great deal more pleasant than the smell of petrol and the fumes of diesel oil today.'

The sad story of 'The High-Mettled Racer' still portrayed in the lavatories of many country houses, was by no means unique. And many speculated on the source of all London's cab horses. The majority of them probably were cast-offs from private stables, hunting stables and the racecourse. Undoubtedly, one or two winners of races ended their days as 'cabbers'. They were usually sold on account of vice or because they were unsound. Hard work cured the former and, in time, finished off the latter. It seems that hansom-cab horses were usually well bred. Those pulling the four-wheeler 'growlers' were lower down in the scale.

There was a good deal of snobbery in the cab world. Outside London clubs like Whites and Boodles you would find only a rank of hansoms. But by the big hotels, both forms of cab would be in evidence. Four-wheelers would be needed for baggage and station journeys. Nevertheless, despite their hard seats, inadequate springing and shabby upholstery, the 'growlers' provided excellent transport, slow but functional, despite the discouraging comment of Sir Alexander Cockburn, then Lord Chief Justice, when summing up in the Tichborne Trial: 'One of those shapeless, rambling vehicles, which are a disgrace to a civilized country, the four wheeled cab.'

9

But a drive in a hansom was something quite different. Roscoe remembers the tinkle of the little bell on the harness, the rhythmic sound of the horses' hooves against the macadam surface or the later wooden street blocks and the faster pace of a better sprung conveyance, all of which were eminently satisfying. Frequently in the residential areas of London, you would come across a section of a street covered for about fifty yards with straw. This would show that one of the occupants of the houses was seriously ill. Over such a carpet the hansom travelled noiselessly.

Despite the popular image of the cab horse, standing dejectedly with its head down, rather over at the knees and probably with one hind leg resting like a running terrier, they had a fair reputation for both courage and stamina. One of the longest runs ever made by a hansom was a journey taken by a well-known journalist called Swears, who had missed the last train from Victoria and had an appointment at the Old Ship Hotel in Brighton early the following morning. For £25 he persuaded a hansom-cab driver to attempt the journey of fifty-two miles which was duly achieved on time.

Although this splendid vehicle vanished from London with the advent of the motor taxi-cab, Roscoe was to encounter it many more times in his life, usually under the new name of a 'gharry' on the streets of Cairo and Alexandria, as well as in India.

Anne Harvey was a wonderful woman. Appreciating that she only had a few years to live, she determined to make her younger son not only a sportsman in every sense of the word, but also sufficiently independent to carry on on his own after her death.

In the summer holiday she sent him up to one or other of his seven Scottish uncles, several of whom were to command Highland regiments but, although a Highlander herself, she was determined that young

10

Charles was to be a hunting man. She must have been a foxhunting fanatic like the magnificent Surtees character who looked out at that morning in November. 'Hurrah! Blister my kidneys!' exclaimed he in delight. 'It is a frost! – the dahlias are dead!'

During her time with the Beaufort, Anne Harvey had bought some good horses from Dick Holborow, described by Roscoe as the most wonderful gentleman horse-coper, who lived in a lovely house close by Berkeley Road near Dursley. He was a large, somewhat fat, delightful character, who had forgotten more about riding and foxhunting than most of us will ever know. At the end of the summer holidays, when cubhunting began in earnest and, particularly, every Christmas holidays, Anne sent her son to Dick and his sister, who was also called Anne, praying that he would be able to live the life which had been denied to her until the end.

The Berkeley country, with the yellow coats of the hunt staff, was an exciting place for young Roscoe. Its splendid, enthusiastic, hard-drinking, hard-riding yeoman farmers really went when following the hounds over the rhynes or vales or across those steep hills and great woodlands. Their marvellous hounds were renowned for their great hunting qualities and their blood was in great demand in other kennels for the improvement of nose and cry.

Roscoe still rhapsodises about the Berkeley as, 'The most wonderful country, the best hunting and the best people in the world.' He has gone back many times since.

Way back in the eighteenth century and just at the beginning of the nineteenth, the fifth Earl of Berkeley hunted his enormous chain of countries until 1807. Originally he had kennels at Charing Cross in London and could hunt on his own land right the way down to

Bristol. His eldest but illegitimate son, Colonel Berkeley, inherited the Castle but not the pack of hounds which formed the Old Berkeley Hunt at Gerrards Cross. To his home country the Colonel added the Cotswolds and hunted from kennels at Cheltenham and Buckland. He built up a new pack which was superb, small, not always straight but with great hunt and great drive.

The Colonel became Lord Segrave and then Earl Fitzhardinge. He tried to establish his legitimacy in the House of Lords but succeeded only in creating a family feud of extraordinary bitterness. His (legitimate) brother Grantley consequently accused him of lechery, rapacity, theft and preferring amateur theatricals to hunting, but the Colonel was one of the most original and influential hound breeders of his time and a very popular Master of Hounds.

The hounds were slightly unusual. They had been, and continue to be, bred entirely to work without regard for appearance. Complete indifference to the Peterborough Hound Show made them increasingly distinctive. They would have been used more as an outcross but for the risk of that unfashionable pale colour. They were real hounds, incredibly savage, bred to hunt and kill foxes, which they did with ruthless efficiency. Nothing changed under the 2nd and third Lord Fitzhardinge except the introduction, which was fully in line with the kennel's philosophy, of Welsh-cross blood from Itton.

In Roscoe's boyhood he hunted under the third Earl, Charles Fitzhardinge, a tall, charming old man who had the hounds until 1916 when they were taken over by the late Lord Berkeley.

Roscoe says, 'I once asked him why he never showed his hounds at Peterborough. He replied, "Little boy, I breed my hounds to kill foxes not to stand on the flags at a dog show!"'

Savage? Well, if you wished to stay alive, you would never visit those hounds in kennel on your own without a

12

really stout whip. Charles Fitzhardinge never took them to the meet past one of their favourite covers. 'I often had to go several miles out of my way,' he said, 'or they would be gone!'

Many provincial hunting people regard this as disgraceful, as appalling discipline. But many years later, when the late James Hanbury was Master of the Belvoir, he told me that his huntsman George Tongue frequently had to make a similar detour for the same reason on the way to a meet with the famous keen little Belvoir bitches.

As a boy, Roscoe's hunting clothes were the same as the farmers'. 'I wore "ratcatcher" clothes,' he says. 'A tweed or cord jacket over breeches, boots and gaiters. I never wore a red coat until I joined my Regiment.'

When Dick Holborow died recently, mourners from far and wide thronged the fourteenth-century Church. Roscoe remembers, 'In those days the Berkeley provided far more sport than any other pack. The "Shires" were no comparison.

'Lord Fitzhardinge,' says Roscoe, 'who owned sixty-five per cent of all the land we hunted over, was a marvellous landlord, who did everything for his tenants, even keeping a stallion at the kennels to serve the farmers' mares free of charge. But woe betide any of his tenant farmers who put up wire. Any man who committed that sin got a month's notice straight away. He was right of course. The main reason for wire was because small tenant farmers could genuinely afford no other sort of fencing. But this did not apply in the Berkeley country where the farmers were men of substance, most of whom hunted themselves.'

Roscoe sometimes rode with Lord Fitzhardinge and, as time went on, started to whip in. 'One day when we were out, he saw barbed wire across a particular fence and demanded, "Whose land are we on? What's that

13

wire doing there? Get off your horse and cut it in about eight places. Tell the farmer he will have a month's notice if he puts up any more wire!"'

'He was quite keen on his pheasant shooting, but fox hunting always came first. After an unusual blank day when he found not one fox, he summoned four keepers to Berkeley Castle and told them, "We seem to be a little short of foxes." They all protested that it had been a windy, rough night which had caused the dearth. Lord Fitzhardinge was not impressed. He said, "Well, I am altering the meet. And, if we haven't had any foxes in three days' time, you'll all have a month's notice!"'

When he was eleven years old, Roscoe went to Downside, the famous Roman Catholic public school at Stratton-on-the-Fosse, south of Bath, only a comparatively short distance from his beloved Berkeley country.

'Downside was a lot smaller than it is now,' he says. 'There were only about 150 boys there. I don't know how good they were educationally and I don't believe that I ever passed an exam, but it was a very good sports school and it was far more important to be able to pass a rugby football than to pass exams!

'I took my Faith quite seriously at that time. We were bound to, as the Benedictine monks who ran Downside were such splendid men that they encouraged you; and they did not ram it down your throats. As a result, I went to communion very regularly.

'Downside had wonderful hockey and rugger teams and I played for both. I was scrum-half to the school from my second year.'

In addition to Roscoe, there were several other boys who were to become amateur jockeys – Oliver Fingall, Billy Filmer-Sankey and Harry Webber.

Those Benedictine monks were, as they are today at Downside and Ampleforth, first-class school-masters, real men who combine discipline with caring friendship. The Headmaster was Sigebert de Trafford from the famous family which has been so closely associated with racing for many years.

Unlike many other monastic orders, Black-Cowl Benedictines were neither exclusively academic nor exclusively unworldly. 'Orare et Arare' is their motto and the rule of the Order commits them to work and to prayer in equal proportion. Their work, be it writing, studying, bookbinding, farming or, of course, teaching is regarded as a form of prayer in itself. The Creator is worshipped not in aethereal or theoretical terms but through His creation.

In consequence, Downside and its sister school Ampleforth boast a staff of experts permanently on site and permanently committed to the welfare of their charges. Although in many regards conventional, they enjoy an unparalleled reputation for friendly relations between staff and pupils. Much to their surprise, they have therefore found themselves now in the vanguard of liberal (rather than ILEA cranky) education.

Just as the monks mixed the spiritual and the temporal, so Roscoe found his daily discipline to be an incongruous cocktail of morning mass, evening prayers, benediction, eight hours study and three hours of sweating and cursing in the mud of the rugger or the hockey field.

Games were taken seriously at Downside and Roscoe, despite his inherited short-sightedness, excelled at them. He says, 'Both my father and grandfather were short-sighted and, later, my son was to suffer from the same trouble. I think mine was made worse when I was struck in the eye one day when we were throwing lumps of soap at each other in the washroom at Downside and I have worn spectacles ever since.'

And always, of course, morning, noon and night – or

15

rather Matins, Nones and Vespers – above the ragged cries of the boys on the playing field, there came from the Abbey Church the haunting sound of Gregorian chant, the strange, magical, male unison drone in which the monastic community had for centuries sung their praises.

Perhaps one other factor lent poignancy in those years to the echoing walls of the Stratton-on-the-Fosse church. Every term, every month, the roll-call of the dead increased. Monitors, friends, heroes who had so recently been fresh-faced boys in the dormitory or on the playing fields, became within months mere gilt names, fallen on muddier, lonelier fields and fallen for good.

Roscoe and his contemporaries believed that they would go to war. They also knew, whether or not they openly acknowledged it, that the life expectancy of an officer in that 'war to end all wars' was somewhat lower than that of a condemned man on death row. It was not in that less complicated, less selfish age, something against which to rebel. It was not even something to question. It was a necessary fact. It was accepted.

Roscoe says typically, 'That side of things really didn't worry me. I wasn't callous, but I was enjoying myself too much! Furthermore, there was no wireless and, in the country, newspapers were scarce, so that we never appreciated the ghastly extent of those appalling casualty lists.'

Roscoe adds, 'We used to bet like anything at school but we weren't allowed to go racing. We used to send off our bets by post to a bookie called Dick Power in Ireland. One day we thought some horse was a certainty. So we clubbed together and collected as much money as we could – about £14. Not only did the horse lose but we were also caught and given a proper ticking off. De Trafford wrote to the bookmaker saying, "I could have you up for betting with minors, but I suppose if the horse had won, you would have sent the money to me!" After that Mr Power would not bet with us any more.'

Roscoe loved Downside but he could not wait to get back to the Berkeley country and that happy home with fat jovial Dick Holborow and his sweet sister Anne. When age finally stopped Dick from hunting, he handed his young charge over to another Berkeley farmer called Hastings Neale who had a big family down in that country. 'He taught me so much about riding to hounds. He had that extraordinary knack of knowing where hounds and foxes were going to go. He never seemed to be in a hurry but was nearly always at the head of the field. When the war started in 1914, we went on hunting all the way through. It was fantastic experience for me because those grand Berkeley farmers were constantly buying horses, hunting them and then selling them on to the Army. I used to ride them and learnt a tremendous amount about horsemanship. They were all different. Some had good temperaments, some had bad, I had quite a lot of falls and wouldn't have missed it for the world.

'A few drinks on board and you couldn't see those farmers for dust! It was all tremendous fun. There was always a fox somewhere, either in a tree or in a drain. One day we bolted one almost in Bristol at Aust down by the side of the Severn River. We took the fox right the way back up near to Thornbury and let it out. It ran back right the way down the side of the river in that lovely vale and we had one hell of a hunt.

'During the First World War when everyone was getting killed and people were naturally sad, it really did not affect me because I did not realize about all the awful things that were happening in France. I was very young and having a wonderful time and enjoying

17

myself too much. My mother died in 1917 and I then had a guardian called William Ferrier-Ker, whose wife was my aunt. He lived in Norfolk but I was seventeen by now and didn't stay with him much. I preferred to stay down with all the people from my youth – the farmer boys and so on – a real country-boy's life. I had a very good horse by this time which Dick Holborow had found for me, and I rode to the meet or went in that old dog-cart. Later at the end of the day, if my driver was drunk, the pony used to find its own way home!'

By now the time had come for Roscoe to join the Army, and he went to the Royal Military College, Sandhurst, while the war was still on.

'The trouble was that I was no good at exams. I think I just passed the School Certificate but I failed the Sandhurst entrance examination. I was no good at French and although I had a French expert sitting next to me in the examination, I was just too far away from him to crib his paper. So I failed that. This meant that I had to go for a "nomination" in front of a Board. Here I was very lucky because there was one man on the Board whom I knew very slightly and knew that he was a very keen foxhunter, but he didn't know me.

'They asked me all sorts of questions and then asked me what sort of sport do you like best, football, cricket? I drew myself up to my full height and said, "Sir, there is only one sport in the world and that is foxhunting!" When I said this my friend brightened up and that is how I got in!'

Chapter Two

The Army

The Royal Military College, Sandhurst, with its mighty buildings set in glorious grounds on the borders of Surrey and Hampshire, has always been a unique English institution. When Roscoe arrived as a Gentleman Cadet, even though for nearly four years the flower of British youth had passed through its doors only to perish in the trenches, it still maintained its own quaint system which was to be preserved for another twenty-one years.

Every GC had his own room and shared a batman with, probably, six other cadets. This was not the luxury that it sounds because there just was no time for bed-making or kit-cleaning up to a very high standard in the tight schedule of lessons, parades and exercise.

The first period of a typical day might well be drill, dressed in ultra-smart Service Dress uniform, collar and tie with every bit of leather and brass beautifully polished. Just under an hour of 'square-bashing' to the staccato screaming orders of a seemingly sadistic Sergeant-Major of the Foot Guards.

'Mr Viscount Tidworth, Sir! Pick up your rifle, you bloody little man! You call me "Sir" and I call you "Sir"! But you're still a dozy little man and, if you do that again, you will be saddled with a load of extra drills, Sir!'

Stamping feet, marching, slow marching. The drill of the Champion Company at Sandhurst was always rated third in the entire Army behind the King's Company of the Grenadier Guards and the Royal Marines. It was brilliant.

Then, finally dismissed, there was a rush back to your rooms to change for PT (Physical Training). Here the quaintest form of dress was adopted. Over his singlet, shorts and stockings, the Cadet had to put on long white flannel trousers, a red and white striped silk scarf and a blazer in thick red and white vertical stripes with polished buttons, the whole outfit surmounted by a red and white striped pill-box hat kept on by a bit of elastic at the back. He then had to run down and grab his bicycle, known at Sandhurst as a 'bogwheel', and form up on parade on the square. This in five minutes, or there was hell to pay.

Then Cavalry drill with bicycles instead of horses. 'From the right, form sections, walk, march. Mount.' The parade then went down to the gymnasium where, after dismounting and leaving their bicycles, the Cadets would rush in and take off their outer garments so that they could be drilled by the Army physical-training staff, the APTS, who were normally considerably more sadistic than the Guards drill Sergeant-Majors.

Back on with the red and white striped regalia and, once again formed up, Cavalry drill again on bicycles and ride back to be dismissed on the square outside your company.

A hectic rush and five minutes to change into ordinary uniform for a lesson in French or perhaps Military History or any of the other subjects which potential young officers were taught so well. Then another hectic rush with five minutes to change for

Riding School. This meant changing into smart Service Dress again, with cap, Sam Browne belt, collar, tie, tunic, breeches, boots, leggings and spurs. Rush down again for the bicycle and, as for the ride to the gymnasium, so now the squad moved to the stables and the indoor school.

In Roscoe's day there were, of course, many more horsed cavalry regiments and he says, 'There was a lot of riding.' Riding School was compulsory, but, on arrival, cadets were asked whether they wished to take part in horse sports during their spare time. They had to undergo fairly stringent tests. There was a Drag Test, a Hunting Test and a Hacking Test. If you had ridden all your life and were really good, like Roscoe, you passed the Drag Test, which meant that you could not only hack and hunt whenever you had the opportunity but also go out once or twice a week with the Staff College Drag Hunt, which provided really good flat-out gallops over well worked-out lines with plenty of jumping on the best horses in the large Sandhurst riding school. Passing the Drag Test meant that you were allowed to take part in all horse activities.

The Hunting Test was not so good. But it did entitle you to go out with the local hunt, the Garth, as well as to hack for pleasure. At the bottom of the scale came the Hacking Test which needed no explanation. It just meant that you were competent to go out for a ride if you wanted to. With such large stretches of heathland like Barossa, the area around Camberley has always provided plenty of scope for riding, as long as you don't ignore the red flags and stray on to the ranges when firing is taking place!

Roscoe had a decent horse at Sandhurst. As soon as the armistice was declared in November 1918, racing got going again. The last substitute Grand National run

21

at Gatwick in the Spring of that year had been won by the greatest steeplechaser of the time, Poethlyn, owned by Mrs Hugh Peel. In the true Aintree tradition, Poethlyn's career had had a humble start. He was sold for £7 to a hotelier in Shrewsbury and then bought for 50 guineas by Hugh Peel, who gave him to his wife. The Aintree course near Liverpool had been taken over by the War Office and closed to racing. The Grand National was transferred to Gatwick and there in 1918 he won the last substitute National.

In April 1919, five months after the end of the war, the country was still celebrating the armistice and huge crowds flocked to Liverpool, wanting to cheer their favourite, Poethlyn, to a second National victory. The field included past winners Sunloch, Vermouth and All Sloper, as well as the future winners Sergeant Murphy and Shaun Spadah.

That year Mrs Peel's brave nine-year-old bay was carrying 12 stone 7 pounds. Only Cloister, Gerry M and Manifesto had carried that weight to victory in the National. Although Poethlyn was sometimes an erratic jumper and needed all his strength to cover those four and a half miles, he had become the course's hero. The huge crowds, many of whom had finally been freed from the horror of the trenches, backed him down to 11-4 favourite and Poethlyn did not let them down. His jockey, Earnie Piggott, who had won on him at Gatwick the previous year, rode a wonderful race and won confidently from the Irish horse Ballyboggan.

A crystal ball that day might have revealed two remarkable facts. Ballyboggan was ridden by Willie Head, father of Alec, who became France's finest trainer, and the winning jockey's grandson, Lester Piggott, was to become the future champion.

Roscoe says, 'I knew the Peels and shot with them several times. And I got to know Willie Head later when he was training in France. A wonderful old man. Never changed right up to the end. Always remained essentially English. You know, rose garden and afternoon tea with silver teapot – right there in France!'

Despite his eyesight which has caused him to wear spectacles for most of his life, Roscoe had already caught the racing bug. Small, but immensely strong with a short back and good long leg for a boot, he was the ideal build for a National Hunt jockey.

While at Sandhurst, he started point-to-pointing. 'The first time I rode, Ken Alexander and I thought we had the race between us but a chap called Jenkinson beat us both. Ken, a great character and friend of mine, was second and I was third. Jenkinson afterwards went into the Life Guards.

'When we went racing, we used to meet a chap called Mr Head, no relation of Willie, who was, I suppose, a sort of professional backer. He looked like a man who would read lessons in church but he knew a great deal about what was happening in racing. We got to know him through Harry Webber. After the war there was a fair bit of skulduggery going on on the racecourse and on one particular day he told us to come and see him. He asked us, "Have you got a lot of money?" We told him that we hadn't very much between us. "Well, you ought to have it on this horse," he said.

'When the race came round, the animal was quoted at 6-4 against. So we put on our all. It was a five-furlong race and after three furlongs his horse was five lengths in front. Marvellous. We were counting our winnings already. But a furlong from home it started to wobble about and went backwards. It finished last and, as it passed the winning post, it fell down stone dead. I suppose it had probably been given strychnine. I never knew if there was an enquiry or any post mortem. I don't suppose there was in those days.'

Whenever possible, Roscoe would slip back to the Berkeley country to hunt and also to ride in point-to-points. He won several but in the Members Race was beaten by the Master, Percy Lister, who had brought a good charger back from the war. This was the same Percy Lister who later became Chairman of the famous family firm at Dursley and was knighted.

When the war ended, Roscoe joined in the celebrations at Sandhurst, and once more the long-suffering big guns were pushed into the lakes. These old-timers had been immersed during the Sandhurst mutiny of 1902 over stoppage of leave, but since that time they have only found their way into the lakes on the nights of big dances like the June Balls and other celebration parties.

Roscoe was now becoming an outstanding horseman by any standards. He was learning still more about foxhunting from the legendary tall handsome farmer Hastings Neale from whom he acquired the knack of always being in the right place at the right time without ever appearing to hurry. Moreover, 'C.B.', as Roscoe was known in those days, was always up there at the head of the hunt when hounds were running over what they called 'the marsh', the country which, in those days, stretched from Berkeley to the outskirts of Bristol, and was all grass with big ditches to every fence, wonderful scenting and no wire. Joan Dunn – a splendid hunting-lady who still lives in the area and who has been a friend of Roscoe for years – writes: 'In those days no farmer was allowed to have wire in his fences and every one of them had to walk at least one hound puppy. Moreover, in those days, car followers were few so that long points were made. Foxes were always plentiful and it was nothing to run all day over the marsh.'

Hastings Neale had a large family. A short while ago

Roscoe went down to the Berkeley country to seek out Dick Holborow's grave. 'I met two of Hastings Neale's sons,' he said. 'They were a bit puzzled when we first met and I asked them if they had heard of a man called "C.B.". "You are not *the* Mr C.B.?" they asked. I told them how much I owed to their father and, after that, we had a lot to talk about!'

As one who for some years rode in a great many point-to-points, I can vouch for the fact that Roscoe's sixty-five winners constitutes a major achievement. 'First through soldiering abroad and then later with my Jockey Club duties, I missed a lot and was never in a position to go around touting for rides,' he says.

On top of that, under Rules in England and India, he notched up a total of forty-five victories. The thick spectacles which he wore strapped to his head must have been an appalling handicap, especially since in those early days they were made of glass that splintered easily. Roscoe says, 'The going in an English winter and spring is frequently heavy and muddy. How often do you see jockeys coming in covered with mud? My vision depended entirely on being able to see through those thick glasses. It meant galloping round with one hand holding the reins and the other desperately wiping away the mud.' It's a terrifying thought. Just imagine jumping the famous Sandown 'treble' in muddy conditions. The fences come so close together that on many occasions Roscoe must have been completely blind when he met the third. Then, of course, he knew subconsciously that, if he fell on his face, he was in danger of smashing his spectacles and losing his sight entirely. But it never worried him. He was completely dedicated, in love with the great sport of steeplechasing. And, with due respect to skiers and Cresta Run enthusiasts, I shall always believe that there is no greater thrill in the world of sport than riding a good horse over English steeplechase fences.

By the end of 1919, Roscoe, who also played hockey for Sandhurst, was finishing his time at the Royal Military College. He had no doubt about the Regiment that he wished to join, the 10th Royal Hussars (Prince of Wales' Own). 'My uncle had a great friend called Hargreaves who was connected with the Regiment, and because of this, and the fact that I knew them to be a very fine outfit indeed, I had no doubt.

'After it had all been decided, Lord Airlie, who was in the 10th and was an instructor at Sandhurst, came to me one day and said, "I think you ought to consider coming into my Regiment."

'I told him, "Thank you, Sir. I am coming into your Regiment. It has all been decided some time ago!"'

So, in *The Times* and *The London Gazette* there contained the information that 2nd Lieutenant C.B. Harvey had been commissioned to the 10th Hussars. His supremely loyal devotion to that great Regiment has remained a major feature of his life and the bedrock on which it was built, for over sixty-six years.

The Passing Out Parade at Sandhurst, presided over by a senior general, was a particularly impressive ceremony. The senior terms, comprising approximately 200 commissioned young officers, were parading for the last time on that famous square, dressed and polished to the nines in their very best uniforms. With them there would be the intermediate and junior terms of gentleman cadets, whose turn would come. The Sandhurst band played for the Inspection, the presentation of the Sword of Honour, and the March Past, watched by admiring families, relations and friends.

The *pièce de résistance* was when the Adjutant, normally a major or captain in the Foot Guards, rode his charger up his steps of the Old Building. This act was always carefully rehearsed beforehand. Because Foot Guard officers are not normally renowned for

26

their horsemanship, in order to get the horse's back down and make him completely docile, the Adjutant's charger would be taken out by the riding-school staff for two hours before the parade. On one famous occasion, however, they had not perhaps done their work as thoroughly as they might. The horse, as I remember, was an old brown thoroughbred called My Lord. On this particular day he stood like a rock throughout as the Adjutant, resplendent in his Grenadiers uniform, bellowed his orders. Then suddenly, with no warning, My Lord upped with his heels and deposited the Adjutant on his hands and knees, still with his sword at the 'carry' and stood stock-still looking down at him. The discipline was such that the quiver of joy that ran through the ranks was momentary, but for all present it was a memory to cherish.

The Regiment was founded in 1715, raised at the time of the Jacobite Rebellion as the 10th Regiment of Dragoons. Even then, although the arms were 'a sword carbine and a pair of pistols,' there was the promise of a light-cavalry role for the Regiment because the horses were soon standardised as 'not above the size of fifteen hands, very nimble kind of horse that can gallop, with short backs, broad fillets and clean legs.'

Indeed, in 1783 six Dragoon Regiments, including the 10th and the 11th, formed into Light Dragoons. At this time His Royal Highness George Augustus Frederick, the Prince of Wales, was twenty-one and his exploits, dashing, dissolute or scandalous, depending on your taste, were the talk of the country. So his father, King George III wished to stimulate 'Prinny's' interest in the Army and the following order was issued:

'29th September, 1783, ORDERS.
It is His Majesty's pleasure that the Tenth Regiment of Light Dragoons shall, for the future, be called the "Tenth, or Prince of Wales' Own Regiment of Light Dragoons."
Signed William Fawcett,
Adjutant General.'

The uniform was changed from scarlet to blue and the Prince of Wales' plume with the Rising Sun and the Red Dragon became the badges of the Regiment with the motto 'Ich Dien'. Not unnaturally his Regiment was frequently stationed at his favourite town, Brighton, and by 1796 the Prince of Wales was appointed Colonel of the Regiment, which he determined to make the crack Regiment of the British Army in bravery, military skills and smartness. As Colonel of the Regiment, he paid for specially tailored uniforms for the soldiers to bring them up to the standard of the uniforms worn by the NCOs. Not for nothing have they always been known as 'The Shiny Tenth' or 'The Shiners'. The Prince of Wales even gave a commission to his young friend George 'Beau' Brummel, who, however, resigned three years later when the Regiment was briefly posted to Manchester on the grounds that 'He was not prepared to go on Foreign Service!'

Soon Hussar Regiments were being formed all over Europe after the renowned Hungarian light Cavalry. So, with his Regiment stationed at Brighton, the Prince of Wales almost inevitably decided to dress his Regiment in the latest fashion as Hussars, even though the title was not as yet officially recognized in the British Army. In 1806 his father, George III, gave permission for the Regiment to be equipped and recognized as Hussars and they were the first in the British Army.

The 10th Royal Hussars (Prince of Wales' Own) had come into existence, determined to be the smartest Regiment in the British Army.

Their record since then, whether fighting or in the field of sport (they introduced polo to England), has been quite exceptional. At the time when Roscoe joined, the 10th had over the years taken the lead in many famous battles, hard-fought campaigners, right through the years down to the Boer War, when they exchanged their gay uniforms for khaki, to the 1914-1918 war from which they had just returned with ten new battle honours, earned while fighting almost entirely dismounted in the trenches of France and Belgium and running up casualties of fifteen officers, 199 other ranks killed, forty-one officers, 528 other ranks wounded. In 1919, when Lieutenant Colonel Archie Seymour had come from the Royal Scots Greys to take command, the 10th, after being abroad for nearly twenty years, returned to Canterbury. However, they had hardly settled down in England before, in April 1920, they were suddenly posted to Ireland. It was here that Roscoe was to join them.

The Gentlemen Cadets dispersed from the Royal Military College for a life of peacetime soldiering, never dreaming for one moment that this state of affairs would last for only twenty years because Germany was not really defeated, just temporarily dormant and determined on revenge.

Maintaining the Royal Family's connection with the 10th, Prince Henry, Duke of Gloucester, joined the Regiment at this time. He was a splendid, dedicated soldier who was to become a great friend of Roscoe's. He was not allowed, to his chagrin, to go to Ireland during the 'troubles'!

Not for nothing did a young man require a substantial private allowance to join a Cavalry Regiment.

29

The uniform alone was a major item by any standards. Full dress and mess kit with all the traditional finery, blue patrols, overalls with the wide yellow cavalry stripe, different types of boots, polo boots, field boots, dress boots, and pairs of spurs in the Regimental pattern. Different caps, Service Dress hats, forage caps, Hussars shako, with its plume. Sam Browne belt, lovely engraved sword (for carrying on service duties), zinc uniform cases, cord breeches for everyday wear, Service Dress tunics and slacks. There were no short cuts. Everything had to be made to the Regiment's individual pattern and from the Regiment's own individual material. Even the khaki shirts were handmade. Every item had to be produced by the Regiment's own prescribed tradesmen, invariably masters of their craft, the finest in the world. Uniform and breeches from Huntsman, boots from Maxwell, hats from Herbert Johnson, leather and steel from Wilkinson. Then there was your saddlery with, for parade work, stirrup slides and ear bosses with the Regimental crest. The Army uniform grant for a young cavalry officer just joining was £60, which just about covered three pairs of Maxwell boots with trees, even in those days!

The fitting drill was complicated. A short while after the initial measuring, you returned first to the tailor who was in the process of making your breeches. Donning these garments held together by tacking thread, you would travel in a taxi the short distance to the bootmakers where a pair of boots in the same unready, tacked together condition would be placed on your legs. Then, wearing both, back again to the breeches maker. You might need a couple of further fittings but, of course, the result was as near perfection as you would expect of an officer in the Shiny Tenth.

At this age most of us had parents to help us. But Roscoe had been an orphan since he was seventeen years old and, even before that, with his mother sick in London, he had necessarily been forced to fend for himself. I firmly believe that this went a long way towards forging his wonderful character.

Now fully equipped, 2nd Lieutenant C.B. Harvey, small, bespectacled, tough and already a wonderful mixer with people of all kinds, joined the 10th Hussars on the Curragh in Ireland – that broad expanse of grass and gorse, heavily populated by sheep, with its wide galloping racecourse and the old barracks which look as though they had stepped straight from the pages of Kipling and are now occupied by the Irish Army.

He was made a troop leader – the best young officer's command in the services, thirty-two horses and thirty-two men. He had two chargers of his own and two servants. His first servant, the equivalent of an infantry batman, looked after the officer and all his personal equipment. The second servant looked after the officer's two horses and his saddlery, as well as his own troop horse.

It was soon after Roscoe's arrival that he was asked by a senior officer to ride a horse at Punchestown at the weight of 10 stone. He had considerable difficulty and finally ended up on the scales at 10 stone 2 pounds. This was when he was told, 'You're a fat little pig. You are as bad as Roscoe Arbuckle!' The name stuck with him ever since.

He says, 'I enjoyed the Curragh during the troubles. There were a few instances when people got shot in typical Irish fashion, returning from tennis parties and so on. But basically there was very little danger. We had as much hunting as we wanted. The only condition was that Archie Seymour, our Commanding Officer, insisted on us carrying pistols when we went out hunting. He was a strict disciplinarian but a very nice chap. I had a tiny little automatic pistol which didn't interfere with my comfort, was not much good as a weapon, but satisfied the Colonel's condition.

'Our job was to pick up Sinn Feiners. As a fully horsed cavalry Regiment, we were like beaters on a grouse moor, stretched for miles, advancing across the country. Each squadron had about two miles width.

'I had a rather fat windy troop sergeant who didn't want to leave the road for any reason, but at the same time I had a very dashing corporal and about six good soldiers. We would leave the troop sergeant with the rest of the troop on the road and set off over those banks. By the time I got back home I had two or three really good hunters.

'We caught a few Sinn Feiners. We had to pick up every man we found working in the fields and so on who was under forty. We rounded them up and they were vetted by the RUR or whatever the equivalent was in those days.'

Roscoe says, 'We were doing a cavalry escort for King George V when he came out to Belfast. I was only a very junior Second Lieutenant and I had to go down a side street because they thought there might have been some trouble, which, in the event, there was not. Anyway, there was I sitting on my horse down this side road when a very old blind man came up, holding out his cup. I have never forgotten this. It is imprinted on my mind. This old blind tramp staggered up, looking half starved. So I dropped a sixpenny piece in his cup, whereupon somebody tapped me on the shoulder and said, "You shouldn't have done that. He's a Catholic." "God save us!", I said. "So am I!" Whereupon the "Loyalist" who had tapped me on the shoulder, went down the street as fast as his horrible little legs could run as though I was the devil with horns on my head. Bloody idiot.

'They blew us up on the train as we were coming

back. Each squadron was returning on three separate train loads. We had so many horses on those trains. In each train we had a couple of fellows in the back with Hotchkiss machine-guns, as we thought there might be trouble. I was in the first train with my Colonel, Archie Seymour. I shall always remember leaning out of the window with him, and seeing a number of workmen on the side of the rail. I thought they were working on the line. We paid no attention to them but the second of our trains that came through was de-railed by a bomb in the most horrible way. We lost the two machine-gunners. They were both killed and so were seventy of our horses. To this day I can't forgive them!'

The Regiment returned from Ireland to Canterbury in 1922 and at last the 10th Hussars were to be allowed a reasonable tour of home duty. Now, Prince Henry, the Duke of Gloucester, a newly promoted Lieutenant, was allowed to join his Regiment after a spell with the 11th Hussars, waiting for the 10th to come back from Ireland.

Roscoe says, 'Prince Henry adored his service in the Regiment. He was not particularly intelligent but a thoroughly good chap. He loved his sport, rode in point-to-points, hunted, played golf and polo. He beat me in the Regimental Race one day. I did fall at the last, but he would have won anyway. He used to come racing with Henry Forester, a first-class polo player in the 17th/21st Lancers who had the best Regimental team at the time, John Verney (later Lord Willoughby de Broke) and myself. The greatest blow for Prince Henry was that he was not allowed to come out to Egypt with us later because of the troubles. He would have loved it out there.

'I remember playing golf with him one day. He bought a new mashie-niblick from the professional. There were four of us and four caddies – quite a body of people going down the fairway. Prince Henry never minded losing but he hated playing badly. He hit one ball shockingly and then hit himself on the head saying, "Keep your head down. Bloody fool!"

'We went on and occasionally, in a rage with himself, he would throw his club into a gorse bush or a bunker. Finally we got to the eighteenth green. Chipping up to the pin from nearby, the ball went straight across the green into a bunker on the other side. He threw his club and it stuck straight up in the green like a spear. The caddie quietly took the club out of the green, gave it back to His Royal Highness and pressed the damaged turf down with his foot. Prince Henry went into the Pro. Shop and confronted the pro. "Damn rotten club," he said. "Its head was loose." The professional said, "Well, Sir, with respect, the way you have been treating it . . ." Prince Henry laughed. "Yes, I suppose you're right!" he said.'

After a short stay in Canterbury, the Regiment moved to Aldershot, where they were to stay until 1928. Roscoe now started riding racing in earnest.

'I had my first ride at Cheltenham,' he says, 'on a horse belonging to Alf James in the National Hunt Chase. I was lying fourth coming into the last and, although I had no chance of winning, I would probably have stayed in that position if the horse had not made a very bad mistake at the last and I fell off. When I got back, Alf James said, "I wish you hadn't fallen off. I had a good bet that you would finish and another good bet that you would finish in the first six. I lost them both!"'

It is always every young jump jockey's dream just to ride at Cheltenham, let alone to win there. This big, wonderful, undulating course above Prestbury village, is set against the scarp of the Cotswolds. The centre of steeplechasing, it has always been a legend to both the

English and the Irish. Here Roscoe's favourite horse, the mighty brown Golden Miller, triumphed no fewer than five times in the Blue Riband of steeplechasing, the Cheltenham Gold Cup. For the Irish, coming to Cheltenham is a religion in itself. They have always travelled across the Irish Channel from the Emerald Isle in their thousands, including a strong contingent of black-coated Roman Catholic priests. The Cheltenham Festival usually comes in the middle of Lent, and March 17th is often one of the days of the Meeting. On St Patrick's Day, the loyal Irishman is allowed to break his Lenten fast and, if he has a winner or two, he does so with a vengeance at Cheltenham!

There was a wonderful old padre at Camberley called Father Twomey, Canon Twomey to give him his full title, who looked after the Roman Catholic boys at Sandhurst and whose brother was a notorious, highly successful breeder and dealer in greyhounds in Ireland. Father Twomey, in dog collar and clerical black, used to ride round Camberley and the Royal Military College on a confidential cob, visiting his parishioners. One Sunday in mid-March he announced from the pulpit, "I must ask you to pray for the soul of Mrs O'Leary who died this morning. It was most inconsiderate of her because she insists on being buried on Thursday, Gold Cup day. Most inconsiderate!'"

Just before he joined the 10th, Roscoe had been awarded his Berkeley Hunt buttons and now he always hunted in a red coat and top hat. Moreover, now that he was riding in so many point-to-points, he registered his colours, white, brown sleeves and cap. 'That was the purpose,' he says. 'Quite often when you were riding in several races during an afternoon, the conditions for the Member's Race, for example, might read, "To be ridden in hunting dress". This meant putting on a light-weight red coat with a white shirt, hunting tie, etc. I could achieve exactly the same effect by slipping the coat on top of my collars with their white body. Very effective!'

The National Hunt Chase is traditionally known as 'The Amateur's National'. It is for horses that have not won a race, and is confined to amateur riders. The distance is four miles – four gruelling, stamina-sapping miles if the going is at all soft. They used to go round behind the stands until a short while ago and the fences were much stiffer in Roscoe's day than they are now; but even today, that open ditch at the top of the hill in the back straight, second time around, and the penultimate fence where every good jockey tries to win his race at Cheltenham are obstacles to be feared. Tim Molony, five times Champion National Hunt jockey, says, 'If you can ping that second last fence, then the final hill will make little difference to you. But if someone else has pinged it and you haven't, then you are struggling!'

On his first ride at Cheltenham, Roscoe certainly didn't ping the second last and he was undoubtedly struggling as he came into the last. Nevertheless, it was a fine achievement for a young inexperienced amateur to get as far as he did and Alf James's bets showed that he had confidence in his new recruit.

In a Cavalry Regiment between the wars an officer could have two months' hunting leave a year and as many long weekends as he wanted, within reason, as long as he spent them hunting or racing. As there were only about thirty officers on the strength and a number of them were away either on leave or on course at any one time, it meant that, to a large extent, the Regiment was run by the NCOs, who *ipso facto* learnt a graver sense of responsibility and became increasingly better soldiers.

The system has often been mocked and derided by

ignorant class-conscious people. 'Carry on, Sergeant Major!' and so on. But, in fact, it proved extremely successful over the years.

The standard of officer in a Regiment like the 10th was very high indeed and any who, despite first-class recruiting, fell below that standard, were quietly transferred to some other branch of the Army. When an officer returned, improved and refreshed from course or leave, he found a highly efficient lot of soldiers, whose personal problems he knew well, who were his friends and who respected him, taking personal pride in his prowess on the racecourse or polo field. Roscoe says, 'Aldershot was great fun. We raced, soldiered and, believe it or not, did a fair bit of poodle-faking! London was not far away. We would go through the list of the deb dances and say, "Well, that one wasn't much good last year. We will give it a miss this time," or, "That was definitely one of the best last season. We will certainly go again."'

'As for soldiering, we may not have done a lot, but of course we were all mounted. I enjoyed the drills. It was a great feeling having three Regiments doing mounted drills with a trumpet.'

In the euphoria of peace, the Army was being reduced. When the 20th Hussars were disbanded, Colin Davy was transferred to the 10th and immediately became a life-long friend of Roscoe's. Slim, lithe, about the same height as Roscoe, capable of riding at 9 stone 5 pounds, he was an outstanding horseman/jockey, featherweight champion of the Army and a racing novelist. Roscoe is convinced that Colin was even better than his successor, Dick Francis.

Colin was older than Roscoe and, by the time he joined the 10th, he had served in the trenches in the last stages of the First World War, as well as in Egypt and Turkey. He was as brave as a lion and had already ridden a fair number of winners. Always amusing and considerably more articulate than most writers, he was credited with the apocryphal cavalry story of a dinner when he was a guest of the Royals, one of whose proud possessions was a complete dinner service in solid silver. It was a glittering night, the Royals in their scarlet mess kit and Colin in his blue. Colin, a naughty twinkle in his eye, chose his moment. In one of those inevitable silences, he said to his neighbour, 'What a lovely dinner service. Extraordinary coincidence. Do you know, in the 10th we have exactly the same service – in gold!'

Colin and Roscoe were riding in point-to-points and under Rules consistently now. Roscoe says, 'On one occasion I rode for a bookmaker called Merrel from Cheltenham. He wanted to know if I was going through Cheltenham on the way to a meeting where this hurdle race was to take place, and would I call in? When I did, he said, "Do you want any money on it?" I asked him if he thought it would win and he said, "I think it might." I did not bet very heavily in those days but had £10 each way on it with its owner, and thought myself very dashing. I won all right at 100-6. I was very happy!'

Colin attended the course at the Cavalry School at Weedon in Northamptonshire, to be succeeded there by Roscoe who also enjoyed the most wonderful eighteen months at this marvellous establishment. This flagship of British equitation maintained the standard which was the envy of the entire world for horsemen and horsewomen to look up to. Sadly, but inevitably, without this firm, superlative standard at the top, British equitation has steadily deteriorated.

An officer fortunate enough to be selected to attend the eighteen-month course would take with him his two fully-trained chargers and would be provided with a half-trained horse and remount. By the end of the course, the half-trained should be fully-trained, capable of winning any three-day event today, and he should have brought the remount up to half-trained standard.

Roscoe says, 'It was a wonderful life at Weedon. You were riding all day long. We were allowed to hunt with either the Pytchley, Grafton, Bicester or Warwickshire two days a week and could always get leave to go away and ride in races. Our normal day's work, riding our remounts, half-trained and fully-trained chargers, was filled with just as much incident and excitement as an average good day's hunting. One afternoon I counted and found that our ride had jumped no fewer than eighty-seven fences between lunch and tea-time!'

Roscoe learnt a great deal about the balance of a horse, placing a horse at his fences when jumping slowly, and a little *haute école*. His seat and all-round horsemanship were improved considerably. But, whenever the instructor's back was turned, he and the other 'racing swine', as those of us affected by the bug have always been called in the Cavalry, would pull their stirrups up four holes and slip their remounts or half-trained chargers down the steeplechase course. Not for them the sedate, accurately timed jumping, but a sharp canter. They liked to crack their horses into their fences with whips singing, if only they could do so undetected.

Among the horses subjected to this indignity was the mighty Broncho himself, who was a demonstration horse at Weedon in those days. 'Lucky my Colonel didn't find out,' says Roscoe. Commanding the 10th in 1923 was Malise Graham, who, sharing the rides with Joe Dudgeon of the Greys, partnered Broncho in many of his famous international show-jumping triumphs. 'But I think dear old Broncho seemed to enjoy pretending to be a chaser for a change. I also hunted him with the Grafton and he was the nicest horse in the world.

'The senior instructor at Weedon was a very good chap, a Gunner called Lucas. Like most hunting and racing people, I've never gone much on this show-jumping lark, but they were very keen on it at Weedon. So, when I got back to the Regiment after my extended course, I was quite pleased to find that in my troop we had two horses who jumped terribly well and my Troop Sergeant Wells was a good horseman. I took a fortnight's leave in London, and Wells and I produced these two troop horses at Olympia for the International Horse Show.

'When I arrived I met the Weedon Chief Instructor Lucas who said, "Good God, Roscoe. What the hell are you doing here?"

'I said, "I'm just doing some show-jumping."

'"You – going show-jumping!"

'"Yes, I am!"

'"Well, Christ, I was going home but when are you coming in?"

'"I'm about twenty-fifth on the board."

'"Well, I'll wait and see you."

'Whereupon I said, "I'll probably do a clear round!" And by God I did. It didn't get me into the money but it wasn't too bad considering that this was the Daily Mail Cup.

'Two days later I was supposed to ride the same horse, Second Chance, in the King George V Gold Cup. I arrived in the ring beautifully turned out as a 10th Hussar officer, in blue patrols and overalls with that famous cavalry yellow stripe, to find that of the fifteen men that had jumped before me, only one Englishman had a clear round. Two or three Frogs had also done clear rounds. So away I went and, believe it or not, went clear! The crowd cheered with shouts of "Vive l'Anglais!" and all that rubbish.

'As I went out of the ring, a pal of mine who had

come to see me jump said, "Christ, Roscoe, this is bloody marvellous. What you must do now before you jump off is come and have a bloody strong whisky to put you right." I needed no second bidding. I was one of ten in the jump-off. But I don't think the whisky made any difference and in the final jump off for the King George, I was clear up to the last double with big gates where you jumped in and out and then straight through to the finish. For some reason my horse refused and so I turned him round and jumped it perfectly, but that refusal cost me a place in what was then the world's biggest show-jumping contest. It made me laugh. That was my one show-jumping venture. Nothing like starting at the top, is there?'

Of course Chief Instructor Lucas's amazement that racing, hunting Roscoe should go show-jumping was shared by others, including Colonel Malise Graham, an acknowledged expert at the sport. He was obviously convinced that he could improve on Roscoe's performance, and anything this young officer could do, he could do better.

Roscoe says, 'As Regimental Equitation Officer I was supposed to be organizing our musical ride. Malise said, "I think it would be much better if Colin Davy took over." So I was relegated! I couldn't have cared less. It was probably because I wore glasses and didn't look as smart as Colin that he never had a very high opinion of me.' It was the Colonel's undoing.

At stables one day he came round Roscoe's troop and stopped at Second Chance, enquiring: 'Do you think this horse would do me?'

'Well, Colonel,' Roscoe replied, 'he has been properly messed about. I ride him one day and Sergeant Wells rides him the next.'

The Colonel decided to take over the horse to ride himself at Dublin Horse Show in August. Dublin, the world-famous show in the huge arena of Ballsbridge, featured a notorious enormous double bank. A rider must jump off the hocks, land on the top, change legs and go away down the other side. A good rider on an experienced horse would have little difficulty. The rider must be sure of giving his horse ample rein so that he may have sufficient freedom to alternate his change of balance when negotiating the obstacle.

Perhaps Second Chance had just not had sufficient experience of banks. Roscoe says, 'The horse made a mistake jumping on to the bank and stumbled so that Malise fell off with his foot caught in the stirrup. For a few desperate seconds the crowd watched aghast the drama on top of the bank as Second Chance, one of the kindest horses I have ever ridden, swayed off balance and then, through no fault of his own, kicked Malise in the head. For the Colonel there was no second chance. He was killed outright.'

This was a dreadful tragedy. Years later, Malise Graham's son Nigs, who was at Sandhurst with me in 1939 was killed with the 10th in the Western Desert.

Chapter Three

Soldier Rider

While he was at Weedon, Roscoe rode out for Dick Payne who trained nearby and he soon acquired a number of good point-to-pointers and two very decent chasers. He also acquired a wife. Biddy Mylne was the sister of one of Roscoe's brother officers who was shortly to leave the Regiment. An officer's future wife always had to be vetted by the Colonel, and officers of the 10th Hussars were not supposed to get married until they were thirty years old. This was a fairly strict rule. In this case, perhaps because Biddy was the sister of a brother officer, permission was granted.

Did he marry too young? Roscoe says, 'No, I don't think so. It was a good marriage right through until we grew apart in the war. What's more, it did produce two wonderful children, Jeremy and Jennifer.'

Throughout his life in peace, in war, on a horse, in a tank and just in the course of everyday living, people have always marvelled at Roscoe's particular unique brand of courage. It seems probable that he inherited it from his grandmother, Granny Harvey as she was known, who died when he was about eighteen. He describes her as 'tough as old boots and a tremendous character. She had ten children, eight sons, several of whom commanded Highland Regiments, and two daughters, one of whom married Ferrier-Ker, who was my guardian after my mother's death.

'Granny Harvey was out in Borneo, in Sarawak at the time of the Boxer Rebellion. Things got pretty tense and people got the wind up so badly that they despatched all the women off to a little refuge in the hills. When the news got worse and the women became over-excited and hysterical, Granny Harvey took charge. She formed them all up and gave them orders. "I want to tell you," she said, "that if a hundred Chinamen come up this hill, a hundred Chinese heads will roll down the hill!"

'She was a wonderful woman. I got to know her well when I was about eight years old and she came to live in London. She ruled everybody with a rod of iron but everybody loved her. She was terribly nice to her grandchildren but not so nice to her own children. She absolutely growled at them, but to me she would say, "Come on, my little boy," and, quite out of character, spoilt me – to the amazement of the rest of the family.'

During this period, Roscoe's two racehorses, Snow Crest and Tiger, were trained by Dick Payne. He was the brother of Bill Payne who trained successfully first near Epsom and later at Seven Barrows, Lambourn, and uncle of young Bill, an unlucky loser of the Grand National on Great Span at the age of seventeen and destined to serve with distinction in the Yorkshire Dragoons through the Western Desert and Italy campaigns.

Snow Crest was a useful mare who had won the Ayrshire Handicap and run well over hurdles before Roscoe bought her. Tiger was a real bargain. Roscoe found the horse in the Berkeley country with one of his farmer friends, John Lewis, whose son had already won on him. This particularly nice animal had won a couple

44

of point-to-points. The farmer was asking an enormous price until Tiger cut himself very badly. 'I took a chance,' says Roscoe. 'I bought the horse from him for just £100 on condition that he was sound by Christmas. He was sound all right. I won ten point-to-points on him and two races at Sandown Park, on successive days. When I went abroad I sold him to Herbert Blagrave, who wanted to win the Foxhunters Chase over the Grand National course at Liverpool. He asked me if Tiger could manage that. I told him, "There is one thing that I will guarantee and that is that he jumps the course. He might not quite get the trip." I was absolutely right. Tiger jumped Aintree beautifully but couldn't quite last out and finished third. Herbert gave me £400 for him, which was big money in the twenties.' Herbert Blagrave, a man of considerable substance who owned most of the town of Reading, was to become a tremendous sportsman and had considerable success as owner/breeder/trainer of high-quality horses.

Almost immediately after Roscoe had bought Snow Crest, he brought off a small coup with her in a hurdle race at Leicester, in which Colin Davy shared. As he was riding her himself, he kept the secret of her ability well and she started at 5-1. The result was never in doubt and the new owner got nearly the whole of her purchase price back in bets. Although she sometimes fell, 'the Old Girl', as they called her, gave Roscoe and his friend Colin an enormous amount of fun and got some nice touches for them in the next few years.

Roscoe says, 'In the ordinary course of events, I would have ridden my mare in all her races but, in the National Hunt Chase at Cheltenham that spring, I had a crashing fall on someone else's horse at the fence behind the stands. It was just about the worst fall I ever had and I ended up in Sister Agnes' Home with such severe concussion that, for a time, she said she even feared for my sanity! I don't remember much about it but Colin said that, while we were waiting for a stretcher, he was digging the glass of my broken spectacles from between my upper eyelids and my skull. I was still sufficiently *compos mentis* to mutter, "You'll ride the Old Girl for me till I'm better, won't you, Colin?"'

The King Edward VII Hospital for Officers, much patronized by the Royal Family, was presided over by Sister Agnes for many years and has therefore always been known as Sister Agnes' Home. For Roscoe, Colin and many other soldier riders over the years, it became a fairly habitual lodging place.

Colin's first ride on Snow Crest was in the Grand Military Gold Cup at Sandown, the race which Roscoe has always wanted to win and, although it was only her second run over fences, she started joint favourite. 'Colin was a very good jockey,' Roscoe says, 'a lovely horseman with beautiful hands. He had plenty of guts. I was always a little surprised that he didn't go right to the top. Perhaps if he had a fault, he was a little weak and that may have prevented him from getting more good rides. On this occasion he had not ridden a winner for some time and he blamed himself for not laying up when the mare fell at the open ditch in front of the stands. However, when he came straight up to London for a conference by my bedside that evening, he was able to assure me that the Old Girl was perfectly all right after her fall. So we decided to run her the next day in the handicap chase. I was damned if I was going to lose her maiden allowance for the paltry prize money of £200 and so I asked Colin to put £50 each way on her for me.'

There was of course no wireless communication with Sandown and you can imagine Roscoe's state of mind as he lay in his hospital bed, biting his nails in frustrated agony. 'When I eventually received a telegram saying, "Mare fell. No bet," I nearly had an apoplectic fit. What the hell had Colin been up to? I was so upset that my temperature rocketed up and I was put back into a dark room for the next three days!

'When Colin arrived at Sister Agnes' that evening, he explained. Dick Payne had two runners in the same race and there was a hitch in the saddling of Snow Crest, so that she was late coming into the paddock. In the flurry of mounting and getting out onto the course after the others who were already halfway down to the start, Colin forgot all about asking Dick to put my bet on. He only remembered when he was cantering down and, realizing that the price was 100-8 against my mare, he didn't know what the hell he was going to do. He was in such a terrible state of indecision that the feeling must have communicated itself to Snow Crest who met the pay-gate fence all wrong, turned over and solved his problem herself!'

Recovering, but still not well enough to leave his hospital bed, Roscoe plotted to recoup. He would put Snow Crest back to hurdles and have a good bet. He chose a race at Hawthorn Hill, the now sadly defunct happy little jumping course near Ascot. On this occasion, all went according to plan. Colin rode an excellent race and duly won. The bookmakers paid up at a good price. As soon as he was out of hospital, Roscoe was back in the saddle again, riding everywhere as often as possible with increasing success. In fact it was now Colin who was paying the more frequent visits to Sister Agnes's.

After their marriage, Roscoe's wife Biddy used to come to watch him ride but daughter Jenny says, 'My mother never really liked the racing and in any case she was soon busy having first my brother Jeremy and then me.'

47

Jenny was not born in 1928 when her father achieved one of his ambitions, a good ride in the Grand National. The horse was a top-class hunter-chaser called Commonside.

We can gain some idea of the standard which Roscoe reached and the respect which his riding had inspired in the steeplechasing world from the fact that the horse's owner in the world's greatest steeplechase was none other than the top horsemaster of the day, Brigadier Geoffrey Brooke, DSO, MC, author of several outstanding books including the first volume of the Lonsdale Library, *Horsemanship – The way of a man with horse*. He had watched Roscoe's progress from Weedon days and it was a great honour to be chosen by him at the age of twenty-seven to ride his horse in the National.

The Grand National in those days was run on a Friday with the Foxhunters Chase over the same course and distance on the Saturday. As was his wont, Roscoe got to Aintree early, walked the course and was once again surprised to find how those big fences seemed to be slanted at different angles across the course, and yet he knew that he would meet them absolutely right. And they were really big fences – much bigger than they are today – upright and tough with no sloping or bushing out on the take-off side.

There was a record field of forty-two runners which was condemned as dangerous. People were alarmed that in the cavalry charge for the first fence one faller could bring down others, endangering both horse and jockeys. The favourite was Easter Hero, trained by Jack Anthony, who was destined to win two Cheltenham Gold Cups with the horse, in 1929 and 1930. In the summer of 1927 the Irish-bred horse by My Prince had been bought by Frank Barbour, a rich, eccentric, extremely shrewd linen-thread manufacturer who had owned and trained the previous year's Gold Cup winner Koko. Easter Hero won eight chases during the 1927/28 season, including the Molyneux and Becher Chases over the Grand National fences at Liverpool, but it was not until the last of these eight victories in the prestigious three-and-a-half mile Coventry Chase at Kempton, where he won with 12 stone 7 pounds, that the pundits really sat up and took notice. Hitherto their admiration had been qualified. It was an age when the top steeplechasers were big, burly powerhouses with enormous quarters like Commonside and most of the other fancied Grand National runners and, although today we have become used to all-quality chasers like Mandarin, one contemporary writer thought that Easter Hero was 'Full of quality but rather lacking in substance,' and another scribe wondered 'where he finds all his power for jumping and endurance'.

However, by winning the Coventry Chase and proving that he could stay a long distance in top-class company, the chestnut had become a star overnight and was to preserve this status for the rest of his brilliant, sensation-strewn career. Briefly, he won twelve more races, including the two Cheltenham Gold Cups, and was an extremely gallant second in the 1929 Grand National under 12 stone 7 pounds, despite being handicapped by a grotesquely twisted plate over the last mile.

He might well have won the Gold Cup also in 1928, but before the Cheltenham Festival that year he was bought for £7,000 with an extra £3,000 contingency should he win the Grand National, for which race his new owner wanted him to be trained to the exclusion of the Gold Cup. The man who paid what was then this astronomical price for a steeplechaser was the Belgian millionaire financier Captain Lowenstein, called 'Low' by his friends at Melton Mowbray. He kept a yard of magnificent horses in the nearby village of Thorpe Satchville and gave investment advice on the hunting field!

As well as Commonside with Roscoe aboard, the 1928 Grand National field included Great Span, ridden by seventeen-year-old Bill Payne, nephew of Roscoe's trainer Dick.

When they jumped off, contrary to expectations, the jockeys galloped at a sensible pace so that, as they came away from the first, not one horse or jockey was down. The relief of the huge crowd was premature. Disasters were to come so that for the second time in the history of the race, only one horse was to get round without mishap.

Easter Hero led the field on the long stretch towards Becher's, which he jumped like the other obstacles, almost effortlessly. Roscoe was lying well up with the leaders, enjoying a splendid ride on Commonside. Easter Hero jumped the fence after Becher's with spectacular ease, looking what he was declared to be, the best steeplechaser in the world. As he approached the Canal Turn fence which was then an open ditch, he gave no hint of what was to come. He seemed to swerve, to think about refusal. Some eye-witnesses swore that he slipped. But the sequence of events was so swift that those gathered near the fence could not be sure of what happened, or why, or exactly when. The favourite crashed on top of the fence and straddled it, apparently stuck, baulking those behind and putting more than twenty, including Commonside, out of the race. Not until Popham Down caused similar trouble in 1967 was there to be another melee like it.

Two fences from home there were only three horses left. Young Bill Payne's mount Great Span was battling it out with the first-class American challenger Billy

Barton, trained by Aubrey Hastings and ridden by Tommy Cullinan. Great Span looked to be going the better but his saddle slipped, to add to the other disasters of the race, dumping Payne and leaving Billy Barton clear. The Americans began to cheer as their horse approached the last, accompanied by the riderless Great Span. The only challenger was Tipperary Tim and few had noticed him in the parade or had even found his name on the racecard. Billy Barton must have won if he had stood up. But fate yet again took a hand and he came down at the last, worried by the loose horse. The rank outsider, Tipperary Tim, escaped interference, got over and then kept plodding on to win the only race of his life. Cullinan remounted Billy Barton to finish second, but no horse was placed third behind the 100-1 outsider.

As their horse had only galloped a mile, Geoffrey Brooke and Roscoe decided to run Commonside again the next day in the Foxhunters Chase, over the identical course and distance. There was no revelry for Roscoe that night. This was serious business and it looked to be justified. 'I was ten lengths in front,' he says, 'at the Canal Turn second time round. My horse was jumping superbly but I had a loose horse with me. I had been trying to fight him off but when we jumped the Canal Turn ditch, my horse was brought down. I remounted but they had gone on about 150 yards. Nevertheless, I was only beaten twenty lengths by the winner.'

All through those halcyon days in the twenties, apart from occasional visits to Sister Agnes's, Roscoe, in addition to point-to-pointing and riding under both rules (there were many more 'bumper' races on the Flat in those days), playing polo and foxhunting, preferably with his beloved Berkeley, had been soldiering with typical enthusiasm and going racing on the Flat

51

whenever the opportunity presented itself. By his twenty-eighth birthday in July 1928, he and Colin were fully involved in racing, well-known members of the tight little racing world, knowing everybody and known by all in that close circle. They were very popular and made many good friends in every branch of the racing industry. Not for the first time this was shortly to stand them in good stead.

The previous year Colin Davy, now a Major, while Roscoe had been promoted to Captain, had re-published the *Tenth Hussars Gazette* as editor. It is significant to note that the first issue made reference to the increased interest in mechanisation. Roscoe already had his little bull-nosed Morris, but the 10th Hussars on their official strength had fourteen motor lorries, three motorcycles and three motorcycle-combinations. Nevertheless, the days of complete mechanisation still seemed distant.

Lieutenant Colonel VJ Greenwood assumed command in 1928 and, as a valedictory feat, the Regiment won two small polo tournaments – shades of greater things to come – before departing for Egypt. Another sign of the times was perhaps that a subaltern, Ronnie King, flew back from leave to Cairo in a Gipsy Moth before the Regiment was later posted to India.

Chapter Four

The Land Of The Pyramids

Taking a whole Regiment of soldiers and horses out to Egypt was a formidable exercise, but in those days it was well organized. The 10th found themselves quartered in great luxury in Abbassia barracks and even the greatest sybarite among them had to admit that they were 'suitably housed'. The mess was excellent and so were the officers' bedrooms. Roscoe says, 'There were any number of baths and scores of Suffragis ready and willing to cheat us of as much money as they could. There was also a charming garden. The only accommodation that was not up to the standard we expected was the stabling. Officers' stabling was non-existent; and as Colin and I had determined to run a joint racing-stable, we set to work at once to build it for ourselves. Of course the stabling for the troop horses which we had brought out from England was good enough. There they were on lines and so on. But Colin and I needed decent stabling for our racehorses. We were determined to make a go of it.

'Colin told me that, when he first went to Egypt, with the 20th Hussars in 1919, he had been terribly disappointed to find that the accommodation was no good. Now, with the whole of the 10th Hussars installed in barracks at Abbassia, he was delighted with the change.'

Fortunately both Roscoe and Colin had plenty of money during 1928, thanks partly to a good stayer called Arctic Star which belonged to their old friend Sir Matthew 'Scatters' Wilson. With typical modesty Roscoe says, 'Not only was I clever enough to back him for the Cesarewitch, but I also brought off the Autumn Double with Palais Royal II in the Cambridgeshire.'

Knowing that they were shortly off to Egypt with the Regiment, the two friends had gone racing as much as possible. I remember that year so well. I was eight years old and, as my birthday is on July 29, my parents had established a new little family tradition by taking me to Goodwood for my birthday treat. It was my second visit, therefore, to that glorious course perched high on the Sussex Downs. It is important to remember that, until after the Second World War, we only raced at Ascot and Goodwood once a year, four days at each. For the rest of the twelve months, those wonderful tracks were unused. Royal Ascot, of course, came at the height of the London season and Goodwood at the very end, a holiday meeting, just before Cowes and then the exodus to the grouse moors of Scotland in mid-August.

If Goodwood cannot lay claim to be regarded as the most ancient of racecourses, it is certainly one of the finest in the world. In some respects, such as the texture of its fine old turf and its lovely scenic surroundings, it is incomparable. Every year, as we drive to the course through the park, we can pause to admire the old-world home of the Dukes of Richmond. The third Duke established racing here on a more extensive scale than had been previously known. On some parts of the original track, the races are run to this day. The building of a wooden race-stand in 1801 was regarded as something of an occasion. A notice appeared in the *Sporting Magazine*, that 'the new racecourse on the Harroway, near Goodwood, the seat of His Grace, the Duke of Richmond, is now completely formed for sport and much admired by the acknowledged amateurs of the Turf.' In the local journal of the time the Duke was praised for having 'munificently and liberally instituted an establishment of most material local benefit from every point of view.'

I personally shall never forget the scene at Goodwood in 1928. We climbed up that long hill and came to a racecourse which was completely dedicated to the sport. Where the 'chalets' are now, there were club tents – White's, Cavalry Club, etc. It was a wonderful scene. The Jockey Club nobles dressed in their holiday regalia, panama hat with School or Regimental colours on the ribbon, smart blazer, MCC or Regimental tie, white or pale trousers and co-respondent shoes. It was a gay, happy, gambling scene. Have I really been on the racecourse for sixty years? Roscoe has been on it for eighty!

1928 had been a funny year in the racing world. It was a fabulous vintage year for champagne but not for racehorses. The Derby was won by a 33-1 shot, Felstead, trained at unfashionable Lambourn by Ossie Bell. It was the year when Brown Jack, then a four-year-old, won the Champion Hurdle and, with 7 stone 13 pounds, took the Ascot Stakes on the course where he was next year to initiate his fabulous run of six successive Queen Alexandra Stakes, which earned him a permanent memorial on the Royal Heath.

Less well known of course, and unrecorded in any reference books, this was the year too when Roscoe Harvey and Colin Davy backed Arctic Star in the Goodwood Stakes.

Roscoe explains: 'If we were going to back him for

the Goodwood Stakes, we obviously ought to back the horse for the Cesarewitch first. After all, if he won at Goodwood, his price for the big race would shorten immediately.'

So together they went to see their old friend, bookmaker Ted Heathorn, to ask Arctic Star's price for the Newmarket race. He laid them 33-1.

'We had a really good bet and then hurried off to find 'Scatters' Wilson. When we told him we had just backed his horse for the Cesarewitch and what a good price we had been given, he came with us at once to Heathorn and backed it himself for a very considerable sum. Arctic Star duly won the Goodwood Stakes and his price for Cesarewitch came down with a rush. By October, however, when the horse ran in the big Newmarket handicap, we were in the middle of the Mediterranean.

'All afternoon we had pestered the wireless operator on our troopship and he had asked all passing vessels if by any chance they knew the winner of the Cesarewitch. Most of them were completely baffled by the question, having no idea to what he was referring. I believe that one Italian steamer, hearing the name Cesarewitch, answered that all the Russian royal family had been dead for years!

'In the end – it was just as we were getting up from dinner – the operator came running into the saloon, waving a piece of paper to tell us that Arctic Star had won. Although we had passed the coffee stage and were well into the port, we a'l sat down again and ordered champagne!'

Arctic Star, trained by Vic Tabor and ridden by a youthful Charlie Smirke, won the Goodwood Stakes at 13-2. Although Roscoe, Colin and 'Scatters' Wilson got 33-1 antepost for the Cesarewitch, he was returned at 9-1 when he scored at Newmarket with Dick Perryman in the saddle. What a coup!

Mention of Smirke invariably makes Roscoe chuckle. 'Charlie is a good golfer,' he says, 'and since his retirement, he has spent a lot of time on the golf course. I like the story of a day not so long ago when, in a foursome against the pro and somebody else, Charlie was partnered by a certain Major X. They started off with a fair bet – £5 corners or something like that – and halfway round Smirke took his partner on one side. "Have you been doing your best, Major?" he muttered out of the corner of his mouth. The Major was suitably indignant. "What an appalling suggestion!" he exploded. "Of course I have!" 'Charlie was quite unmoved! "Well, I haven't. Let's double the stakes." They did and they won!'

Egypt between the wars was a delightful place for peacetime soldiering. Most of the year the weather has always been what millionaires pay enormous sums to find; even in the summer the heat is not unbearable. Every Regimental officer automatically received three months leave every year and England was only four days journey away. There was excellent polo, cheap racing, good tennis, golf, swimming and, although Roscoe was not interested, shooting. Colin Davy was a good shot and made the most of it.

In addition, there was a very considerable social whirl in Cairo during the winter and – unlike in India – they were not everlastingly dining and wining in the same small circle. Apart from all the interesting and amusing British and foreign residents, there was always new blood arriving in the form of visitors from England and America. Cairo was very amusing indeed and the residents very hospitable. Says Roscoe, 'I would be sorry to have to count up the number of mornings when I changed straight from my dress clothes into my uniform without going to bed at all!'

Racing took place at Heliopolis and Gezira in the

winter and at Alexandria in the summer. There was a three-months break in the autumn so that the horses could have a rest and the trainers could go to Europe in search of fresh blood.

On an ordinary day's card, there were about two races for English thoroughbreds, one for countrybreds, the combination of Arabs and European thorough-breds, and the remainder were confined to Arabs. The Arabs were divided into four classes – beginners, third class, second and first class. Beginners ran weight for age. When they had won, they entered the third class, also at weight for age. When they had won twice in the third, they were put into the second class and hand-icapped. The handicapper then decided when a horse had won sufficient races in the second class to be pro-moted to the first. There were a few amateur riders' races and most of them for Arab horses. But the offi-cials and trainers told Colin and Roscoe that as soon as the officers in the different Regiments began to collect horses and show that they were keen to ride them, these races would be increased.

Much later I myself discovered the disadvantages of riding Arab horses. They are so short in front and have such little necks that there is nothing to 'scrub' and you always feel that you are falling over the handlebars!

Colin and Roscoe immediately began to look around for horses and canvassed the other two Cavalry regi-ments to do the same. It was obvious that they would have to confine their purchases to Arabs, because they had not got the wealth of people like Mrs Chester Beatty and others who brought English thoroughbreds out to Egypt to run each season.

Roscoe says, 'It was fairly obvious as soon as we arrived that racing in Egypt was going to be cheap. There were none of those grizzly financial problems that faced an owner in England. There were no travelling expenses. You could walk your horse from the stables to both Heliopolis and Gezira. The horses themselves were inexpensive. You could buy a decent sort of beginner off the desert for about £50 and a fair second-class handicapper for between £100 and £150. The stakes were good. The winner of a beginners race got £60, of a third class race £80, and a second-class race £100. The place money was much better than in England. Second money in a second-class race was £30. The entry fee was only one per cent of the value of the race. We kept a rough account which showed that wages, forage and shoeing worked out at about £6 a month per horse. That meant that a horse had only to run second in a second-class race to pay for his feed and keep!

'The first horse we bought was our best. He was a grey Arab entire horse about seven years old called Bareed. We paid £130 for him and he looked awful. His coat was staring, his teeth were in a terrible state and his feet turned up at the toes. Yet, even in that state he had run consistently well in second-class handicaps and we both decided that even though he would need time, we would be thoroughly ashamed of ourselves if we could not improve him at least a stone.

'We were a little worried that our new purchase might have been doped because there was a fair bit of doping going on in Egypt at that time. However, luck was on our side and Bareed began to pick up well. Of course, as a fully horsed Cavalry Regiment, we had the call on expert professionals in the shape of our Regimental vet and his team of farriers. So we physicked the little grey horse and the farrier Sergeant did excellent work on his teeth and feet. Before long he was a different animal, putting on condition daily and full of the joys of spring.'

The next addition to the string came from an

unexpected source. The racecourses were always crawling with Egyptian racing spivs or touts, on the look out for 'baksheesh' in the form of information or a back-hander. Sidling up to the two soldier-trainers in their little stable, he insisted that he knew of a really good young horse which had been given by a desert sheikh to an Egyptian army officer, who was terrified of the animal and would be only to willing to sell. 'He told us he could get it for us really cheap – £100, provided we gave him a nice commission,' says Roscoe. 'I told him that if he halved the figure, we might think about giving him something for his pains. Then came a surprise bonus. We could have the horse on trial for a fortnight! This meant that we could try a maiden beginner against a proven old handicapper. If the new horse, Deban, as he was called, could go with Bareed, he should be a good thing in any beginner's race and we ought to be able to manage a really good touch.

'A few days later, at first light, when there was not a soul about on the racecourse, we staged this trial, riding the two horses ourselves. Sure enough, we discovered that Deban could lay up with Bareed for five furlongs. Not a word to anyone, even our brother officers in the mess. Dreams of untold riches! That evening we did our horse-coping act, struck a hard bargain and bought the new horse, whose owner had no idea whether he could gallop or not, for £65, including the spiv's commission!

'We bought the third member of our string, Goha, for £100 after he had won a seven-furlong selling race. He was snow-white and looked in appalling condition, with all his ribs showing, rather like the pictures of "the High-Mettled Racer" or "Uncle Tom Cobleigh's old grey mare". It was amazing that he could raise a gallop at all!

'Two other horses, belonging to friends, one called Safwan made up a total of five.'

The big trainers like Ferguson and Marsden, who

trained for the King of Egypt, were most helpful and so were the senior professional jockeys like Barnes, Gibson and Lister, who would often ride work for Roscoe and Colin. In addition, Roscoe was playing quite a bit of polo and was developing into a very passable Number One.

They had another stroke of luck and once again had reason to thank their many contacts in the racing world at home when the famous Ogbourne trainer, Marty Hartigan, with whom Sir Gordon Richards had served his apprenticeship, came to Egypt for his winter holiday, visited the Regiment and was able to give our young trainers some priceless advice. He informed them of the dangers of galloping on sand, a very tricky surface which takes much more out of an animal than you think. A sharp canter on sand is the equivalent of a good three-part speed on grass. Horses are apt to get soured off and spoil their actions. Marty told Roscoe and Colin, 'I should gallop on the sand as seldom as possible. Let them do only their slow work, trotting and hack-cantering, on the desert. After all, since it only costs £1 to run, you can give your horses their fast work in races every weekend on grass. In addition, you'll have the fun and experience of riding them yourselves.'

So that was exactly what they did. They ran and rode them, themselves, in every amateur race and, in other races, put up one of the good professionals. This had a two-fold effect. First, the horses were not seen and reported on the gallops by the touts and secondly, they were given one fast gallop a week on grass and in colours. Just before Christmas they brought off their first coup – with Bareed in a seven-furlong selling race at Gezira. Barnes was engaged to wear Roscoe's white, brown sleeves and cap, and the friends engineered a decent bet. The outsider of all, untipped by any paper, Bareed, after appearing to have absolutely no chance, came from behind under strong pressure and got up on the line to win by a head. Roscoe, hoarse from shouting his charge home and looking almost exactly the same as he does today nearly sixty years later, was photographed after the race with Colin and their first big Egyptian winner. The trainer 'Fergie' Ferguson was delighted. He sent them a copy of this picture for Christmas with, scrawled across the bottom, 'One of the old sort. 22-1, and not a pal on!'

The next planned coup with Deban just failed. He was unlucky enough to run up against the best beginner in the country, owned by the King of Egypt, and was narrowly beaten. However, he won a fortnight later and then old Goha, still looking like a woebegone hatrack, justified their confidence by winning a seven-furlong selling race easily at the wonderful price of 10-1!

It didn't seem to matter what distance they ran over. On the last day of the season Bareed, who had won that seven-furlong race earlier, carried Roscoe into second place in a two-mile amateur race. Although the press and the professionals were still not taking them seriously, the little venture had already been a great success. Three of their horses had won and their owners had made themselves a tidy sum of money while deriving the maximum enjoyment out of it all.

That summer, Colin went on leave to England and Biddy, with two little children and a Scottish nanny, joined Roscoe in Egypt. Roscoe says, 'My wife and I decided to go on a grand trip in my open Lancia car to Costanza on the Black Sea, right across Europe. We sent the two children and their nanny off to Cyprus and set off. When we landed up in Vienna, I went to the famous Spanish riding school with their superbly trained Lipizzaners and rode there for a fortnight. Their first reaction was, "He rides too short – like a monkey!"

'So they made me let my stirrups right down and ride like a policeman. I got the horse doing a Spanish trot and a few other of the simpler tricks, but I never got round to doing things like Levade, Pirouette, or Grande Passage, etc. They told me, "You must come back for two years, then you will be able to ride properly!" It was all rather fun.

'I had brought with me some jodhpurs and some polo breeches and boots. When they told me that I had permission for a fortnight's riding in the famous school, they said, "What are you going to wear?" I told them jodhpurs. "Jodhpurs?" They didn't understand that. "You must have breeches and boots to ride in the School of Vienna." So I put on my polo breeches and boots. I used to leave the Bristol Hotel and walk to the school in white breeches and polo boots!

'It was a wonderful trip. Budapest, Bucharest, Vienna, they were all marvellous in those days. We ended up at Brioni, where I played polo. It was a nice place with a very good hotel and a golf course.

'Mind you, we were frightfully lucky. I had brought two spare tyres with me. We had already used one of them and, when we were right up in the lonely hills of Yugoslavia, miles from anywhere, the other tyre went. It could have been very tricky. You never saw any other traffic up there but our luck was obviously in. Before we had been waiting for more than a few minutes, a bus came along. They helped me to mend the tyre. Then they saw my golf clubs in the open Lancia and asked, "What is that?" I got out a golf ball and teed it up on the ground. Then, thank God, I hit it properly and it soared away. They had never seen a golf club or ball before. "Very good! Very good!" they applauded. They were delighted.'

The holiday was over and Roscoe and Biddy returned to the Land of the Pyramids to be reunited with their little children, with the Regiment and with the racehorses, which had now been augmented by a very classy, young grey Arab entire colt called Safwan, which belonged to Hermione Howard Vyse, the wife of their Brigadier.

The social round was as happy as ever with those wonderful hotels, Shepheard's and the Continental in Cairo, Mena House by the Pyramids and the Cecil in Alexandria doing thriving business.

For Captain C.B. Harvey, enthusiastically enjoying every minute of his life as ever, it was back to the polo ground and, in particular, to the racecourse.

This time the horses were fit for the start of the season and, although Deban had turned sour, he was still a useful lead horse. He played an essential part in the strategy of amateur races. 'We had a lot of fun in this way,' says Roscoe. 'Supposing that Colin was riding Bareed. We took it in turns. I would set off to make the running, flat out on Deban, and get myself a place on the rails. As we reached the final turn, Colin on Bareed would be closing up behind. Deban, at this stage, would naturally be fading and the fancied horses in the race would be coming up on his outside. I would take a quick look back over my shoulder to see where Colin was and then, for some strange reason, it often happened that Deban would go a bit wide, carrying out the horses who were lying up with him. The other riders were screaming abuse at me, and Colin would slip old Bareed through into the place on the fence that I had just left, and there he was in the most perfect position, at exactly the right stage of the race. My steering must have been bad! The ploy worked well. After finishing second in the first two amateur races of the season, we won the third one at Gezira.

'Then, after Christmas, Colin and I decided that we would bring off another little coup. Goha, who had the reputation of being unable to get more than seven furlongs, had shown us that he was a really good stayer. One morning we got up again at first light when there were no touts about and galloped him a mile and a half with Bareed and Safwan. What's more, we had the ungenuine but speedy Deban jumping in at the six-furlong mark to bring them along to the end and make sure that it was a really good gallop. Goha, dear old ribby grey, had gone every bit as well as the other two.

'There was a selling race at Gezira over a mile and five furlongs which might just have been designed for him. Colin and I entered both of the Arabs, Bareed and Goha, for the race. It was a professional contest and so we engaged Barnes for Bareed and Gibson for Goha. By now, it seemed that the touts and the press reporters were taking a little more interest in our stable and the night before the race, in Shepheard's Bar, I was approached by a French racing journalist who asked me which of our two we were going to run. I told him that both would run.

'Next day, in his racing selections, he made Bareed his nap for the day and, on his own authority, informed the avidly curious, greedy public that Goha had been left in the race to make the running. His fault, not ours!'

Colin, with plenty of people standing around in the paddock, gave Barnes his orders. 'You must ride a waiting race,' he said. 'Lay well behind on old Bareed, sit into him and don't move until you're well into the straight for home. Then get at him. Have a real go and get as close as you can. I think you'll win. Don't worry about Goha. Don't pay any attention to him. He's there to make sure it's a good race. He'll go dashing off in front because he has been pulling like the devil on the gallops lately. I wouldn't wonder if he doesn't run away with old Gibson.'

'Me, I just said quietly to Gibson, "Make every post a winning post", and put him up in the saddle without any further talk!

'As planned, Goha jumped off in front and, before half a mile had been covered, he and Gibson had a lead of about twenty lengths. Barnes on Bareed stayed behind and the other jockeys, seeing that he, one of the champions, made no attempt to go after the leader, stayed with him. Passing the stands, we could actually hear the jockeys laughing. Barnes had said, "Fancy Gibbo bein' run away with by an officer's horse!" It was a good joke.

'After a mile Goha was twenty lengths in front. Every now and again we had seen this situation happen in England. Some of the other jockeys were a bit anxious but, even so, the danger was obviously our second string Bareed and Barnes and Bareed seemed quite happy to be in the position they were.

'Half a mile out, they all began to chase after Goha and the gap between them and him obviously began to get smaller. But Gibson on Goha was only sitting up against him, allowing him to enjoy his race and giving him a breather. As soon as he heard them closing up behind him, he just said to the old grey hat-rack, "Away we go!" and Goha, having the time of his life, came into the straight leading by ten lengths and won in a canter. As so often happens, the others gave up the unequal struggle. It was a real coup!

'The next morning, I telephoned Colin to ask if he had seen the morning papers. Nearly all the papers in those days were published in English. One carried a banner headline saying, "WHEN WILL THIS FARCE CEASE?" It seemed that the gentlemen of the sporting press were taking us seriously at last!'

Roscoe looks back on those days with nostalgic happiness. 'All the good luck followed,' he says. 'We won another professional race with Goha, Bareed won two good amateur races and on the last day of the season Safwan trotted up for Colin.

'We finished up our little Egyptian expedition with a splendid profit in stakes alone – let alone the money I had won in bets!'

Chapter Five

India

The troop ship which left for Bombay, carrying the 10th Hussars to their new station at Meerut, contained Captain C.B. Harvey, his wife Biddy, their two children, Jeremy and Jenny with their Scottish nanny and entourage. That entourage was considerably increased when the family moved into one of the attractive, white-washed bungalows at Meerut, with its thatched roof and garden full of flowers. In the days of the British Raj, both officers and soldiers in a crack cavalry Regiment were wonderfully looked after. Roscoe says, 'While I was in India I actually had no fewer than forty servants. Of course I had my usual first and second soldier servants, the one looking after me and the other after my horses. But then there were boys or "wallahs" for everything. The nanny not only had nursery maids but a nursery boy! The cook had to have an assistant. The gardener had to have two assistants. The dhobi wallah, who did the laundry, had to have assistants. I had a sort of major-domo butler chap, who commanded a team of houseboys. Then there were umpteen maids of different kinds. As for the horses, I had five polo ponies and each one had its own syce. Forty servants to look after one small family. It was a

68

wonderful life! I think I enjoyed my six years in India more than any others of my life.'

As this wonderful enthusiast says that about nearly every period of his long life, we can just assume that India with all the wonderful opportunities for sport was tremendous fun. He says, 'Perhaps the hot weather was a bit oppressive for some. Colin Davy hated it, but then he got prickly heat. When it was very hot, some of the families went up into the hills of Kashmir. I went there twice, but I never really minded the heat.'

For much of the time, the weather was perfect and there was plenty to occupy everyone. Roscoe was Adjutant and Equitation Officer for most of the time that he was in India. For the last two years he was promoted to Major and had a squadron.

Lieutenant Colonel 'Chatty' Greenwood, who had brought the Regiment from Egypt, retired shortly after to be replaced by Lieutenant Colonel Willoughby Norrie, a keen and capable racing enthusiast.

Since in my own Regiment, the Royal Scots Greys, we had all grey horses and therefore had to take them with us wherever we went, I never realised that other cavalry Regiments would simply leave their horses behind for their replacements and, when they moved into a station, would take over the horses of the Regiment which had just left. In this case, the 10th took over the horses of the 4th Hussars. In Meerut, they unexpectedly found an old 10th Hussar already there. The horse, known as 'Old Timer', had first joined the 10th in 1908. Left with the 21st Lancers in 1912, he had served in action and been wounded on the North West Frontier, subsequently proving a fine showjumper and winning many prizes. On the arrival of his old Regiment he appeared to recognize the Regimental call, but by this time he was retired and allowed to roam at will around the barracks, being a great pet of all. He finally died two years later aged 34, still with the 10th.

Roscoe says, 'Such soldiering as we did was a real pleasure. The mornings were spent in Squadron and Regimental training, followed by stables, and there was polo, tennis, golf, shooting, racing and every other form of recreation to fill in the afternoon. Of course, as Adjutant, I had to spend a certain amount of time in the Orderly Room, but I was always heavily involved in the Riding School. We had equine and human recruits to train. Rough remounts used to come over from Australia, and some of them were very rough! We had every possible facility, a magnificent indoor school and a wonderful outdoor riding school area containing every form of obstacle. Every Saturday morning we would leave the soldiers in a "jolly", galloping around the area over all those fences. It was tremendous fun.

'Thanks to the horde of followers and syces who cleaned the saddlery and equipment and did all the menial services and fatigues, there was no such thing as "one man to four horses".

'You never saw a man who had "joined the Army to see the world" spending all his time with a dung barrow and shovel. As far as the rank and file were concerned, they led a gentleman's life. The tea-sellers brought them their early morning tea to their bedside; hordes of little Indian boys sat on the verandas cleaning their buttons and equipment; syces and sweepers sped to do their bidding; and they went to the pictures in the evenings in tongas like swells.

'We, the officers, did everything we could contrive to make their surroundings more in keeping with their position as masters of men. The days were past when Trooper Brown turned over his plate and ate his pudding off the reverse side. He had table-cloths, plenty of crockery and glasses, and native waiters to serve him. Each Squadron had its sitting-room carpeted and curtained, and equipped with ping-pong, card tables and a gramophone. The barrack rooms were decorated and gardens laid out on every square foot of land which was in reach of water. Unlike some people who suddenly find servants at their beck and call and themselves surrounded by a higher standard of luxury, the British soldier remained a modest and kindly gentleman. The standard of turn-out and their pride in the Regiment was almost fantastic. There was hardly a man in the 10th who did not buy himself a blue undress uniform out of his own pocket and I don't believe there was a member of the Sergeants' mess who did not own a dinner coat. Even in the hot weather they wore them walking-out and to the pictures in the evening!

'The polo was the best in the world. On those hard grounds, and with no boards to slow up the game, it seemed about fifteen miles an hour faster than in England. When we arrived we were a very poor side with a total handicap of four. We worked so hard at it that, after a comparatively short time, we were a twenty-five goal handicap team. We won the Inter-Regimental Cup twice, the first British Cavalry Regiment to do it since the war, and when we returned to England we won it there. We were competing a double which had never been done before – India and England – and of course, can never be done again.

'Our team consisted of Charlie Gairdner, David Dawnay, Mike McMullen and myself. Charlie Gairdner's handicap went up to eight. He should have been ten but he had been wounded in the leg in the First War. He was a splendid man, standing six foot one, a two-handicap golfer who had played hockey for Ireland. I played Number One and even my handicap went up to five. I may not have been very good at hitting the ball, but I was fairly good at marking and riding-off the opposing back. In our first Inter-Regimental final, against an Indian Regiment, they had one

71

very good player, a chap called Denning, who played back. I was told, "You have got to take Denning out of this game." I did take him out. He got more and more angry. He said, "You're like a bloody mosquito. If you don't leave me alone . . .!" I never left him for a second. I hadn't a great eye but I could do this all right and everyone was roaring with laughter!

'One day Charlie Gairdner sent the ball up to me and I missed an easy shot at goal. He was furious. David Dawnay was the peacemaker. He told me, "Don't get angry, Roscoe. There'll be another chance."

'How right he was. Next time the ball came up it was a frightfully difficult shot but I hit it absolutely dead right and it went straight through the goal: I turned round to Charlie Gairdner and said in a loud voice, "Did that one go a bit better?"'

These were the days of the Maharajahs. They lived in the greatest conceivable luxury and entertained in the most lavish and generous manner. Roscoe was lucky enough to enjoy not only their hospitality, but also their company. Their loss is India's loss. The majority of them were very fine men, wonderful landlords and tremendous leaders. Some like Jodhpore and Jaipur, whom I too was lucky enough to know and admired tremendously, were among the finest polo players the world has ever seen. Roscoe says, 'The grounds were absolutely true – beautiful and very fast. The Indian teams were top-class and Jaipur, in particular, led by the late Maharajah, were magnificent, with a team handicap of thirty-three goals. Possibly our greatest triumph was in a match against the full Jaipur side. The Maharajah "Jai", invited our Regimental team for a fortnight to play polo. The Jaipur team suggested that we had an eight-chukker match on handicap. They were thirty-three goals and we were twenty-five. So we had the whole handicap of eight goals. As we were

72

playing eight chukkers it was rather hard on our polo ponies. Anyway, after a tremendous game we beat them by two goals. The Jaipur side were very upset, not at being beaten, but because they thought that our handicap was either too low or theirs was too high! They said, "It's all wrong. How did you beat us?" It was their full side and this really was a bit of a triumph for us. Each member of our team was given a lovely silver cigarette box with the Jaipur arms on it.'

On another occasion the late Winston Guest, the American international polo-playing brother of Raymond, who won the Derby with Larkspur and Sir Ivor as well as the Grand National with L'Escargot, came out to India for the tiger-shooting, a sport which Roscoe did not like.

'I was asked to go down to Calcutta to play polo. It was a mixed side called The Gladiators, including Ginger Anderson who was about eight handicap, Claude Pert, the Number Two – about seven handicap, and myself. The trouble was that for the final against Jaipur they invited Winston Guest to play and Winston, as was his wont, started to shout. He went on shouting. We were tied six all in the last chukker and the final throw-in was vital. I can see it now. I was Number One. As the ball was about to be thrown in, we all rushed forward. The umpire shouted, "Get back! Turn round!" I wish I hadn't followed his instructions. We did turn our ponies round, whereupon the umpire threw the ball straight onto the stick of the Jaipur Number One, Prithi Singh a super player, who picked it up and away he went straight down the ground to score a goal. Old Anderson was furious. So we were defeated. I don't think the umpire, Mahboob Kushra Jung, did it on purpose but he just lost his bloody head!

'We worked so hard at our polo, constantly practising on the field or on the wooden horse, and took the game so seriously that they stopped me riding steeplechasing in case I should hurt myself.'

Roscoe's rough-rider groom in charge of his polo ponies was a very fine ambidextrous nagsman who could play his polo right or left handed and thus was invaluable for schooling ponies. He was a good horseman and a good servant. In one particular match Roscoe had wanted to try out a young pony. 'But it turned out a much closer run affair than we had expected. We were a goal down and I obviously needed an experienced pony. So, when this chap brought out the young pony, I said, "Christ, you bloody fool!"

'When I got back in the evening my bearer said, "Sahib, there is your stud groom to see you." I wondered what for. In he came and said, "I go back to my village. Sahib called me a bloody fool." I wondered how I was going to get out of this one. So I turned to my bearer and said, "How many times a day do I call you a bloody fool?" He answered, "About fourteen times a day." Everyone laughed and the stud groom stayed!'

Roscoe was tremendously fit. As well as playing and practising polo, he rode with Sergeant (later Sergeant Major) Fraser McMasters, who had come from the Royal Scots Greys and was a pillar of strength in Colonel Joe Dudgeon's famous Irish riding school. Roscoe's other activities in India, which he pursued with his usual tremendous enthusiasm, were race-riding and pig-sticking.

On the racing front there were the big meetings where the standard was high and the prize money good. The discipline was tight and they were comparatively straight. The Gymkhana Meetings were exactly the opposite. They were very necessary from the financial point of view and Roscoe said there was certainly not a racecourse 'up-country' in India which could pay its way without the Gymkhana Meetings, which took place weekly or fortnightly and which were patronised in their thousands by the Indians. Thumbing through a 1932 issue of *The Tenth Royal Hussars Gazette*, I came across a fascinating anonymous piece describing these events and Roscoe's participation, which might perhaps have come from the pen of the *Gazette*'s editor, Major Colin Davy.

'Every station in India has a Gymkhana Club and in the old days the race meetings of the Gymkhana were purely amateur affairs when polo ponies and hacks ridden by their owners competed for small prizes. In the small stations the Gymkhana races remain the same to-day; but in Lahore, Lucknow and Meerut the Gymkhana season is a more serious affair. When the Lahore season ended this year there arrived in Meerut some 150 horses and ponies most of whose owners are Indians and race for profit and not for sport. When the Meerut season ends these strings will move on to Lucknow for another joust with fortune. Some there will be left on the wayside as tonga ponies since their owners have been "warned off", or have failed to meet their financial obligations.

'In order to draw the line between "Gymkhana Racing" and "Open Racing" it is decreed that the winning stake be limited to ninety-nine rupees. Anyone who has any experience of racing and the cost of training racehorses exclaims at once: "How can they race for profit with a winning stake of only seven pounds? It is well nigh impossible to show a balance chasing in England for stake of seventy, eighty and a hundred pounds."

'The answer is that it is not possible – without betting. Forage is cheap, travelling expenses are reduced to a minimum, syces' wages are low, but a horse would have to win two races each month before he could balance his budget on stakes alone. For those

75

who like statistics: there are upwards of 180 horses in training in Meerut and about 45 races per month. So it would seem that about 160 horses will be left by the wayside at the season's end. But thanks to the elastic consciences of their owners, the wherewithal will be found somehow to move the majority to Lucknow at the end of the season.

'The whole matter can then be summed up by the fact that in Gymkhana racing nowadays "the bet's the thing". Without betting the sport as it is today would die a sudden death. And so when one leaves one's bed at three pm on a June afternoon to attend the races, one must leave behind one's principles (along with one's collar tie and jacket) and attend in the spirit of a grandmother visiting the Folies Bergere or Major Walker attending a supper party given by Al Capone – expecting to be shocked but hoping to get some fun out of it.

'Ninety-nine per cent of those who attend the races are Indians and the remaining one per cent are British, acting as officials who give their services gladly despite the grilling heat – Colonels and magistrates in the stewards box, Officers and gentlemen at the starting gate and at the scales. But all the members and officials of the English Jockey Club working together could not cleanse this Augean stable so long as only "ninety-nine" chips repose at the winning-post and horses continue to eat.

'"Old Taylor", 40 years in the "Shiny" and never been sick ("I always eat onions for me breakfast, Sir") has urged the last horse from the saddling boxes (and incidentally forestalled a syce from administering a bucket of water to one of them) and twelve equine specimens have reached the paddock. Now there are ten, for the stewards have ordered the removal of a colt which is lame and a mare that is obviously in foal.

76

Captain Harvey is riding one at the request of the owner since the stewards have become restless as regards the eccentricity of its recent performances. Major Davy delighted to find he can "do".9-3 has reluctantly agreed to ride a mare that the boys are frightened of. He seems apprehensive and is sweating profusely. Three English professional jockeys and five Indian riding boys prepare to mount the remainder. The race is a four-furlong affair and after a short parade they are gone to the start.

'By the bookmakers' stand – there are six bookmakers – the crowd stand waiting. They make no move, there is no "picking one's fancy". They wait and watch the trainers and the trainers' friends. On form Lovesick is a certainty. She won hard held by twelve lengths last time out – a novice would rush in and take the seemingly liberal odds of two to one which is inscribed opposite her name, but today may not be the day. (If we know the trainer it certainly won't be today.) Suddenly there is a rush forward. By a prearranged signal six individuals have advanced each to a selected bookmaker. The crowd follow. They are backing Lovesick. The bookmakers have shortened the odds to even money. But where the novices may follow suit, the experienced punter hangs back. This is probably a blind. If J . . . was really betting, Lovesick would have no quotation by now. It is certainly a blind and the bookmakers know it too. Lovesick returns to two to one and drifts out to three to one and fours. Lovesick is a dead'un.

'From another corner there comes another rush. The expert punter follows this. They are backing Hopeful Annie. Hopeful Annie has not been placed this year but they have backed her "off the books". The expert punter succeeds in getting three hundred rupees to one hundred at odds on.

77

'Meanwhile the starter has called over the names. His assistants SSM Willis and Corporal Bradshaw have taken up their positions, the former behind with a hunting whip, the latter in front with the recall flag.

'Captain Harvey and Major Davy and two of the English jockeys seem desirous and capable of beating the gate but the remainder, though they wail "No, Sir, not yet, Sir", "Just a minute, Sir", in broken English and Urdu, make no attempt to approach the barrier. They are either incapable or unwilling to gain any advantage over their fellows. But as they cavort and caper before the Sergeant Major's whip, a small breathless native appears by the rails and shouts some unintelligible sentence to one of the Indian jockeys. This man suddenly becomes more proficient and an eager light dawns in his eyes. He is riding Hopeful Annie. In the paddock he was told to "let the mare run her own race" but the messenger has brought a counter order. "Crack-her-out, the guv'ners-going-for-a-packet-and-you're-on-to-a-hiding-if-you-don't-win."

'A furlong from the winning post Hopeful Annie is out with a two lengths lead and the spectators are shouting her home joyfully. Major Davy is kicking his boots off to maintain third place – the remaining jockeys are watching "the good thing materialise". But Captain Harvey has been playing polo all the winter and is driving his animal with more determination than she has known in all her life. He is feeling for his whip too, and if he hits as hard as he kicks, she had better do something about it.

'The Indian jockey hears him coming, panics thinking of the hiding, draws his whip, lets his horse swerve across the course and is beaten by a head.

'The good thing has come unstuck. Of course the owner may object, although the horses were never within five yards of each other but Captain Harvey is a

78

steward . . . Better wait for another day . . . After all, if the bookmakers don't win sometimes, they would leave Meerut and there would be no more racing.

'Lovesick finished last, tailed off, but Major Digby is marshalling jockey, owner, and trainer before the stewards room. There is an expression of pained bewilderment on their faces.'

Roscoe says, 'I learnt one hell of a lot from those Gymkhana Meetings. It was to stand me in good stead for the rest of my life. But the cheating was amazing of course. They did the most dastardly things. It was not at all uncommon for an owner or bookmaker to be caught sending a small boy on a bicycle to give the jockey orders "Not today" because someone has stolen his market. Once a horse was seen to be walking rather feelingly. We took the bandages off and found them filled with stones and pieces of scrap-iron. On another occasion a jockey who had orders not to win won despite his efforts to pull the horse. He galloped straight on after passing the winning-post and rode straight to the bazaar, where he let his mount loose. Of course he was disqualified for not weighing in. He was obviously more frightened of what his owner might do to him than anything the stewards might inflict.

'The stewards, handicapper and other officials worked like beavers to try to keep the game a little straighter, and since at Meerut the Gymkhana season lasted right through the hot weather, they fully earned their reward of free drinks in the stewards' room. But it was a hopeless task. If you warned off a native owner for life, they only handed their horses over to a brother or brother-in-law or uncle and continued their scoundrelly machinations from behind the scenes. The native riding boys too ran the risk of a frightful beating if they didn't do exactly what their employers told them. After all, they were only trying to scrape up a living, and I am sure there was no word in Hindustani for "fair play". If there was they would not have understood it.

'When Colin and I were stewards in Lucknow we tried to introduce a rule that when a horse's running became scandalously inconsistent, the horse itself was warned off. This punished the owner, trainer and rider in just proportion. The owner had to keep his horse without running him, or sell him cheap; the trainer lost his training fee and had one less horse to punt on; and the rider had one less riding fee. The best part of that plan was that if one could not actually detect the scoundrel, one put the blame on the horse itself, and only it could complain about the injustice of the stewards!

'Nevertheless Gymkhana racing was tremendous fun, and riding, say, four flat races in an afternoon when the thermometer stood at over a hundred in the shade had a remarkable effect on weight and fitness.'

Here, for those not familiar with the racing scene in India, it is necessary to point out that the meetings where the good English jockeys spent their winters were at Bombay and Calcutta. But these were like the big Paris tracks in France. Horses were frequently imported from England, and racing was of a very high standard.

Nevertheless, the 'up-country' courses which correspond to the French provincial ones were very good. Roscoe says, 'Lucknow and Meerut had excellent racecourses and I was second – perhaps unlucky not to win – in the Indian Grand National at Lahore. Stakes were good. There were seldom less than 1,000 rupees (£75) as the Winner's share and there were races of 2,000, 3,000 and even 5,000 rupees. The Grand National was worth 7,000. Now when you consider that the average horse running 'up-country' was not worth

80

more than £150 to £200, this made racing a paying proposition. There were usually two steeplechases and two hurdle-races at each meeting. There were a few horses which had been brought out from England, especially for hunting, but the majority of runners were horses which had run on the flat, had lost their speed, or become sour. The stakes for jumping were very good. Much better than the class of horse attempting to negotiate English-style fences warranted!

At this stage Roscoe met one of the most amusing characters of his life. Indeed, Tommy Thompson, a Yorkshireman who served his apprenticeship at Newmarket, was a real character. A great gambler, a wonderful loser, and a fine stableman with a tremendous sense of humour who had forgotten more about racing than most of us will ever know, he had a wonderful fund of anecdotes. He was a bit of a rogue and everyone loved him. Roscoe says, 'In the first year, before the Regiment stopped me riding over obstacles because of the polo, Tommy Thompson asked me to ride an animal which he said was a good jumper, but he did not think it would win because it was not quite straight in condition. I was determined to do as well as I could to make an impression during my first year in India and, as we came to the last fence but one, I was upsides with another horse which jumped a bit better. At the last it was mine which jumped better and we had a desperate struggle up the straight. Suddenly the other jockey came veering across and pushed me into the rails. One of the stewards, Brigadier Miles Thompson, later a member of the Royal Household, came into the weighing room and said to me, "I suppose you will object. You are bound to win," whereupon Tommy exclaimed, "Oh, no objection, Brigadier. The right one won." It was then that I realized that he had trained both horses!'

81

Tommy Thompson was a tremendous admirer of Roscoe. And I think that there is no doubt that this admiration was justified. Roscoe was certainly one of the finest amateur riders of his or any other time. What's more, he was a genuine amateur too. 'Plenty of people offered me money for riding winners,' he says, 'but I can honestly say that I never took a penny. I have always felt very strongly about this.'

His great friend Colin Davy paid him this tribute: 'Roscoe, being a star polo player, was not allowed to risk his precious bones over fences, but he had the most remarkable success in all his races on the flat. A very strong horseman and always as fit as a prize-fighter, in a race he was possessed with an almost bloody-minded determination to win. What was more, he was able to use a whip as no amateur that I have ever seen could use one. He was terrific in a finish, and managed to impart his own desperate determination to his horse, however much the latter wanted to shirk and funk. Whenever it was a case of heads and necks, it was Roscoe's mount who poked his in front. They had no choice with Roscoe. It was the same as with Gordon Richards or Carslake in a finish; they just *had* to win.'

One of the oldest sayings in racing is 'Keep yourself in the best class and your horses in the worst.' In the Gymkhana races, where the horses were graded, the trainers would naturally try to obey the second precept, particularly when horses were rarely of a higher class. Roscoe says, 'One day, a chap asked me to ride a horse for him because he was in a higher class than he should be. He said that he ought to be in the fourth class and not the third. I agreed to ride and, when the owner was talking to the clerk of the course and the handicapper, he said "I have got Captain Harvey riding this horse for me, so you will know that it is doing its best and it will be able to prove that it is in too high a class."

'So I went down to the start of this six-furlong race, jumped off and before we had gone very far everything was getting very quiet. I realized that I was at least five lengths in front. We remained there and won on the bridle in a canter. The trainer came running up and said, "There you are. Those black boys riding for me have just hooked them up. They were quite right to keep him in the third class after all. He is quite a decent little horse." Of course he had had a really good bet at a good price on a horse which in fact should have been in the first or second class! I had quite a few punts. I loved it! It was a great education! We had a well-known bookmaker up there who used to come round to my bungalow and either pay me, or I paid him. A few days after this race he came round and said, "You did me a very bad turn, Captain, winning that race the other day. They took more money out of me than had been taken out of me the whole bloody meeting!" It wasn't a bad little racket, was it really?

'Then another day Tommy Thompson, for whom I had ridden a winner the week before, came round to the bungalow. I gave him a drink, and eventually said, "What the hell do you want, Tommy?" "It's like this," he said, "I'm going bad, real bad. You know that little horse you rode for me last Saturday. Well, he is better than the mare, isn't he?" I said, "Of course. He is sure to beat her any time."

'Tommy said thoughtfully, "I suppose he would. But, if you rode the horse again on Saturday, and I ran them both in the same race, I could let it be known that I was backing you and the stableboys and everyone else would follow suit. Then I could have a really good bet on the mare and make an awful lot of money."

'"What you are really asking me to do is to pull the bloody thing", I said.

'He said, "If you put it like that, I suppose I am."

"'I'm very sorry," I replied, "but I am not going to do it, not even for you, Tommy. I never have, and I am not going to start now at my age."

'Tommy said resignedly, "I didn't think you would, Captain, but it was worth trying. And you won't ride for me on Saturday!"'

After two years the 10th moved to Lucknow, which was every bit as good a station if not better than Meerut where they were relieved by the Royals (Royal Dragoons). This was great for Roscoe and Colin because, with that Regiment, came another great friend, Babe Moseley, a fine strong forceful amateur rider who had enjoyed considerable success and, when Colin was badly injured from a last-fence fall in the Indian National, rode their mare Offence to a splendid victory in an important chase. Babe, who was later to do much to organize the Badminton three-day event, became a life-long friend.

So to the pig-sticking. Roscoe says, 'Which is my favourite sport, race-riding, polo- pig-sticking or fox-hunting? I have never wavered in my answer. Hunting is definitely the winner, the pig-sticking a good second.'

From time immemorial the wild boar has been a coveted prize for hunters. Even in the legend of Venus and Adonis, the handsome young man was killed by one of these brave, fierce, bad-tempered creatures, clearly the most dangerous animal known to the ancient world. There are plenty of known instances of a big boar, standing, say, 36 inches high and weighing no less than 300 lbs, killing a leopard or a tiger. He has a vicious bite, and those curved, razor-sharp tusks, which Roscoe has today as a mascot on his car, can easily disembowel a horse or a man.

In olden times the pig was hunted with hounds and speared on foot. The sport of pig-sticking or hog-hunting appears to date from the nineteenth century. It entails galloping flat out over rough country, which is apt to suit the boar better than your horse, in competition with two or three other hog-hunters. Your great ambition should be to kill your pig with one spear. This, however, is very rare because you are galloping after a jinking or charging animal at high speed and the target, just behind the shoulder, is small. In the Kadir Cup, the Blue Riband of pig-sticking, it is not the man who kills the pig who wins, but the one who can show first blood on his spear.

With its rough terrain, the broad river valley in the Kadir country resembled a sea of high grass, looking more like a snipe bog than hunting country. But it was no bog. The ground underfoot was as hard as iron, uneven and covered in tussocks. Usually you could not see more than two yards in front of you. Moreover the pig-sticker knew that the ground contained many hidden dangers, such as nullahs, native wells, small precipices and deep fissures in the ground. To the novice the prospect of galloping *ventre-à-terre* over this country is terrifying indeed.

The boar, not the man, chooses the ground where hunting takes place. He is a wily animal and knowing that the horse is more handicapped by rough going than he is but that on smooth ground the horse has the legs of him, he will take good care to select a line where the ground is as rough and the cover as thick as he can find. And over this blind, bad and even treacherous going, the horse will have to follow and carry his rider safely.

As an outstanding horseman and horsemaster, Roscoe trained his pig-sticking mounts well. 'I used troop horses from the Regiment,' he says. 'Remember that quite a number of them were Australian walers and, if I had done my job well, as Equitation Officer, the horses of the 10th Hussars were well-trained in the first place. It is important to leave your horse's head alone when riding over bad going. You need a strong enough seat, a good enough balance to be certain of being able to do this under all conditions of pace and ground, and to be able to use your legs properly to guide and control your horse. I found that it was best to lose contact altogether, throw your rein at him and use your legs to guide him rather than risk interfering with his mouth. If well trained, in answer to the leg he would follow the pig without much guidance from the reins, although he would have to be steadied and kept in hand when the pig began to come back to you.

'Riding in ordinary heats with brother officers, in which there was no rivalry, was tremendous sport. We combined together and took the pig on in turns, no-one caring who got first spear as long as we accounted for him in the end. One hunt with Colin Davy and a keen pig-sticking doctor nearly ended in disaster. We had all speared, but the doctor had fallen and I was left with the pig pinned, but not very securely pinned. "Quick, Colin!" I shouted. "Come and finish him or he will wriggle off!"

'Colin jumped from his horse and with his spear at the advance like a pikeman of olden days, rushed towards the boar. The ground was hard and slippery and as he lunged, his feet slipped from under him and he fell flat on his face on top of the pig! Luckily I was able to hold the animal off till Colin got on his feet again and we accounted for the boar. Otherwise Major Davy might have met an untimely end!'

Chapter Six

True Tenth Style

The Tent Clubs in India organised the main competitions. The Tent Club was to pig-sticking what the Hunt Club in England is to fox-hunting. It was managed by an Honorary Secretary, who corresponded to the MFH in an English hunting country, and in his hands were all the arrangements for providing shikaris (hunting guides), preserving the country, arranging meets and attending to finance and the collecting of subscriptions. In the field the Secretary's word was law. He arranged the composition of the heats, where each heat was to go and decided, in consultation with the shikaris, on how the country was to be beaten.

His first duty after arranging the beats, was to decide on the number and composition of each party of spears or 'heats'. As a rule a heat was composed of three spears, although it might sometimes consist of four and sometimes only of two. One spear was detailed in each heat to take charge of it. The Secretary gave each heat its instructions and told them whether they were to move along with the line of beaters, or whether they were to stand near some particular point and watch for a boar breaking cover. If the latter, he usually pointed out zones to each heat in which any pig that appeared

87

belonged by rights to them, and left the details of taking up their positions to the spears themselves. When a boar went away, the spear who was in charge of the heat gave the signal to ride, when he thought that the right moment had arrived, and the whole heat started together in pursuit. On the other hand, if the heat moved along with the line, it would spread out so as to divide up its own part of the line equally among its members. If a boar got up, the nearest spear at once started after it and the rest of his heat joined as soon as possible.

The rules and etiquette of hog-hunting were practically the same everywhere. No spear might be delivered on the near side (they were generally in-effective and dangerous to other riders and horses). No bumping or boring or riding off was allowed and no one might cross or interfere with the man who was on the line of the pig or cut in front of him, if by doing so he caused him to check his pace to avoid a collision. What this amounted to in practice was that the man on the line of the pig must be left alone and not interfered with as long as he was close up to the pig.

Everyone made as little noise as possible when moving along with the line or waiting outside covert, but, when a member of a heat started after a boar, it was his duty to shout at once and go on shouting as long as he was on the line of the boar, so as to help and guide the rest of his heat. If the boar jigged and another spear took up the running, it became his duty to shout as long as he was on the line. 'On, on!' the man on the line would keep shouting. To this day, Mrs Diana Spicer, whose father, when in the 15th Hussars in 1906, won the coveted Kadir Cup, always calls Roscoe 'On, on'!

The first spear to draw blood entitled the rider who delivered it to the boar's tushes. Today, when so many members of the horse world have car mascots of horses or hounds, Roscoe's proud car mascot of a boar's tushes is very distinctive.

To compete on the top level in this thrilling, dangerous sport, you had to know it well. The first spear to draw blood would be fined by the Secretary if a sow were speared in mistake for a boar, or if the boar turned out not to be up to standard height and weight. When riding with the line, you had to keep your eyes skinned for any sign of a pig on the move. If you could be the first of your heat to get onto the boar, you would begin the hunt as hot favourite and your horse would go much more freely and kindly through thick grass if it could see the boar in front and use him as a pilot. It would not be nearly so easy or pleasant for the other members of your heat, who had to push along through the same sort of covert on your right and left with nothing to lead them, and you enjoyed your hunt twice as much if you were cutting out the work. 'On, on!'

When you had picked up a boar and were fairly on his line, you had to press him hard. When he began to come back to you, you had to steady up and collect your horse so as not to override the pig and be ready for the jink that was almost certain to come. Now was the time when the pig was at its most dangerous. As it got slower, more tired and blown, it might well turn and charge. It was always important to go as fast as you could when spearing or meeting a charge. If you were going fast, it was long odds against the pig being able to get in and cut your horse, even if you missed him.

Roscoe says, 'The Kadir was the Blue Riband of pig-sticking. It was a highly competitive, individual contest. All the pig-stickers congregated from all over India. The competition was organised by the most prestigious pig-sticking organisation in India, the Meerut Tent Club.'

He paints a picture of a life we will never see again.

'On the day before a big hunt, you would go out and have the tents put up. You would go out in the morning, just as it was getting light, when it was still cool. I shall always remember all those birds down by the Ganges river, where the Kadir Cup was held. You finished at about twelve o'clock, midday, as it got too damned hot then. You slept all afternoon, if you could, in your tent, or sat in the bar. Bearers used to come up, bringing the ice. In the evening, later on, you probably went out shooting quail or sand grouse.

'The night before the competition started, the draw took place and heats of four were drawn and given numbers. Most competitors entered two horses and the average number of entries was about 130.

'The most memorable, spectacular feature of the Kadir Cup was the elephants, who were kindly lent by the Rajahs, the rich landowners, for spectators, competitors and officials in the Kadir Cup. If you went out in the grey twilight or the mist of dawn on the great day, you would get quite a shock as you suddenly met them moving in from about forty miles away. An unforgettable sight of huge, black shapes moving slowly, but steadily. Their attendants, the mahouts, would be sitting on top of them and the little baby elephants would come trotting along with their mums, seeming quite happy.

'On the great day about thirty elephants would form a line about three-quarters of a mile wide. They just had pads on them, apart from one or two for the officials, which had howdahs. About three-quarters of a mile in front of the elephants was a line of beaters. They were not paid much money, but they quite enjoyed it. Behind the elephants came the horses, the ones which were waiting to go out on the next lot. Between the beaters and the elephants were the four heats, about four people in each, who were on the line

90

for any pig that came up. The beaters were beating away from us and, when a pig got up, we would gallop between them.

'As the lines started to move, I always felt the same feeling as going to the first draw at the Opening Meet.

'The beaters would spot the pig sitting down like a hare and shriek *"Swer,* Sahib! *Swer*, Sahib!"

'You always had an umpire in the Kadir Cup for each heat. They were experienced pig-stickers, who were specially selected. I used to umpire quite a bit. All four in the heat would gallop towards the pig, more or less in line, and, as umpire, you would shout, "Have you seen that pig?"

'One fellow out of sight would say, "No, I haven't. No, sir, no!"

'"Can you see him now?"

'"Yes!"

'You would drop your flag and away they went.

'The Muttra Cup was a team event, which the 10th won several times. The winner was the team which killed the greater number of pigs. The Kadir Cup was something different. The winner of each heat was the one who stuck the pig first. You didn't have to kill it, just show the umpire the blood on your spear. You had to be first to show blood in the Kadir.

'I actually did get first blood in the final of the Kadir Cup in 1934, but, after going down the pig's side, my spear stuck in the ground and was wrenched from my hand, so Douglas Gray was able to move in and show first blood to the umpire.

'The most we ever had in the Kadir Cup was 142. 130 was the normal number. We had a knockout competition and at the end of the first day, there would be thirty competitors left. They went in the next day and probably had only ten heats. Then there was the semi-final, followed by the final. The semi-final may have

91

been two heats or three. The final was usually only two or three competitors. I ought to have won that Kadir Cup, but once you had dropped your spear, that was that. I was just unlucky really.

'At times when hunting the pig, you would just see the grass moving – grass three to four feet high. You might not actually see the pig. Then there were the open bits when you went as fast as your horse could gallop. The pigs slowed a bit. After that, the bigger ones would turn and have a go at you, charge you. No wild beast would take on a pig. A tiger would not take on a pig and the elephants were frightened to death of them. A funny thing, but on this line of elephants in the Kadir Cup, sometimes the pig broke back through the beaters and through the line of elephants. When it did that, the elephants would trumpet like mad. I don't know whether it was the smell of the pig or just sheer fright of this heavy, fierce animal. The Kadir Cup would take place in March and it was staged, as I said, on the banks of the Ganges. When the Ganges flooded over in winter, the pig went somewhere else.'

Lieutenant-Colonel Gray, later Director of the National Stud at Newmarket, was an officer in the famous Indian Cavalry Regiment, Skinner's Horse. He wrote to me from his home near Basingstoke in Hampshire. 'At 76 I am a generation younger than Roscoe, but I was a pre-war regular soldier and competed against and with him in several fields – steeplechasing, polo and pig-sticking. I would like to offer you a few personal reminiscences about Roscoe, who is certainly the most complete all-round horseman that I have ever known.

'In 1932 Skinner's Horse and his Regiment, the 10th Royal Hussars, were stationed together in Lucknow. The 10th had come on from Egypt and arrived in India with a lot of young officers. Roscoe was one of the few middle-piece ones and he, with the great Charles Gairdner, also Mark Roddick, set the pace and the tone for their many successes in the horse world of India.

'Led by the dashing Willoughby Norris, they just about "farmed" all the competitions and in the van in everything was Roscoe.

'He was unusal in that he was a very light weight, so was able to ride many winners on the flat as well as over fences and, at the same time, he was their Number One in the polo team, playing off a five handicap – in an era when the Indian Cavalry and the Maharajahs, as well as other British Cavalry teams, were tremendous competitors in all the tournaments.

'As a spear, out pig-sticking, Roscoe was really brilliant, aided, of course, by his light weight. He rode very fast horses across country on a loose rein and he seldom had a fall because he really did leave it all to his mount, finding a 'fifth leg' when the country was blind or treacherous.

'The remarkable thing about him was that his eyesight then, as now, was bad and he rode in thick glasses taped behind his head.'

Roscoe was still riding in and winning a lot of races. On one particular occasion he was booked to ride a high-class horse from Calcutta in a big Flat event. 'The owner had a good bet,' he says. 'This was something quite different from the usual run of rides in India. I didn't just win. I won by twenty lengths on the bridle. After the race the owner came up to me with an enormous handful of notes. God knows how much money there was there. He was absolutely flabbergasted when I refused to take it. I told him that I had never taken money in my life and was not going to start now. When he asked me what I would like as a present I told him that the only thing I really wanted was a good whip because I had lost mine. So, astonished, he bought the best whip obtainable with a silver band from Swayne and Adeney.'

A great friend was Babe Moseley, then a Captain in the Royals. Babe was a very good, extremely popular jockey. Colin and Roscoe had a very useful hurdling mare called Offence and, when Colin was laid up, after a crucifying fall in the Indian Grand National, Babe rode a tremendous race to win a good prize and land a decent bet for Colin and Roscoe on the mare. Babe had some difficulty with his weight, which was later to increase considerably. There is a picture of him being led in, overflowing on both sides of the tiny lightweight saddle and looking awful from wasting, but nevertheless he won.

In 1932 Trooper Roger Willetts, an outstanding horseman, joined the 10th in India. At the start of his career this splendid man was not with Roscoe. He says, 'I was in A Squadron – the best squadron in the Regiment but the Brig was commanding B Squadron at the time. I teamed up with the polo team as one of the remount riders. I was polo groom to Major Mike McMullen and of course the Brig was in the polo team all the time. We won six cups out of seven. We beat the 12th Lancers in the final and I don't think they ever got over it!'

Later he was to leave the Regiment for a while and return on the Reserve when war began. War and peace he has been with Roscoe now for thirty-seven years.

In other sports such as football, cricket, boxing, swimming and rugby, the 10th remained in the forefront. Regular concerts and entertainments were also arranged in which the band provided some outstanding performers, amongst whom was Bandsman Norman Wisdom, later to become the famous comedian, who ran seventh in the Inter-Regimental cross-country race in Lucknow.

In 1935 Lieutenant Colonel 'Bobo' Hutchinson took

over command of the Regiment. When their Colonel-in-Chief King George V died early in the following year, the 10th had already learnt of their forthcoming return to England and imminent mechanisation. They gained a final farewell victory Inter-Regimental polo cup before leaving India and their horses forever.

Owing to the Colonel being ill, Colin Davy commanded the Regiment during the last Divisional exercise. It was the last time that the 10th ever turned out at full strength as a mounted unit. As luck would have it, the commander of their force employed the whole Regiment in a mounted attack on a grand scale on the last afternoon. Their task was to make a big encircling movement and attack the supposed enemy's supporting troops and lines of communication front their left rear. They had a great ride – 'far better than many hunts I have ridden in,' says Roscoe – and the Regiment covered itself with glory.

At the beginning of this exercise they had heard of the King's death and two days later, even before the last troops of the Regiment had reached barracks, they were asked to provide a Guard of Honour for the Proclamation Ceremony in Lucknow of King Edward VIII's succession to the throne.

The horses were as yet ungroomed and the men still dirty and dusty from four days in the open. Somehow Sunday-best uniforms were got from the dhobi (laundry man) and best boots polished. A rehearsal in slacks and shirt sleeves was staged on the football ground and at four that afternoon the Guard of Honour was on parade.

Colin showed Roscoe a private letter to him from the District Commander General Milward which said, 'I want to express my appreciation to your Regiment of their sterling work during the last three days. On manoeuvres every officer and man down to the youngest worked with tremendous keenness and efficiency. Today within an hour or two of your return from four consecutive nights bivouacking, you were called upon to furnish a Guard of Honour. The Guard turned out spotless and the whole ceremony went without a hitch in the true "Tenth style".'

Roscoe says, 'By this time we were used to what we called bouquets from generals, but the expression "true Tenth style" was as pretty a compliment as we could wish. What was more, we had the satisfaction of knowing it was true. Whatever job the Regiment was called upon to do, we did it thoroughly, and the pride the men and the NCOs took in putting on a good show was enormous. Whether it was the visit of an inspecting officer, a boxing tournament or a horse show, we rehearsed every detail over and over again until it was perfect. We never left anything to chance.'

'As Equitation Officer I had to make sure that the horse which a visiting general would ride was completely bombproof, to use the modern expression. It was no unusual thing therefore to see a trooper on a charger at Lucknow Railway Station, sitting hour by hour while trains whistled, coolies ran and shrieked and taxis blared all around'him. When anyone asked him what he was doing, he would grin and say "I'm General Chetwode this afternoon, sir. This is the horse he is going to ride when he visits us next week!"'

That summer the Colonel went on leave to make arrangements for the Regiment's arrival in England and Colin was left to look after it during its last half of the hot weather and bring it home in October.

Roscoe says, 'We had considerable trouble now trying to disentangle soldiers from various matrimonial affairs. The half-caste women of Lucknow considered that there was no finer future for their daughters than marriage to an English soldier. They preferred a 10th

Hussar because they thought they were all officers! They were not all very scrupulous as regards their methods in this design. It was necessary for me and the other squadron leaders to harden our hearts and push our moral scruples to one side on many occasions. For, even though the soldier fancied the girl in question considerably, had obviously enjoyed the "fruits of love" for some time and was not averse to the idea of matrimony, the girls for the most part made very bad wives and the lot of a half-caste wife in married quarters in England at that time was not an enviable one.

'On one occasion, the soldier did not fancy marrying the girl but he was terrified of her mother, a big, fierce Eurasian weighing about twenty stone. She had threatened to beat him up if he did not marry her daughter at once.

'"But we sail in a week's time," I told him. "The best thing for you is not to leave barracks."

'He shook his head miserably. "Even then, sir, I wouldn't be safe. She says she'll come here and fetch me."

'"That's easy", said I. "You can go to prison. Seven days confined to barracks. The Provost Sergeant will protect you."

'He went off whistling happily to the guard room!'

'Then the day came for the final parade when the District Commander bade farewell to the 10th Hussars. Speaking of their coming mechanisation, he said that the horse was a very hard taskmaster but even so it brought out all the best qualities of manhood – including courage and patience. Now that they were about to deal only with machines, they would miss not only the bondage of the horse but the bond also. Colin, Roscoe and the others were moved by his words, appreciating so well the truth of them. The British public have shown that they also are aware that the horse brings out the best qualities of the human. Otherwise there would not be equitation schools springing up on every available plot of land and every father and mother who can afford it insisting on their children being taught to ride. They recognise that the horse is a hard taskmaster and riding a difficult and dangerous science. It's because they wish to see courage, patience, self control and sympathy for animals fostered in their children that they allow them to risk their precious bones. That, of course, and the fact that if little Mary next door starts riding, then Lucy must surely do so too.'

Roscoe, serious for once, added: 'The bond of the horse between officers, NCOs and men was the whole secret of why all cavalry regiments such as ours were such a happy family and why we were able to work together with that perfect combination which makes for efficiency. Standing in stables for an hour and a half every day, superintending the men grooming, watering and feeding their horses, discussing the problem of B25's prickly heat, B39's rubbed tail, B69's failure to put on flesh, the young officer got to know his men personally. So when B8 kicked Trooper Snooks in the most painful part of his anatomy and the soldier in a moment of blind passion kicked him back, the officer understood and sympathised. When at riding school he saw the same Trooper Snooks dropped three times and get up smiling, he would say to himself, "He may have a quick temper but by God he's got guts."

'It is the same from the NCO and the trooper's point of view. They saw their spotty-faced young Troop Officer play a really dashing game of polo or ride a very bad horse bravely into the last fence in a race and immediately readjusted their impressions of him. Thanks to the horse the officers were not dolled-up figureheads whom the trooper had to salute whatever his opinion of them. Nor were the soldiers just a troop of permanent nuisances, whose health and conduct was the bane of the officers' lives. They knew each other, respected each other and were friends.'

My own Regiment, the Greys, were still horsed for the first eighteen months of the war, so I was privileged to be able to appreciate the truth of Roscoe's words. In peacetime no tank or armoured car can ever establish the same bond as between men and horses but, in wartime, the enforced proximity and camaraderie of tank life proved an adequate substitute.

After winning the Inter-Regimental polo cup for the tenth and eleventh times, the 10th Hussars left their horses behind forever and sailed for home.

Roscoe says, 'We were going to Tidworth, but when the soldiers and their wives asked us what sort of station that was, we had not the heart to inform them that it boasted fewer shops and cinemas than Lucknow. For some time now soldiers had been recruited for the most part from the cities and ninety per cent of them knew little about country life and country sports.

'Their idea of heaven was a city of endless, brightly lit streets, crowded shop windows, cafés and cinemas, football matches and a comfortable "civvy" fireside where the parents of the girl they were walking out with would welcome them. Tidworth could not provide any of these delights in large quantities! Nevertheless we produced every sign of gaiety as, on a wet November morning, we sailed into Southampton. We had the band playing, the trumpets sounding fanfares and the largest regimental flag in history flying proudly. It was 1936. We all cheered like mad to be home.'

Chapter Seven

Back Home

November was a wonderful month for Roscoe to return home. It was the start of the hunting season. He immediately rented a house down in his beloved Berkeley country and set about buying first-class ponies for his children, Jenny and Jeremy. Before leaving England he had bred a splendid horse called Santick.

'As I knew I was going to be abroad for some time, I left him in the more than capable hands of my old friend Perry Harding in the Skins (the Inniskilling Dragoon Guards). Perry, small and immensely tough, is sadly no longer with us. He was not only one of the original "shamateurs" but also, arguably, the finest amateur rider of all time. Suffice to say that he was as good as any professional rider at the time and was the only amateur before the war ever to beat the pros in the Champion Hurdle at Cheltenham. In later years, although the Army considered him good enough to be a Brigadier, the English Turf authorities never made him a member of the Jockey Club or of the National Hunt Committee because, as a young man, he had ridden for money.

'Although he was frequently given a present in cash, he had a nice idea which helped to substantiate his amateur status. When he won a race and was asked by the grateful owner what he would like as a present, Perry would say, "Well, I have seen a gold cigarette case which I would very much like in the window of a famous jeweller in Bond Street. If you would like to give me that, I would be very pleased." Now Perry already had one of these cigarette cases. So when the owner went off to the famous jeweller to order the present, it would really be credited to the account of Captain Harding!

Roscoe adds, 'Perry was so strong that, whereas you and I have to screw out a champagne cork, he could pull it straight out with two fingers. I always told him, "No wonder you can pull them up so well."'

'Perry Harding,' says Roscoe, 'did very well with Santick – too well in fact. In a big race at Cheltenham he rode the race of his life on my horse to beat one of the great star pre-war chasers, Morse Code, ridden by Evan Williams. It was a tremendous feat but sadly it incurred a penalty of an extra stone for the Grand Military Gold Cup, for which he must have been a certainty. Unfortunately that weight just told the tale and we were beaten, the one race I really wanted to win. As it was he was third, with Perry riding.'

Roscoe won several more chases with Santick but unfortunately, the handicapper never forgave the horse for beating the mighty Morse Code.

As soon as the 10th had arrived home, Roscoe and his friend Tony Wingfield, went to a mechanisation course at Bovington. Tony writes: 'It was a driving and maintenance course. Roscoe and I found Peter Dollar of the 4th Hussars in our syndicate. I felt desperately sorry for the Tank Corps sergeant who was our instructor!' At the end of the course Roscoe's report read: 'This officer shows absolutely no aptitude for mechanisation whatsoever.' Soon after the Regiment's return to Tidworth, HRH the Duke of Gloucester was appointed their new Colonel-in-chief, a post which gave him immense pleasure as a true professional Shiner.

Roscoe says, 'I went straight back to the Berkeley country as soon as we returned from India. I took rather a nice little house down there near Thornbury and we had the stables of a big house that was empty. They were very, very good stables. I had two soldier grooms and we had six or seven horses and two kids' ponies. Both my children were riding very well now. For Jenny I bought a little bay show pony called The Nut, a little cracker who had won the 12 hands class at the International Horse Show, Olympia, the year before and still cost me only £100. She had tremendous fun with The Nut, not only in the show-ring but also in gymkhanas and in the hunting field.

'My son had a hell of a pony standing, about 14 hands, which would go over almost anything. It would creep down to the bottom of those big rhynes in the Berkeley country and then lunge forward and up on to the top again. We had two months' hunting leave a year and, as long as you were going to spend your time hunting or racing, an officer would get any long weekend off – probably from Thursday to Tuesday. The Earl of Berkeley was Master of the Berkeley at that time. When Charlie Fitzhardinge died, Lord Berkeley at last came into the property but he had to sell off a lot of it to pay death duties. The hunting was marvellous though, right up to the war.

'I don't know what it's like now, but of course there is the motorway running right through and also the Severn Bridge. They used to hunt miles beyond and on into the Beaufort country. It was wonderful hunting on the left of the Severn Bridge as it is now. We would gallop about four miles up, and on two or three

102

occasions hounds swam the Severn. There was a bridge further up in Gloucester and there was a ferry to take you across but we never hunted on the other side. One of our best coverts was Aust Cliffs. As you start across the Severn Bridge today and look left towards Bristol, there is a drop down to the foreshore which never failed to provide a fox. There used to be an awful lot of foxes, usually eating crabs and other bits of garbage on the shore. You could pick one up and then it was "tally ho" and back into the country again down the famous Berkeley Vale. It was wonderful scenting country but now sadly most of it is ploughed up.

'The hounds were a wonderful pack, all going back to that marvellous dog Berkeley Cromwell. We had a hell of a hound called Whipcord who had only half a tail because it had been bitten off by a rat. There were an awful lot of white hounds in the Berkeley – nearly all that white-lemon colour. Other packs used Berkeley hounds, although they never went to Peterborough, because they had a tremendous reputation for cry and agility.'

Of course Roscoe is talking of a world that has almost ceased to exist. Before 1914 the wealth of the fox-hunting fraternity, who were in the main the upper classes or the genuine landowning aristocracy, was phenomenal; but after four years of bitter conflict had brought the deaths of many true fox-hunting men, followed by a background of industrial unrest, the General Strike and the Depression, in many cases the wealth, although still there on the surface, was in danger of disappearing. This was not obvious to the regular soldiers like Roscoe who were able to work hard and play hard and enjoy what remained of those golden years.

This was the age of cocktails. Young people find it hard to believe that right up to the war the Flying

Scotsman, which left Kings Cross for Scotland sharp at ten o'clock every morning, carried a beautiful green and chromium bar with bar stools and a Ritz-type barman with black crinkly hair and spotless starched white coat standing in front of his drinks and his barman's diplomas, using his shaker and dispensing cocktails with superb skill. And on the alternative route which started at 11.15 and went up to Edinburgh via Leeds, there was in the 1930s a cinema coach? Neither was just for first-class passengers. How times have changed!

Most Sundays while the 10th were at Tidworth, Roscoe and Colin Davy used to go over to Ogbourne to drink White Ladies with that great trainer Martin Hartigan, with whom Sir Gordon Richards served his apprenticeship. Sir Gordon, that wonderful little man, was Champion Jockey no fewer than twenty-six times and rode more winners in a season than any English jockey has before or since. 'There is no comparison between Gordon and Lester Piggott,' says Roscoe. 'I will always believe that Gordon was superior.'

On one occasion when the two friends went to Ogbourne on a Sunday morning, Roscoe had been disqualified in a point-to-point on the previous day. He says, 'When I arrived, Martin, an incredibly handsome and delightful man as well as being a very fine trainer, met us and said, "Come on in then, Colin." Turning to me, he said, "I don't want you. You're a crook!"'

'I took no notice but Gordon had heard. He said, "What's he talking about?" I explained that I had won by a neck, was had up in front of the Stewards and disqualified. Gordon, amazed, said "What did you say to them?" I said, "I told them I had jumped the last fence and come straight up the middle of the course and never touched anybody." Gordon said, "You shouldn't have said that. You ought to have said you'd jumped the last fence and the second came boring into you all the way up the straight!"

'Much later, I was Stewards Secretary at Ascot one year when Gordon was had up before us. He came in and was asked by the Stewards, "What have you got to say for yourself?"

'Do you know, he actually said word for word those words he had told me all those years ago? "Your Grace, My Lord, all the way up the straight, the second was boring into me." Of course, Gordon got off scot free. Some years later I was at a shooting party with Gordon and I said between beats, "Do you remember coming in front of me at Ascot a couple of years ago? I could hardly keep a straight face! You told us word for word what you said that I should have said to the Stewards in my point-to-point!" Gordon looked at me with those large open eyes and said, "I kept the race though, didn't I?"'

Roscoe values his friendship with Sir Gordon Richards very highly.

There were two greats in Roscoe's racing life, Gordon and Golden Miller. As it happened, the year that the 10th returned from India was the year when Golden Miller won his fifth and last Gold Cup.

We do not see the likes of Golden Miller today. Among those who still cherish his memory is that fine jockey and outstanding trainer, Fulke Walwyn, who rode the big, handsome, powerful horse.

The Miller was bought by Charlie Rogers for Dorothy Paget, the fabulous patron of National Hunt racing who became a legend in her own lifetime through her dress – that famous everlasting old grey coat – and her constant entourage of secretaries, her immense appetite, her habit of living at night and her rudeness, which probably stemmed from shyness. She would lock herself in the lavatory at a race meeting

105

until all the people had left. Then she would emerge to eat a dinner as large as Henry VIII might have enjoyed, firing questions at her trainers and her attendants.

A tall popular Irishman, Charlie Rogers was one of the finest judges of a horse in the world, and managed the Paget breeding and racing interests. Incongruously she called him Romeo and he was one of the few men for whom this unique character had any time.

Charlie bought horses for other owners as well, and invested wisely when he acquired Thomond II in Ireland on behalf of Miss Paget's American cousin Jock Whitney. Roscoe, who was home on leave in the Spring of 1935, describes the race for the Cheltenham Gold Cup that year between these two chasers as 'Probably the greatest race I have ever seen.'

The record crowd that gathered at Prestbury Park on that fine, overcast day, backed Golden Miller down to odds on in the five-horse field on perfect fast ground. The previous year Golden Miller, superbly ridden by Gerry Wilson, had achieved the remarkable feat of winning the Cheltenham Gold Cup and the Grand National only a fortnight later. He was now aiming for his fourth successive Gold Cup.

Thomond II was ridden by the local hero Billy Speck, one of the best jockeys never to win the Championship, and the two rivals dominated the race from the start. Flying the fences at a record-shattering break-neck pace, neither jockey gave an inch. Down the hill Speck seized the rails so that the champion jockey had to round the final bend into the straight on the opposite side.

Later Gerry modestly described that never-to-be-forgotten finish. He told me: 'We fought it out neck and neck. There was never an inch between us as we headed for the last fence. We took off together and the two horses didn't jump the obstacle . . . they flew over

106

it and flew the distance of the run-in too. It is a short run in from the last fence to the winning post at Cheltenham . . . but it is an uphill climb and any horse the least bit short of stamina falls back beaten, as so many do year after year. Golden Miller and Thomond were thorough stayers, Speck as well as myself could ride a strong finish, but my horse found rather the better speed and we won all out by threequarters of a length.'

In fact it was the strength and superb horsemanship of the only man ever to remain champion National Hunt jockey for seven successive seasons that won this epic struggle for Dorothy Paget, who had been furiously demanding of Charlie Rogers, 'Why didn't you buy me the other horse too, Romeo?'

Golden Miller's subsequent dislike of Aintree is now legendary, but he won a fifth Cheltenham Gold Cup and Roscoe says, 'This is not just the argument of an old man. If Arkle deserves a life-size statue at Cheltenham, then Golden Miller should have one twice as large as life. After all, he won the Grand National as well, when the fences were really big, straight and tough. He won five Gold Cups against the three that Arkle won (even though, of course, he was deprived of another attempt through injury) but Arkle was never risked at Aintree. For me, Golden Miller will always remain the greatest steeplechaser of all time.'

Many years later Germany's Hans Winkler, who was once again searching for likely young showjumping re-cruits, visited the famous Irish yard of Nat Galway-Greer. On this occasion he did not fancy any of the horses produced for his inspection. Finally he got up to leave, keeping his cheque book firmly in his pocket. With a deadpan face, he pointed to an un-named photo-graph on the wall. 'Find me a horse like that, Nat,' he said, 'and I'll buy him. Make no mistake. I'll buy him.' It was Golden Miller!

Roscoe remembers the great jump jockeys of his time. 'I think the greatest of them probably were George Duller over hurdles and Frank Wootton as an all-rounder,' he says. 'Fred Rees and Jack Anthony were tremendous, as was Fred Winter much later. My word, those old-time jump jockeys were tough. They were incredible characters. I remember Percy Whitaker telling me about the time he took Easter Hero to Auteuil in Paris to run in the French Grand National. He said, "I told Fred Rees that he could do what he liked after the race but he must keep sober before, and I actually saw him into the weighing-room. Imagine my horror and surprise when he came out so tight that he could hardly stand. I put him up on Easter Hero and he nearly fell over the other side. On the way down to the start he aimed the horse the wrong way round at the water, the famous Rivière de la Tribune in front of the stands. When the horse refused, he fell off into the water. He stood up and, facing the crowd, actually peed in the water! Needless to say, being French, the crowd were not in the least dismayed but thought it a wonderful joke and cheered. The horse was withdrawn and Rees was packed straight off back to England.'

If we do not see the likes of Golden Miller today, who is to say that we will ever see the likes again of Sir Gordon Richards? The admiration that Roscoe and Gordon had for each other is evidenced by the fact that one of the last things that the great jockey did in his life was to write the short foreword to this book, in tribute to his great friend. Sir Gordon died while this book was being written, and Roscoe does not think it inappropriate therefore that I say a few words about the great jockey as his tribute in return.

Chapter Eight

All Sir Gordon!

One Monday in 1953 was the most glorious first of June ever. It was the eve of the Coronation and the entire country was en fête. After a lovely fresh hazy start, the sun was already blazing down when the training fraternity returned from first lot to breakfast and the newspapers, to read that racing had been honoured at last. Gordon Richards, champion of champion jockeys, had received a knighthood in the Coronation Honours List. This was the very same Gordon who coincidentally was riding the author's little filly Mirabelle in the second race at Leicester that afternoon. A week earlier, ridden by my apprentice, she had finished second at Warwick. Now she was tipped by all the papers to win the Billeston Plate for the new Knight. He had four other fancied rides, but it was still quite a responsibility for a small trainer like me, particularly since this beautiful tiny little brown model two-year-old was one of my bargains. I had paid only a hundred guineas for the daughter of Mirza II at Ballsbridge in September.

We drove fast to get to 'the Oadby track', as the more fanciful journalists called it, in good time. We need not have worried. As always, the little champion was a complete master of the situation. Any excitement he may have felt was quite hidden behind the big, twinkling eyes and the charming self-deprecating smile as he received the congratulations showered on him from all sides.

He finished fourth in the first race and, when I put him up, he admitted that he would dearly love to ride at least one winner on that memorable day.

It is hard to explain the extraordinary sense of confidence a trainer felt when he put Gordon on a horse. When the animal belonged to someone else, you knew that your owner would be extremely happy, that you had done your best and that, if you did not win, it would be because the horse was just not good enough.

The late Lord Rosebery shared Roscoe's opinion of Gordon, saying that of all the jockeys in his long and wide experience Gordon was the one who lost the fewest races that he should have won. So, when he strutted into the paddock with that characteristic walk, square-shouldered, upright, neat and crisp, you felt a curious satisfaction and pride, knowing that your rivals were jealous of your jockey. Instead of fretting and worrying as you went back to the stand, you walked away from the paddock serenely happy and at peace with the world.

When it was your own horse, as on this occasion, the feeling was of course intensified. I have a splendid photograph of Gordon, when he had just got on Mirabelle, adjusting his 'jerk' – the length of his stirrup leathers – and it is fascinating to see how long he actually rode. It is almost a good hunting length. In the paddock we had not talked about the race – just about the Coronation the next day, to which we were all going. Gordon had received special seats from St James's Palace.

Mirabelle and her jockey were admirably suited.

Starting at 5-2 on, she flew out of the gate, made all the running and won by eight lengths to tremendous cheers. She was the new knight's only winner that day and when I thanked him, he typically thanked me more, as he did the following year when I gave him the only winner on his fiftieth birthday, Mabledon in the Rose Stakes at Sandown.

We saw the papers early the next morning in London while we waited for that wonderful Coronation ceremony. Despite the approach of the Derby, space was naturally short for racing and most of it was devoted to that little race at Leicester. My favourite headline read: 'ALL SIR GORDON!' And that, I suppose, just about sums up the racing scene from the start of 1925 – when, in his first year as a fully-fledged jockey, Gordon Richards took over the championship from Steve Donoghue – to 1954, when he retired.

He was a Shropshire miner's son, of eight children – twelve, if you count the others that died. It is too easy to romanticise and so to exaggerate the rags-to-riches angle. By the time Gordon was born in 1904, his father Nathan and uncle Matthew were both mining contractors, doing well, employing labour and earning good money. They had a great pride in their work, which they instilled into their men and into their own children.

Nevertheless it was Gordon's mother, a highly intelligent woman with a strong business sense, who kept the family going in troubled times by buying land, building and renting a few houses, erecting stables and hiring out ponies and traps, which her children looked after and drove. She kept Gordon out of the mines and sent him, when he left school at thirteen, as a junior clerk in a warehouse near home.

Although strict Primitive Methodists, whose children went to church four times every Sunday, his parents did not object when Gordon applied for a job and was accepted as a racing apprentice by Martin Hartigan, who was then training for the financier Jimmy White, way out on the Wiltshire downs at famous Foxhill. The stable jockey was the champion – lovable, carefree, brilliant Steven Donoghue.

Foxhill was unique among the mighty training establishments that still held sway in those days. No expense was ever spared in anything. Martin Hartigan, the trainer; Jack Fallon, the head lad; Lang Ward, the travelling head lad; and of course Steve Donoghue, the stable jockey, were each one of them right at the top of his profession.

Gordon was very good from the beginning. Under Steve's enthusiastic, sympathetic instruction, he was soon riding gallops and had a ride in public in his first year. In his second season he rode several winners, including a double at Lewes, before Paddy Hartigan fell to his death from his hotel room at Liverpool and Martin moved to Ogbourne to take over his brother's stables and marry his wife Norah, daughter of the great theatrical impressario George Edwards.

Although Jimmy White offered Martin £3,000 – a fantastic figure in those days – for Gordon's indentures, the trainer refused. This turned out to be a happy decision in every way. Under these kind people's care and expert tuition, Gordon's talent flowered, so that by the time he had finished his apprenticeship in 1925, he had ridden 114 winners.

Transferring to Tommy Hogg nearby at the other great training stable, Russley Park, Gordon, weighing only 6st. 11lbs, rode 118 winners to finish champion in his first season as a full jockey. It was a truly remarkable performance.

However his triumph was short-lived. When the 1926 season started, he was found to have TB and was out of the saddle for the remainder of the year.

Happily he made a good recovery and, returning to his same retainers, began his remarkable sequence of twenty-seven years as champion, broken only by Freddy Fox, who beat him by just one in 1930, and by illness in 1941.

His loss of the title in 1930 was compensated by his first two classic successes, the Oaks on Rose of England and the St Leger on Singapore.

Although Freddy Fox won the Derby for Fred Darling in 1931 on Cameronian, Gordon not only regained the championship but was also given Fox's job as first jockey to Darling's wonderful Beckhampton stable. He entered the most coveted job in racing, backed by his devoted wife Margery, whom he had married in 1928 and who remained at his side, a constant comfort and support until his death.

In 1933 he shattered all records. After winning the last race at Nottingham on October 3, he won all six races on October 4 at Chepstow and the first five on the same course the following day – twelve consecutive winners, easily defeating the world record of nine.

On the anniversary of Fred Archer's suicide, Gordon equalled Archer's record of 246 winners and he went on to finish the year with a total of 259, which has been beaten only twice since – by Gordon himself, in 1947 and 1949.

To get these figures in proportion we must remember two things. First, there were fewer race meetings (and no evening meetings), and travelling was inevitably more strenuous. Secondly, to balance that, Gordon never had to waste and was always considerably lighter than Lester Piggott, who had to watch his weight all the time. As a result, the opportunities are levelled out and comparisons between the two great champions become as odious as ever.

Fred Darling, the little martinet of Beckhampton,

was Gordon's hero. In all things he was a perfectionist, a training genius, who tolerated mediocrity in neither man nor horse. That Gordon and all his employees loved him was no great measure of his charm – he had so little – but rather of his genius. Gordon said: 'He was absolutely ruthless with horses and men. Mr Darling was always right in everything he did.'

He taught Gordon so much. Above all he instilled in him punctuality, planning, organisation and realism with horses – never to overrate an animal or put it on a pedestal, but to treat a horse as a horse.

When Gordon retired he had won fourteen classic races. A lot was made of the fact that the Derby eluded him until 1953. People even said that Epsom did not suit him, but that was quite wrong. Gordon rode Epsom better than anyone except perhaps Steve Donoghue and Lester,

Riding Easton in 1934, he ran up against a rattling good Derby winner in Windsor Lad and was beaten a length – form which was confirmed to an inch twelve months later in the Coronation Cup over the same course and distance.

1936, was, in his opinion, his first unlucky Derby. The Aga Khan had three runners and, as Gordon was not required by his retaining stables that year, he was available to ride a very good little pony called Taj Akbar. Charlie Smirke, who had ridden Windsor Lad the previous year, was on the same owner's Mahmoud, unlucky short-head runner-up to Pay Up in the 2,000 Guineas.

Waiting to produce Taj Akbar's tremendous finishing burst, Gordon had just started to move to overhaul Smirke in the straight when a tiring horse rolled on to him and knocked all the stuffing out of his little colt. Inevitably unbalanced and checked in his stride, he did remarkably well to finish second, beaten

114

three lengths by his grey stable-companion. 'Without that piece of luck,' said Gordon, 'I am as sure as I can be that I would have won.'

In the early part of the following season the champion was trying to help Michael Beary, who was suffering one of those bad patches that most jockeys have to endure from time to time. He got him some rides and some winners. So, when Fred Butters was looking for a rider for Midday Sun in the Lingfield Derby Trial and in the Derby, Gordon suggested Michael, who won both races on the colt, while his benefactor was still waiting to win the world's greatest race.

Next year was a vintage one for Beckhampton. Gordon won his first 2,000 Guineas very easily on Pasch for 'Manna' Morriss. While they were preparing the colt for the Derby on the replica of the Epsom course, which Fred Darling had laid out on the Downs, Aly Khan bought the Prix Juigné winner Bois Roussel for Peter Beatty and sent him to be trained at Beckhampton.

Prevented from riding in the final gallop before the Derby, Gordon had to rely on Fred Darling's verdict that there was nothing between the hot favourite Pasch and the 20-1 outsider Bois Roussel. There was really no choice in the circumstances. Any jockey would have selected the winner of the first classic. But Pasch failed to act down the hill at Epsom and could only finish · third, while Charlie Elliott, coming from behind with an irresistible run, swept Bois Roussel past the tough, staying Scottish Union to win easily by four lengths.

Behind Blue Peter in the last pre-war Derby, Gordon showed once again that it was just the horses and not the Epsom course or the big race, which prevented him from achieving his ambition. The champion somehow squeezed a remarkable performance out of the

Beckhampton colt, Fox Club, to finish second to Lord Rosebery's splendid chestnut.

Turned down by the services on account of his TB, Gordon bought a farm, worked on it, flew his racing pigeons for the Home Guard and kept on riding. Throughout the war he was an inspiring nostalgic pin-up for all lovers of racing temporarily engaged in other activities, usually abroad.

Even when the Derby was run at Newmarket during the war years, the hoodoo still remained. In the spring of 1940 there was nothing to choose between Tant Mieux and Pont L'Eveque until the final workout at Beckhampton, when Gordon rode the former and beat his stable companion by a hundred yards. Naturally he decided that this was the one to be on in the big race, but he was wrong again. Tant Mieux failed to stay and Pont L'Eveque won easily, ridden by Sam Wragg.

The jinx struck in a different way the following year, when Gordon had already picked Owen Tudor out of Fred Darling's four-strong Derby team. Asked by the Duke of Norfolk at Salisbury in May to help instruct a new Arundel apprentice at the start, the sympathetic champion was complying with typical conscientiousness when the boy's filly whipped round, lashed out and broke Gordon's leg, putting him out for the rest of the season.

He missed riding a Beckhampton classic double – the Derby on Owen Tudor and the Oaks on Commotion. Billy Nevett rode the colt and Harry Wragg the filly.

So the Derby losing saga continued. Even that remarkable year of 1942 was to prove no exception. Of course Gordon had lost his title in 1941. His Beckhampton substitute, Harry Wragg, a superb horseman and one of the coolest, most intelligent jockeys of all time, had taken the championship. The same year Fred Darling had topped the trainers' list,

116

helped by two outstanding two-year-olds – Big Game and Sun Chariot, both of whom finished the season unbeaten.

In 1905 Colonel Hall Walker, later Lord Wavertree, had presented his stud at Tully, Co. Kildare, to the British nation for the purpose of forming the National Stud. As well as the rich land and excellent buildings, the gift comprised four stallions, forty-five top class brood mares, yearlings, foals, hunters, cart-horses and 600 head of cattle.

This strange man, who organised his actions and the running of his horses by the movements of the stars, even included all the furniture and pictures in the house and, of course, the famous Japanese garden.

For a short while my old guv'nor Atty Persse was Wavertree's trainer at Russley Park. He told me: 'One day at Ascot when the King was there, we had a runner which was strongly fancied by me. I told my owner it would win.

'Unfortunately Jupiter was interfering with Venus at the time, so when Edward VII, who after all was not averse to a flutter, asked Hall Walker if he fancied his horse, he forgot my advice and replied: "No, sir, he has no chance."

'Always prepared to back my certain knowledge against the forebodings of any astrologer or soothsayer, I had a good bet, which was shortly returned to me, with interest, when the animal won by three lengths.

'As he left the winner's enclosure, Hall Walker had the misfortune to meet the King again. In very acid tones His Majesty thanked him for his most excellent information, adding: "I shall not ask you again!"

'My owner was so upset that he left the racecourse immediately.'

A few years later Hall Walker made amends most handsomely by leasing to the King a colt of his own

117

breeding, the 2,000 Guineas and Derby winner Minoru. Indeed Tully bred many great horses, including Blandford, the sire of four Derby winners. But Minoru established a precedent which was to have an enormous effect on British racing thirty years later when the sport was in desperate need.

In 1939, five years before the entire stock of the National Stud was to be transferred to England, a colt by Bahram and a filly by Hyperion were foaled at Tully. Until the death of Lord Lonsdale all the produce of the National Stud were leased to 'the Yellow Earl', as he was known, for their racing careers. When he died, it was decided that they should be leased to the Monarch and run into the royal colours.

So, in 1941 just as racing was at its lowest ebb, King George VI appeared as the owner of the two best two-year olds in training. It was a tremendous boost to the sport and to the morale of racing people.

When Gordon returned, fighting fit, at a natural riding weight of eight stone, there were only twenty-seven horses at Beckhampton, instead of the usual seventy, but they included the colt and the filly, who were hot favourites for the classics.

Hopelessly out of form to begin with, Gordon was suspected of having lost his nerve. Even Sun Chariot suffered the only defeat of her life on her re-appearance. But then he won a little race and swiftly dispelled all fears as his confidence returned.

Big Game and Sun Chariot won the two Guineas races with such contemptuous ease that it was impossible to anticipate anything other than another royal double in the Derby and the Oaks.

Fred Darling and his jockey however had their problems. Sun Chariot was as temperamental as any daughter of Hyperion. Those who knew her vary only in the word they use – cow, lady, bitch – but the sense is

118

always the same. Yet all agree that she was utterly brilliant. So, although she constantly refused to go onto the gallops and, when finally persuaded, misbehaved outrageously, even going down on her knees and roaring like a bull, it was a battle worth fighting.

If Gordon was worried about Sun Chariot's temperament, he was even more concerned about Big Game's stamina.

'I can hardly explain it even now,' he told me, 'but he gave you rather a hollow feeling, and you sensed that if something came up alongside, there might not be much left in him. He was brave enough and he had plenty of guts. I suppose it was the suspicion that, if really tackled, he could not quite get the one and a half miles.'

In The Oaks Sun Chariot spoiled three starts and then, when the gate went up, ran away out to one side, so that the field had gone a furlong before she had covered fifty yards. Even when she decided to race after the others, she was so far behind that Gordon, in deep despair, thought his chance was hopeless.

After a mile, however, she had sauntered up to the others and a quarter of a mile out she joined the leaders to win very comfortably by a length. 'It was one of the most amazing performances that I have ever known,' said her jockey.

Big Game was the odds-on Derby favourite, but some shrewd judges shared Gordon's qualms. Indeed that outstanding judge of classic trials, the late William Hill, risked his all laying against the royal colt and, by so doing, made a fortune and laid the foundation of the Hill bookmaking empire.

Gordon himself described the historic race. 'My own feelings,' he said, 'were more hopeful than confident. As a matter of fact, Big Game would have had more chance if the race had been run normally at Epsom.

Here at Newmarket, apart from a small short-cut just where the horses come round into the straight, it was necessary to canter the whole one and a half miles of the course in order to reach the start, and this did Big Game no good at all. By the time we reached the gate, he was sweating and had taken quite a lot out of himself already, before the race had started.

'I purposely let him go out of the gate slowly, but he still fought me for a while. However, we settled down in a nice place about fifth or sixth, and so far things were going reasonably. Approaching the Rails, where we always normally begin to move on, Big Game was right up in front with Hyperides. But his head began to nod a bit, and that made me desperately anxious. Then, abruptly, the bottom seemed to fall out of everything: he just blew up, and was completely finished. Harry Wragg challenged on Watling Street, and got up to beat Hyperides by a neck.

'Mr Darling thought I had come a little too soon, but behind that opinion was his conviction that Big Game stayed the full mile and a half. I am equally convinced that this was one of the few occasions when Mr Darling was wrong. Big Game could beat all but the best over that distance, but he was not a genuine stayer. You can tell because when this type begins to tire, they blow right up and have not got a kick left. Some horses, even if they do not quite get the distance, will battle on. But others just can't, and this is nothing to do with their guts or courage. Big Game was game enough, and there was no finer battler over a mile, but he was one of those who are incapable of any extra effort if tackled after he had already gone much over a mile. If that happened, he was done.'

Although the colt had lost condition and had been somewhat soured off by the Derby and his preparations for it, Darling's inspired training revived his interest so

Roscoe (left) and Colin Davy, Egypt 1928

The Tenth Royal Hussars Polo Team which defeated the Maharajahs
l.to r. Back row – Baria Prithi Singh, David Dawnay, Abbhey Singh,
Mike MacMullen
Front row – Roscoe Harvey, Maharajah of Jaipur, Maharajah of Jodhpur,
Charles Gairdner, Rao Rajah Hanut Singh

Kadir Cup,
the Blue Riband
of pigsticking

Roscoe jumps the last fence on Santick to win the Crookham Open Cup at
Aldershot, 1939

HRH Prince Henry, Duke of Gloucester,
with Lt. Col. C.B. Harvey in the
Western Desert, 1942

Regimental
orders, 1942.
Roscoe is pictured
in the middle

Race meeting
near Tripoli,
January 1943

Aquilo (with Roscoe up) being led
in by Willetts after winning the
Meynell Open Race for the
third successive year

Roscoe with General Pip Roberts in Normandy

Roscoe's Brigade HQ at Antwerp

Triumphal Liberation of Antwerp by Brigadier C.B. Harvey's
29th Armoured Brigade, September 1944

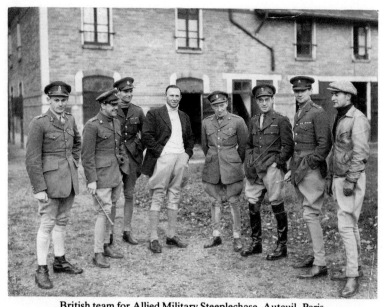

British team for Allied Military Steeplechase, Auteuil, Paris,
11th November 1945
l. to r. – Lt. Col. Cecil Blacker, Capt. Jack Bissill, Capt. Tom Hanbury,
French trainer Guy Pastré, Capt. George Archibald, Brig. C.B. Harvey,
Major Peter Herbert, French amateur M. Hovelacque

Roscoe receiving the Grand Military Gold Cup from the Queen Mother,
March 1987

December 12ᵗ

Dear Roscoe -

My very sincere congratulations to you on your Bar to the D.S.O.

No one has ever deserved it more than you have.

Yours ever M.W...

A much prized personal letter from the Army Commander,
Lieutenant-General Sir Miles Dempsey

				Date recommendation passed forward	
				Received	Passed
2nd Armd Brigade	1st Armd Division	30 Corps		Brigade	10/6/42
Schedule No.	Unit 10th Royal Hussars			Division 19.6.42	
Army No. and Rank 18516 Maj (T/Lt.Col.)				Corps 9.7.42	14 JUL 42
				Army	
Name L. B. C. HARVEY Charles Barnet Cameron					

Action for which commended (Date and place of action must be stated)	Recommended by	Honour or Reward	(To be left blank)
Almost continuously and without rest Lt.Col. HARVEY commanded and fought his Regt and a Bty Gp placed under his command from 27 to 29 May 42. When his Regt was reduced to three tanks I was compelled to withdraw him to refit. Throughout, his courage and endurance and energy has been an example to all who saw him. Throughout he has shown conspicuous skill in handling the combination of the three arms. In particular on 29 May 42 his dispositions, orders and direction were responsible for the destruction of at least eleven enemy tanks and several anti-tank guns in the vicinity of Barrel 201. Confronted by superior numbers and under considerable anti-tank and heavier shellfire his complete control, his absolute disregard of personal danger, his grasp of the situation, were largely responsible for the stemming of the panzer advance from the MAABUS ER RIGEL feature. His handling of the evacuation of wounded and of damaged tanks whilst he was still in action was an example of what courage, determination and direction can effect.	Brigadier R. Briggs. Commander 2nd Armd Bde	General Commander-in-Chief, Middle East Forces. D.S.O. (Immediate)	

Citation by Brigadier Raymond Briggs

Army Form W.3121.

Date recommendation
passed forward

	Received	Passed

8 Armd Brigade. **2 NZ** Division **10** Corps

	Brigade	
Schedule No.	Division	
(to be left blank)	Unit **8 Armd Bde**	
Army No. and Rank **T/Brigadier W/Lt-Col**	Corps 28 JUN 1943	8 JUL 1943
HARVEY, CHARLES BARNET CAMERON	Army	
Name ~~R. HARVEY~~ D.S.O. (late 16ᵗʰ Hussars)		
(Christian names must be stated) 73RD (RAC)		

PREVIOUS AWARDS	Action for which commended (Date and place of action must be stated)	Recommended by	Honour or Reward	(To be left blank)
Mention 30.12.40 D.S.O. 13.8.42				
Mention 16.12.42	Brig R. HARVEY commanded 8 Armd Bde Gp during the time that formation was under comd 2 NZ Div, from 10 Mar 43 to 16 May 43. During that period he carried out several difficult operations with skill and coolness. In the outflanking movement and subsequent battle for the HAMMA Gap, he led his Brigade with outstanding courage and determination and his personal example was an inspiration to all ranks. In the subsequent pursuit he led his Brigade with the greatest skill, and his thrusts greatly assisted the force to drive the enemy back on to his final position on the ENFIDAVILLE line. Every task given to Brig HARVEY was cheerfully and expeditiously carried out, and at all times he showed the greatest devotion to duty.	BAR TO DSO		
	H.R. Alexander General, G.O.C-in-C., 15 Army Group. *Awarded Bar to D.S.O.* L.G. 26.11.43	*B.L. Montgomery* LT-GEN. Comd. 2 N.Z.E.F. G.O.C. Eighth Army	*Strongly recommended B.S. Horrocks* Lieut-General 10 Corps 16341	MS. 20.7.43

Citation by General Sir Bernard Freyberg

Army Form W.3121

Date recommendation
passed forward 14 Nov 44

29 Armd Brigade **11 Armd** Division **8** Corps

	Received	Passed
Schedule No.	Brigade	
(To be left blank) Unit **HQ 29 Armd Bde**	Division	14 Nov 44
Rank and Army or Personal No. **S/Lt-Col T/Brig 18516**	Corps 14ᵗʰ Nov 44	16 Nov 44
Name **Charles Barnet Cameron HARVEY, DSO.** RaC	Army 17 Nov 44	1 Dec 44
(Christian names must be stated)		

Action for which commended (Date and place of action must be stated)	Recommended by	Honour or Reward	(To be left blank)
During the advance of this Division to the VENRAI area between 16 - 19 Oct 44, Brigadier Harvey's Brigade was severely held up by boggy ground in addition to receiving heavy casualties from shelling and mortaring. Brigadier Harvey, who was determined to get forward, succeeded by his own personal leadership in overcoming these difficulties and pressed on with such effect that in 48 hours his Brigade took 700 determined enemy prisoners and inflicted casualties on many others. This action had a decisive result on the whole operation and was undoubtedly due to this officer's fine leadership, military skill, and offensive spirit which permeated to all ranks.	*G.W.E.J. Erskine* Maj-Gen, Comd, 11 Armd Div. (G.P.B. ROBERTS) *Roberts* Lt-Gen, Comd, 8 Corps.	Bar to DSO (Immediate) 2ⁿᵈ Bar to DSO 1. 3. 45	
	31 Oct 44 *B.L. Montgomery*		27485
		LIEUT-GENERAL. COMMANDER, SECOND ARMY. P.T.O.	

Citation by General Pip Roberts

that he won the Champion Stakes and was promptly retired to stud, defeated only once – in the one race that really mattered!

Sun Chariot was a very different kettle of fish. She continued to improve in ability, if not in temperament, and from the way in which she won the Leger, slamming the Derby winner and runner-up, she confirmed herself as one of the greatest fillies of all time.

'I have no doubt,' said Gordon, 'that she would have won the Derby just as easily. She was certainly the greatest filly I ever rode.'

So ended an incredible year, when Gordon won no fewer than four of the five classics in the royal colours – but not the Derby.

The following year the champion was presented with another problem horse, one who was to prove himself probably the greatest of all international stallions, Nasrullah.

Gordon believed that the best mover he ever rode owed his outbreaks of temperament chiefly to the zoned racing of the war years, which necessitated his being kept at Newmarket, training alongside the July course, where he had to race.

'If only he could have been taken off the Heath for a change, I am sure it would have altered his outlook completely,' he said. 'He hated the place. We had terrible times with him in the early morning work. He would frequently hold the whole string up and we had to dodge between the Banks and get up to all sorts of tricks with him in order to get him to work at all.'

So many horses, particularly those of the Nearco line, seem to dislike our wide, straight, staring courses. Dr Edouard Pouret, probably the world's most famous racing vet, himself a fine horseman and former amateur rider of note, has no illusions about it: 'It is not lack of courage which makes horses develop a hatred of such courses,' he says. 'It is just not natural for them. They like going round bends. You will notice that on a turn an animal will frequently catch hold of his bit again and try to run away with you.'

Despite all this, Nasrullah, who had shown his dislike of the straight mile by running in snatches to finish fourth in the 2,000 Guineas, ran a good race in the Derby, just failed to stay and was beaten a length and a head by Straight Deal and Umiddad. Towards the end of the season he won the Champion Stakes in grand style. The Aga Khan then sold the future champion stallion to Joe McGrath, who was later to pass him on to the United States, where he is now a legend.

The following year was one of those arguments for Lester Piggott's freelancing. A recurrence of Gordon's TB initiated a long persistent bout of terrible depression and nervous trouble, relieved by the end of the war in Europe and a consequent return to his beloved St Moritz, where the air and the curling restored him to form. Even so it was not until the end of 1945, the year of Dante and Court Martial, that he fully recovered. He still managed to top the list yet again, with 104 winners.

1946 produced his first post-war double century (212), and in 1947 he finished with the incredible score of 269 winners. This time his Derby loser, however, excited bitter resentment and harsh criticism from the multitude of 'sportsmen', who talk through their pockets.

Fred Darling had been very ill in the previous year and now returned to Beckhampton for what was to be his last season. Tudor Minstrel had won the 2,000 Guineas for him in a common canter by eight lengths. He was one of the easiest-ever winners of the classic and Gordon said: 'On that day he was the best miler I rode in all my career.'

Trouble started when Darling began to prepare the hot favourite for the Derby. Gordon was not happy with the horse after riding him round the stable's replica gallop of the Derby course. 'This fellow's not right,' he told his guv'ner. 'He can't get on his other leg. If he does, he's all at sea.' The implication was that Tudor Minstrel might not act well on the left-handed course at Epsom. Gordon also had some doubt about the horse's stamina over the Derby distance.

'I did not know how to ride him,' he admitted, 'and neither did Mr Darling . . . I have never, in my whole life, had such an uncomfortable ride at Epsom. Every time I held him up, he fought me. Every time I let him down to go, he shot off to the right. Either way, he was making certain that he lost the race. The whole race was a nightmare, but he still finished fourth.

'Then the letters began to arrive. Hundreds of them, and telegrams as well. Some incredibly impertinent people even telephoned. I was told that I had pulled the horse's head off. The kindest suggested that I was incapable of riding a donkey.

'As a matter of fact,' Gordon added characteristically, 'I find donkeys very difficult to ride.'

Gordon told me an amusing story of how Lord Woolton, Chairman of the Conservative Party, made reference to the unfortunate selection Gordon had sometimes made in choosing his Derby mount. Gordon had collected quite a nice sum from his fellow jockeys for the Conservative Fighting Fund then being raised. In his letter acknowledging Gordon's cheque, Lord Woolton wrote: 'It is most encouraging for me to know that you of all people are backing the right horse.'

One of the more exasperating events of that year happened at Chepstow, where Glendower, a good horse, opposed by only one other runner, started at 20-1 on, whipped round at the start, unseated Gordon and took no part. Gordon learnt afterwards that one man had a system whereby he picked the champion's most likely mount every day and backed it to win him £1,000. There were no overnight declarations at that time and the punter was not to know that the field would cut up so badly. When the results came in, he discovered that he had lost £20,000!

Fred Darling was now very ill indeed and decided that he must retire. He sold Beckhampton to Mr J.A. Dewar, the owner of Tudor Minstrel, and persuaded the other patrons to stay on. Noel Murless, who had been recommended by Gordon, was appointed the new trainer.

Trainer and his jockey started well. They won the 1,000 Guineas with Queenpot and would surely have completed the Newmarket classic double with The Cobbler if a bruised foot had not prevented that handsome speedy colt from having a preliminary race. As it was he was beaten by a head by My Babu.

Despite the change of trainer at Beckhampton, Gordon won his twenty-first championship with 224 winners. In 1949 he finished with 261 winners, but still no Derby winner. Royal Forest started favourite, but sweated his race away in the Epsom preliminaries, as so many horses have done before. Even so he finished fourth behind the three concerned in that first-ever Derby photo-finish, Nimbus, Amour Drake and Swallow Tail.

Time was running out, but at the end of 1949 Gordon took a fifth retainer – for Jack Clayton, who managed the stable at Newmarket where Fred Darling's former travelling head-lad, Norman Bertie, was installed as trainer. But for this, the great champion would probably have had to retire without ever winning the greatest race.

1950 was a year when all the classics, except the 2,000

Guineas, went to France. The Beckhampton three-year-olds were extremely moderate, but Gordon won 201 races. Far from flagging with age, he went from strength to strength, winning 227 in 1951, including the 1,000 Guineas on Belle of All, and 231 in 1952. But he had still not ridden a Derby winner when he came to his forty-ninth year in 1953.

He was champion again in 1953 with 191 winners. It was to be the last time, but that did not matter because that total included the one winner he had always wanted.

Newly knighted, he took a house at Worthing for Epsom week as he had done so often before.

'Norman Bertie,' he said, 'asked me to come and ride Pinza for a canter round Tattenham on the Friday morning. I met him in the paddock about seven-thirty. We had one of our own lead horses, and Mr Wootton kindly lent us one of his. I told the riders to keep increasing right into the straight so that Pinza could get the feel of the ground and the roads which cross. We set off at the seven-furlong gate at the top of the hill, but neither of the lead horses was any good to me. Pinza swept along with his ears pricked, doing nothing, and he finished like that.

'There was a great change on the Saturday, the morning of the race. For such a big horse, he came down round Tattenham like a bird.

'I went back to George Duller's house for breakfast and, if possible, a sleep. George was one of my best friends, and I had been doing this for years. But there was something about this year's Derby which had me even more tensed up than usual. Her Majesty's Aureole had put up a really sparkling show in winning the Derby trial at Lingfield, and there was no doubt in my mind that he was my great danger. The fact that Aureole belonged to Her Majesty, and that she had just

125

knighted me in the recently published Honours List, added piquancy to the situation.

'Later, as we jockeys started to walk to the paddock, Her Majesty was standing with the Duke of Edinburgh and some of the Stewards, and she stopped me. She gave me that wonderful smile as she shook hands with me, and said: 'It's all terribly exciting!' The Duke also shook hands with me, and said: 'You'd think there were only two runners in the race. Nobody talks of any of the others.' Her Majesty wished me luck, and I wished her luck. Then I went on to the paddock.

'Pinza was of course a grand horse, but he was a real man and he took all the upsetting preliminaries in his stride. He seemed to be enjoying the noisy crowd. He was on his toes, but he was perfectly happy. I have an idea that he was far less nervous than I was.

'I was drawn number five, which is not really a good draw because the Derby course bends out to the right after a little and so the runners are apt to bunch when this point is reached, with the result that the low numbers may get buffeted. But as it turned out, Pinza could have been drawn anywhere for the difference it made.

'After we had gone about three furlongs, I was maybe twelfth, but I was nicely tucked in on the rails. With about six furlongs to go, on top of the hill, I had managed to work my way into fifth place, without having to leave the rails. Smirke had now taken up the running on the Aga Khan's Shikampur. As Smirke began to go on, I found myself just in fourth place behind Star of the Forest, who I realised was tiring. I had two or three horses outside me, and my only chance was to go between Star of the Forest and the rails. I gave Pinza a little kick and he went through like a lion. I found myself, right in the middle of Tattenham, in second place about four lengths behind

Shikampur. Pinza came down the hill, and round, quite perfectly, just as he had done that morning. Although I was still four or five lengths behind Shikampur, I already knew that the race was over. I let Smirke lead me until just under two furlongs from home, and I went by and we won as we liked.

'For such a big horse, I have never known such an active horse as Pinza. Most big horses need to be driven, but not Pinza. He did it all by himself, a quality which Mr Darling used to call class. Pinza was a terrific racehorse, brimful of class.

'I have been told that my expression never changed, that I seemed to take that tremendous moment unnaturally quietly, even when I was being led in. This seems to have surprised some people, in view of the fact that I had just won my first Derby after all those years of disappointment. But I am not surprised myself. Frankly, my mind was in a turmoil, and my brain perhaps a little numbed. Everyone was being so tremendously kind; the reception which the crowd gave me was something out of this world.

'Her Majesty sent for me after the race, and there was no sign of disappointment in her face. Aureole had finished a gallant second, but the fact remained that – good horse though Aureole certainly is – he never had a chance with Pinza, who was one of the greats of all time. Still, before the race everyone had thought that Aureole could win, and you know how hopeful an owner always is! But Her Majesty seemed to be just as delighted as I was with the result of the race.

'After she had congratulated me, the rest of the Royal Family gathered round. We talked about the race, about Pinza, and about Aureole. The Duke of Edinburgh suddenly asked me if I was going to retire now that I had won the Derby. Before I had time to reply, the Queen answered for me. She said: "Of course not! He's going to ride for me in the Derby next year, on Landau."

'I went back to Marlborough that night a very tired but a very elated man. Not only had I been trying to win the Derby for years, but so had that grand supporter of racing, Sir Victor Sassoon. And at last we had both done it!

'One final story about that Derby. Ever since I had first gone to Newmarket, as a little boy unable to reach up to her door-knocker, I had always stayed in a house run by a Mrs Seaman. She was a great person, who was a mother to us all, and we soon got to calling her Ma. She was a grand cook, who used to taste everything as she was cooking it in order to be certain that it was right. She loved cooking, and had been a cook in private service of the great houses in England. She was proud of that.

'She made me so comfortable that I never wanted to stay anywhere else in Newmarket, and I very seldom did throughout all the years that followed. She and I were great friends. After her son got married, she bought a house and called it Myrobella, and moved into it. Sometimes she used to get nervy or something, and would complain about her tummy, and then I told her that I sometimes got the same. She then always felt much better, and seemed delighted that I also suffered!

'Towards Derby time, and when I was up staying with her for one of the Pinza's work mornings, when she was very old and very sick and bedridden, she called me to her bedroom as I was leaving the house in the morning. I am afraid that I had been singing in the bath, and she had heard me. "I could kill you," she said, "getting up singing when I'm lying in bed here." And she meant it, she hated inaction so much.

'Only a few weeks before she died, she asked me if I was going to win it. "Win what?" I asked. "The Derby, of course," she said. It was almost an obsession with her. When I told her I had been knighted, she did not approve at all, because she thought it might upset me for the race! "They might have left it till after the Derby," she said almost angrily.

'She was a great old lady. I discovered that she had asked her doctor to keep her alive until after the race, because – as she told him – she had waited nearly thirty years for the great occasion when I should win.

'She did live to know that I had won. And then quite peacefully, she gave up the trouble of trying to stay alive.

'Just as Mr Fred Darling died, a few days after knowing of the triumph of the horse he bred.'

Gordon won the King George VI and Queen Elizabeth Stakes at Ascot on Pinza but the enormous bay, who had the St Leger at his mercy, predictably broke down before that race.

Landau, the horse that the Queen wanted Gordon to ride in the 1954 Derby, was one of those National Stud horses leased to her for its racing career – an unreliable animal, a son in fact of Sun Chariot. Gordon rode him in the Derby trial at Lingfield and thought he should have won. 'It was the same old tale again, when you asked him to do something he either would not or could not.'

Soon after this, in a race at Salisbury, an apprentice in front of the champion touched the heels of another horse and came down, bringing Gordon with him. The champion was badly concussed and, in fact, was unconscious until he woke up in Salisbury Hospital.

He was now fifty years old, and reluctantly he had to decide that he would not be well enough to ride Landau less than a month later in what was to have been his last Derby. This was the race that Lester Piggott won on Never Say Die.

Gordon came back just in time for Royal Ascot where, riding Rashleigh, he had an unhappy contretemps with Lester on the same horse, which resulted in Lester's suspension.

Gordon had ridden fifty-four winners and was well ahead in the jockey list by July 10 at Sandown, when he was riding a two-year-old called Abergeldie in the Star Stakes. This one, like Landau, on whom he had just finished third in the Eclipse, belonged to the Queen.

He was riding in a one-pound dock and the filly may have felt it a bit cold on her back. She half reared up and then went right up on her hind legs as they went down the gravel track to the course. A colt will not come over backwards unless he is pulled over, but a thoroughbred filly will flip onto her back without a moment's hesitation.

Unfortunately, on this occasion Gordon was underneath. When he was X-rayed in hospital, it was found that he had fractured and dislocated his pelvis.

It was the end of the great champion's racing career.

As I said before, comparisons between different times should be avoided. It is fair to say, however, first that with the opportunities provided at the time he was riding, Gordon rode more winners than any other British jockey. He holds the record total of winners with 4,870 from 21,834 months – not a bad average!

He himself said that his secret was the will to win and concentration on the job at all times. As one who knew him well for many years, I can vouch for both those things, as well as for his wonderful, open, honest attitude towards life.

Atty Persse used to say that Gordon's secret lay in the great strength of his legs, in that he could squeeze a horse so tight with his knees and hold it balanced so effectively that it would run dead straight however much he threw the reins at it and however vigorously he rode. The champion himself did not believe this to have been the case. I remember when he rode VC for me when she was only half fit and still quite fat at the beginning of her career. She won all right very comfortably, but for the next week she had a large bump on either side of her withers.

One thing is certain. I cannot possibly argue with Roscoe when he says that there never has been and never will be a greater champion than Gordon Richards and I doubt if anyone else could have kept the racing scene as happy through all those troubled times.

Chapter Nine

No Arms, No Armour

Roscoe has always lived for the present, enjoying life to the full and taking the slings and arrows of outrageous fortune squarely on the robust shield of his own character. If war should come, it was just too bad. He was a regular Cavalry officer and, as such, while regretting the interruption to his sporting life, he would devote all his considerable energy and enthusiasm to defeating the enemy as quickly as possible, so that he could return to the task of rearing his young family against a background of the racecourse and the hunting field. But for two years, from the arrival of the Regiment at Aliwal Barracks, Tidworth, in the autumn of 1936, there was no suggestion of the approaching storm. Sadly, even after Munich in 1938 and Neville Chamberlain's infamous piece of paper – 'peace in our time' – those in high places, with a very few notable exceptions like Winston Churchill, thought it couldn't happen again. The holocaust would never come. In just twenty years the Services had been allowed to run down to such an appalling extent that, even with the obvious evidence of Germany re-arming and bent on revenge, Britain was to be caught with her trousers down.

When I went to Sandhurst in January 1939 at the age of eighteen, I found that it was just the same as when Roscoe had been there twenty years earlier. We hunted, raced, played polo and enjoyed our parties. There were the same red and white pillbox hats, the same PT parades, the same archaic uniform, the same sense of fun in all we did; but there was no intensive training for war for young officer cadets who would shortly be facing the greatest test of their lives.

For the 10th at Tidworth, mechanisation was in name only and could scarcely be called a fact, because only a few 15-cwt trucks were issued with which to convert horsemen to mechanics.

By 1937 experiments in mechanisation in the Army as a whole had reached a stage at which it was decided to form a mechanised division. Thus the Mobile Division was formed, consisting of the 1st and 2nd Cavalry Brigades, two RHA Brigades (later to be termed Regiments), two motorised Infantry Battalions, one Field Squadron Royal Engineers, and certain other divisional troops. Attached, but not under its organic composition, was the Tank Brigade.

The two Cavalry Brigades were given little more than a handful of obsolete light tanks, while the Tank Brigade was equipped with medium tanks, which were eight years old and scarcely less obsolete than their lighter counterparts given to the Cavalry.

The Regiment now joined the Bays and the 9th Lancers in the 2nd Cavalry Brigade and the fact that these three Regiments remained together throughout the forthcoming Second World War, knowing each other intimately as a team, undoubtedly played a vital part in the final victory. No other cavalry or armoured brigade had the good fortune to maintain such cohesion.

Despite all the cavalryman's natural adaptability,

133

mechanisation was a slow job without proper equipment. Old horsemen had to become equally skilled drivers and mechanics, or learn the intricacies of wireless or tank gunnery. Tank commanders had to master all these and learn to direct the driver and gunner while map-reading and choosing ground across country at speed. Troop Leaders had to learn to control two other tanks as well as their own and make instant tactical appreciations, while remaining alert for orders from their Squadron Leaders. The cavalryman's natural eye for a country helped, but the transition from commanding a troop of thirty horses to commanding three or even four tanks was a hard one.

Meanwhile those last halcyon days before the war provided some of the finest sport ever. There was plenty of money around still in the hands of those who knew how to enjoy it.

Carrying on from where they had left off in India, the 10th, led by their new Colonel, Charles Gairdner, and Roscoe, remained in the forefront of all horse sports.

Not only did the Regiment win the Inter-Regimental Polo Championship, but Mark Roddick created a nice record, riding three consecutive winners of the Grand Military Gold Cup: Buck Willow in 1937, Kilstar in 1938 and Fillip in 1939, all trained by himself. This was the one race which eluded Roscoe, who was impressed with Mark as a jockey.

Nevertheless Roscoe was winning more than his share of other races and, in addition to his polo, was hunting like mad with his beloved Berkeley.

His old friend, Mrs Joan Dunn, writes from Dursley: '"C.B.", as we all called him, was a great man to go over our marsh, the country stretching from Berkeley to the outskirts of Bristol – all grass, big ditches to every fence, wonderful scenting and virtually no wire.

'I remember Roscoe, who hunted regularly with us.

Nobody went better and he was always ready to help anyone in trouble. This was the era of bliss and the best of hunting. As there were no hedge-trimmers, the country took a bit of crossing. Moreover, as it was dead flat, one really needed to be right up in the field with hounds or you could neither see nor hear them because the fences in many parts were full of thorn and briars and very thick. C.B. had very good horses, had a great eye for a country, was always in the forefront and was a great man to follow.'

She added amusingly: 'I hunted with him for ten years before I discovered he was married!'

Of course, our fathers, who had given their all in that first terrible 'war to end all wars', just couldn't believe that it would ever happen again. The wishful thinking of those who had endured the nightmare of the trenches is only too easy to understand. Unfortunately their thinking was shared by those in authority.

Politicians, with a few notable exceptions, have always been notoriously ignorant, pigheaded and full of their own importance, to the exclusion of all else. They and the Higher Command between the wars stand condemned by history for the criminal wishful thinking that resulted in this country's unpreparedness in face of the obvious menace of belligerent Nazi Germany.

Typical of the breed was the Minister of Defence during this vital period, Leslie Hore-Belisha, who will best be remembered for orange balls on black and white poles, known as Belisha Beacons, marking pedestrian crossings, introduced during his term as Minister of Transport.

One afternoon at Tweseldown Racecourse, Aldershot, the Minister of Defence was presenting the prizes for the big 'chase. He was introduced to the winning rider, Major C.B. Harvey of the 10th Hussars and, as Roscoe turned away with his trophy, Hore-

Belisha remarked in a loud voice: 'He's quite well spoken for a professional jockey!'

With this sort of man in the highest places, it was small wonder that, when the late Field Marshal Lord Ironside went to the War Office in 1939 as Chief of the Imperial General Staff, he was, in his own words, 'flabbergasted' at the appalling deficiences in the equipment of the Army and at the very long time it would take to make them good.

He revealed in his diary*: 'There were not enough battle tanks for our one and only Armoured Division and only two battalions of army tanks for the Infantry Division!'

By 1938 the Regiment had acquired some obsolete eighteen-year-old Mark IV tanks and a number of Bren Carriers (both death traps) and were becoming accustomed to tactical manoeuvring and otherwise operating in their new sphere.

The equipment throughout this year remained unchanged, but theoretical training, at least, exposed certain deficiences in the organization of the under-staffed Mobile Division. There was insufficient holding power and the fact that the heavier Tank Brigade was not a permanent part of the Division, reduced its effectiveness.

Early in 1939, while the Regiment was starting to train National Service militiamen, a certain reorganization of the Mobile Division was agreed. This reorganization looked a lot better on paper. It comprised the provision of two armoured Brigades entirely equipped with the new Cruiser tanks, which were just beginnng to arrive and, with the necessary supporting arms and administrative services, was to be renamed the Armoured Division.

*The Ironside Diaries 1937–1940 (Constable 1962)

However, owing to the rate of production of tanks, it was thought that the new organization could not be completed until the summer of 1940. As an interim measure therefore, the 2nd Armoured Brigade, as the 2nd Cavalry Brigade was now called, was to remain on a light tank basis, except for one Squadron per regiment, which would be equipped with Cruisers. The 3rd Armoured Brigade (late Tank Brigade) would replace the 1st Armoured (late 1st Cavalry) Brigade and would be equipped entirely with the new Cruiser tanks.

Thus the interim Armoured Division comprised a light and heavy Armoured Brigade together with a support group and Divisional troops.

It was while the 1st Armoured Division was thus organised, though by no means fully equipped in accordance with the new interim measure, that war was declared against Germany in September 1939.

The scandal was that even the Cruiser tanks had quite inadequate armour and were equipped with peashooters, two-pounder guns, virtually useless against strong armour and, of course, hopeless in a high-explosive artillery role.

Roscoe says, 'After the war I went to a rather dull cocktail party in Derbyshire. I didn't know anybody, but my kind hostess was trying to introduce me to as many other guests as possible.

'She said, "You must meet Mr So-and-So, because he is with Rolls Royce up here and had a lot to do with designing tanks during the war."

'I said, "He did, did he? I would certainly love to meet him." When we were introduced, I said, "You're the guy I've been wanting to meet for years." I felt very strongly about it and this obviously showed. He asked, "What's the matter?"

'I told him, "If you had anything to do with our British tanks during the war, you ought to be crucified."

'He was taken aback and said, "What do you mean?

Let's go and have a drink." So we went to the bar and, over a drink, I told him, "If you had anything to do with tanks in the war, starting at the beginning and going through to the very end, you're a disgrace to your country. There's no excuse."

'"All right," he said, "first tell me what sort of tank you would have liked."

'I left him in no doubt! I would have liked a tank with a lot of face armour, comparatively light side armour, a 17-pounder gun and a decent engine.'

'"Right," he said, "if you feel so strongly with all your experience, come to my office tomorrow and I'll show you a blueprint dated 1936, which exactly fits the description of the tank you have just described to me."

'I went along next morning and there it was, just as he had said. "Why the hell didn't we get it?" I asked. He replied, "I don't know. The Treasury might have thought it too expensive or some of your military boys perhaps didn't think it was the sort of tank you wanted. But there's the blueprint."'

The unions were probably as guilty as anyone. Under the dictatorship of Germany, the production line could be stopped at once. A Mark IV would replace a Mark III; a Mark V and then a Mark VI would be made to order. But in England, it was alleged that the unions refused to stop the production lines, even though there was a desperate war in progress. The vast stocks of unused Matildas and Valentines, all equipped with those ludicrous 2-pounder guns, costing at least £30,000 each and never even issued, gave credence to that story.

Roscoe says, 'In a recent book, Field Marshal Lord Carver claims that the British troops were badly trained. Balls! They were very well trained. It was just those awful death-trap tanks. Montgomery wouldn't have won the Battle of Alamein if it hadn't been for the

138

American Sherman tanks. It's not too much to say they won the war for us in the desert.'

In the run-up to the war, no racing man who was ever there is likely to forget the racing season of 1939. We were to carry that Form Book around with us for so long in so many places that it became old, dog-eared and dirty. It still provided comfort and memories as we read those pages far from home.

It was a year for favourites in the Classic races. Lord Rosebery's Blue Peter, a supremely handsome rangy chesnut son of Fairway, had won the Two Thousand Guineas and the Derby in the style of a champion. The St. Leger looked like being one of the races of the century, because Blue Peter was due to meet his arch rival, the French champion, Pharis II, who had won not only the French Derby, but also the Grand Prix de Paris for Marcel Boussac.

There was a Classic double for the fillies too. Both the One Thousand Guineas and the Oaks were won by Galatea II, owned by American Robert Stirling Clark, who had made his fortune from Singer sewing-machines and who was much later to win the Derby with Never Say Die from the same family. Galatea, who won the first Classic easily, won the Oaks by only a head because her jockey, Bobby Jones, had not realised the danger of White Fox's challenge and had dropped his hands. She looked a certainty in the Coronation Stakes at that unforgettable Royal Ascot, but, like so many favourites at the meeting, she was beaten.

By now we all knew that war was inevitable, and Royal Ascot was characterised by a sort of frenzied gaiety – 'Eat, drink and be merry, for tomorrow we die!' The champagne consumption and the gambling reached new peaks.

On the opening day of Royal Ascot a great cheer had

gone up which was thought to herald the arrival of the Royal Procession, but in fact it was the bookmakers greeting Kim Muir and another inveterate gambler, James Hanbury! Kim, after whom the Kim Muir Memorial Steeplechase for amateur riders is named at Cheltenham's National Hunt Festival, was a young officer who had joined the 10th on their return from India. A fine horseman, he was immensely popular. His charm was matched only by his wealth, which was considerable even by the standards of the 10th Hussars, and he enjoyed nothing more than a tilt at the ring. The bookmakers' rapturous welcome was fully justified on this occasion. Kim and James suffered a disastrous day at Ascot. Even the Gold Cup was won by a rank outsider, Lord Milford's big, strong chesnut Flyon, trained by Jack Jarvis, which started at 100-6.

The biggest gambling race at Royal Ascot, the Royal Hunt Cup, on the Wednesday, had been won at the satisfactory price of 100-8 by Caerloptic, ridden by Michael Beary and trained by Harry Cottrill, whose son Humphrey is one of Roscoe's oldest friends.

The four days of Royal Ascot were not followed at that time by a fifth day on Ascot Heath that does not enjoy Royal status, so on the Saturday, Kim and James, licking their wounds, went in with their heads down at Windsor in a vain attempt to recoup their losses. Roscoe didn't need any 'getting out stakes'. He had enjoyed an excellent Ascot and was in splendid mood to play a first-class game of polo on Saturday afternoon.

That last, languid, lazy summer rolled on. Blue Peter strengthened his claim as European champion by winning the Eclipse Stakes at 7-2 on. We could not believe that the French had anything that could beat our colt. What we did not know was that the forthcoming war would prevent the two champions from ever meeting.

Goodwood came and went with its club tents, women in summer frocks, men in boaters, blazers, white trousers and co-respondent shoes. Life went on as normal – Cowes, buckets and spades, the grouse moors, and the York August meeting – but over everything hung the spectre of war.

In the Autumn of 1938 officers and non-commissioned officers of the 10th Hussars had hurried back to Tidworth from Mike Morley's wedding in order to dig slit trenches during the Munich crisis. Early in 1939 the Regiment had formed a special squadron under the command of Tony Wingfield to train the National Service militiamen. In July and August 1939, Tony had conducted a secret billeting reconnaissance in the Wimborne area of Dorset.

And so it was no surprise to those gathered round the Tidworth Officers Mess wireless on Sunday, September 3 to hear the Prime Minister, Neville Chamberlain, announcing that England would fulfil her guarantee to Poland and must consider herself at war with Germany.

Chapter Ten

Comfu

Reactions to the news among the regular officers varied from 'We'll fix those bloody Nazis!' to a quiet contemplative 'I wonder how long it will last.'

No one in his wildest dreams could have guessed we were under starter's orders for an epic contest lasting six long years, which would involve nearly every major nation in the world and leave Britain, for so long the solitary freedom-fighter, as the bitter-sweet, impoverished victor, with her economic and social structure completely changed; nor that, once it was all over, there would emerge another threat to freedom in the shape of the Soviet Union and its far-flung legions of Left-wing rodents.

For Roscoe, as a hard, fit, regular officer with twenty years' service, the outbreak of war was, in the first place, a nuisance in that it interrupted his adventurous sporting life; but, on the other hand, it promised a far greater adventure in which he could use those twenty years' experience to defeat a much deadlier adversary than our six-times champion jump jockey Gerry Wilson.

Mobilisation had already been in process for some days and many familiar faces were now rejoining from the Reserves, including Major Colin Davy, who had quickly become the Dick Francis of his time and was now one of Collins' leading thriller writers, and Lance-Corporal Roger Willetts, who was to see so much service and is still with Roscoe to this day.

Of course, the majority of the reservists were only horse-trained and would require extensive mechanical training before they could take their place in a tank crew.

The Regiment soon settled down to routine training of reservists and the building up of equipment to war establishment. It sounds grand on paper, but in fact a shameful situation existed. The 1st Armoured Division, of which the 2nd Armoured Brigade was part, was not nearly fully equipped. The Tank Brigade had only one squadron of the new Cruisers and otherwise was still equipped with a pathetically small number of the wholly obsolete Mark IVs, armed only with heavy machine-guns. Due to this and to the return of the reservists, who were still largely untrained, the 1st Armoured Division did not join the British Expeditionary Force.

Now, suddenly, the whole country was in uniform. Tin hats and gas-masks were necessary additions. Racing stopped temporarily and the cancellation of the Doncaster fixture meant that Blue Peter was never to meet his Continental rival, Pharis II. Nevertheless, as the phoney war persisted, the racecourses opened their gates again.

During the first few months of the war it was difficult to get the business of rank into perspective. So many prospective officers were temporarily serving as cadets, or had joined up as troopers and were, for the time being, dressed as Other Ranks. One such was popular Tom Hanbury, whose son Ben is now doing a fine job training at Newmarket. Tom, an excellent all-round horseman, well-known in Leicestershire, who was to finish the war as a Major of the Lifeguards with a Military Cross, was, at this stage, a trooper in the Blues. Roscoe's own home-bred steeplechaser, Santick, was still going strong. He says, 'At the Newbury October meeting there was a 'chase in which Tom was to ride a horse belonging to Kim Muir called Gowran Ranger; Kim was riding another called Tea Tray and I was on Santick, who had only recently come up from grass. Jill Muir was training all three of them. Gowran Ranger was the best of the three at the time.

'When I got to Newbury I saw Jill trotting up Gowran Ranger and asked whether there was anything wrong with him. She told me that the horse was perfectly all right and that Tom was going to ride. I said, "You must be crackers. Gowran Ranger is bound to beat Tea Tray; and mine, even though he's unfit, should beat Tea Tray too." Anyway I had a fiver on Tom and Kim had a very big bet on his own mount Tea Tray. Tom jumped off in front and made all the running, although we did have a bit of a go at him at the last fence, pushing and shoving. Nevertheless, he came away again on the run-in and won, with Kim second, and I was third.

'Now at that time, Tom Hanbury was a trooper in the Blues and a condition of the race, which had not been noticed by most people, was that it was for horses ridden by officers. As we rode in, Kim, who was behind me, said, "You can object, Roscoe!" I thought, "Christ, that will be a good thing. Everybody knows that Kim has backed his and if I object, he will get the race. A pretty sort of carve-up!" So I told him to keep his mouth shut and not to be such a bloody fool. I did not object. In the end it all came out and both Kim and Tom were had up in front of Lord Rosebery and each fined £50 and given a serious ticking off. Tom kept the race and Kim lost his money!'

This race had improved Santick considerably. He was in again at Taunton a fortnight later. Roscoe says, 'He was a better class than any of the others, but somehow I don't think he liked the course very much. He preferred a galloping track like Newbury or Sandown. I think that was why he jumped very crookedly. I didn't take the lead until quite near the end. Then I went on and we were quite a long way in front as he jumped the last, crookedly again. There was an objection and I was had up in front of the Stewards. The Senior Steward was a Captain – in uniform, of course. I had put my tunic and cap on before going into the Stewards' room. As I walked in, I thought I'd better do something and so I saluted. The Senior Steward blushed and said, "That's the first time I've ever been saluted by a Major!" Anyway, the objection was over-ruled! I was very proud of Santick. He was a damn' good horse.'

In the second week of November, the Regiment moved to Newmarket. The 1st Armoured Division had a Home Defence role in East Anglia. It is interesting to note that this one Division, stripped of its Royal Horse Artillery, which alone had been sufficiently equipped to accompany the British Expeditionary Force to France, was given the task of guarding the east coast from the Yorkshire Wolds right down to Harwich. This proved an embarrassing task for a formation whose primary requirement at this period was to be left in peace near the training equipment which it had been able to collect in lieu of tanks during the previous year. Newmarket, however, proved a good station where life in billets and requisitioned buildings was experienced for the first time. The country round the town proved quite good training ground for tanks, by the standard of those days, and many day and night exercises were carried out in the area of Thetford Heath.

Roscoe says, 'We were lucky because we moved up to the east coast to repel Hitler. Even luckier when we drew Newmarket, so that when we arrived there you can imagine what the local inhabitants thought of our tanks, even though they were not very big! They were aghast, but luckily we had a lot of horsed soldiers still and as soon as they saw a string of horses, they pulled up automatically out of courtesy and to look at the horses. Every morning we trundled up the Bury Road but kept strictly off the gallops. We were billeted for our Officers' Mess in Oakfield House, which used to be the Calcutta Turf Club. It made a lovely Mess with eighteen bedrooms and a swimming-pool. The soldiers were billeted where the stable lads used to stay for the races, so they had a pretty good time too.

'We were royally entertained also, by the trainers like Basil Jarvis, who always gave Colin and me a bottle of champagne on Sunday morning. Both of us used to ride out for old Tom Leader every day and how well I remember working up Warren Hill. We stayed in Newmarket for five or six months and before we left Newmarket we gave a large cocktail party to all our friends who had been so kind to us. I was talking to Fred Darling when a Colonel Joe Kingston, who had been in the 1914–18 war and had two rows of medals to show for it, walked past. Fred said, "Who's that?" I told him and he said, "He has ridden some winners, hasn't he." I always remembered this remark with much amusement when I saw some of our generals, particularly our allied ones with rows and rows of medals .

'I had a lot of hunting with Kim Muir. We had two horses each. So we moved them to the Crown Hotel at Oakham, where we had rooms for our soldier servants as well. To begin with we were not allowed to hunt. Our Colonel said, "If Hitler arrives and you're away hunting, what do you think would happen?" I said, "He'll probably win!" Eventually everything quietened down and we hunted with all the packs in Leicestershire, the Belvoir, Cottesmore and Quorn. We would meet at 10.30. No wire and only fifteen people out. It was fantastic hunting.'

The landowners of the district were extremely hospitable and the officers enjoyed several days' wonderful shooting in what is possibly the finest pheasant country in the world. The racing fraternity spent hours in the stables and on the Heath at the invitation of their many friends among the trainers.

Round about Christmas the weather turned bitterly cold. The country was still snow-bound at the end of January 1940 when the 10th moved from Newmarket to the Wimborne area of Dorset. On the way they took part in a Divisional exercise, directed by the War Office, spending one night at Dunstable in what in those days was considered extreme discomfort. This exercise, nevertheless, had the effect of stimulating interest in the 1st Armoured Division and caused a redistribution within the Division to equalise the proportion of light tanks and Cruisers between the two Armoured Brigades.

At Wimborne the Regiment began to take shape for action. More tanks arrived and transport was built up to war scale. This was fortunate, for it was not long now before the 10th were to enter the active war.

On the Continent there was an extraordinary sense of false confidence, and at the end of April the 1st Armoured Division was ordered to proceed on May 13 to a training area at Pacy-sur-Eure, south of the Seine, merely to complete training and to equip.

But on May 10, before the first flight of the Division had left England, the long-delayed German blow fell on the Western Front. However, instead of a frontal assault on the Maginot Line, in which the French plan put so much trust, Hitler launched an airborne assault on Rotterdam and attacked the Dutch and Belgians along the Meuse. After a few days the Dutch were forced to capitulate while further south the enemy captured bridges over the Meuse at Sedan and Maastricht, thereby outflanking the main Maginot key defences.

The first flight of advanced units of the 1st Armoured Division actually left England for France on May 16 and, owing to the situation, the Division was warned to be ready for immediate action. Orders for training at Pacy were therefore cancelled. It was now hoped to concentrate near Arras, but again, owing to the rapidly-developing situation, this was changed to Bolbec in the Havre peninsula. However, only a small portion of the Division arrived at Bolbec before it was finally decided, after all, to concentrate south of the Seine.

Moreover, at this stage, while the Divisional Commander, Major-General R Evans, was already over in France, the only divisional Infantry (the 2nd King's Royal Rifle Corps and the 1st Rifle Brigade), and one of the Armoured Regiments were removed from his command and retained in England for a special task, which eventually turned out to be the gallant defence of Calais, that was to see many fine men killed or in prison for the rest of the war. So the Division was by no means complete in units, apart from deficiencies in equipment, when it embarked for France.

May 21 was the day the main body of the Regiment embarked at Southampton. It was also the day on which the Germans captured Amiens and, having encircled the BEF and the French First Army turned their attention southwards. In fact the whole thing was a Comfu (for the benefit of the uninitiated: Completely Organised Military Fuck-Up), from which it is incredible that we ever emerged. That this country was not sunk without trace will always remain one of the most amazing facts in history. The pre-war politicians and the Higher Command should all have died, like Queen Mary, with Calais engraved on their hearts.

Lieutenant-Colonel Derek Hignett had taken over command from Charles Gairdner in April. Roscoe was second-in-command of the Regiment and Colin Davy was commanding A Squadron, Jack Archer-Shee B Squadron and David Dawnay C Squadron when the 10th sailed from Southampton.

Frantic efforts had been made to complete the Regiment's equipment, but when they finally embarked, many 2-pounder guns for the Cruiser tanks were still in their crates and had to be lashed onto the tanks until there should be time for their fitting after disembarkation. The Division sailed at 4 o'clock in the afternoon in two ships, the *Amsterdam* and the *Vienna*, which formed convoy in the Solent at midnight and set a course for Le Havre. During the night the course was changed for Cherbourg, as it was reported that the Germans were approaching Le Havre. The two ships carrying the Regiment then berthed at the same quay at Cherbourg before daylight and unloading began at once. As they were slung ashore, tanks were driven off to an assembly area nearby where the guns were fitted and calibrated and ammunition stowed.

During the day of disembarkation two long RAF trailers arrived at the docks loaded with Rolls Royce engines and driven by crews of exhausted, but tough, young non-commissioned officers who were determined to prevent these precious power units from falling into the hands of the enemy. Although the reason for their haste was not yet apparent, the 10th helped them load the engines on board one of the ships, and they have always believed that possibly these contributed to the winning of the Battle of Britain four months later.

Roscoe says, 'We soon discovered how bad our tanks really were. They wouldn't even stop a rifle bullet. We moved up as far as the Seine and Amiens and had a very bad battle. We were the only Regiment in the Brigade to attack. The other two Regiments, the Bays and the 9th Lancers, had received orders calling off the attack, but the message never got through to us and we attacked on our own. So, instead of having three Regiments in line, the enemy were able to concentrate solely on the 10th Hussars. My tank was put out of action. A bullet had made a hole in the petrol tank. I didn't realise that and thought my tank driver had lost his nerve, so I told him to start the bloody thing up and get across the road. He said he couldn't because he'd been hit. I said, "Don't talk such balls!"'

There was plenty of unorthodox fighting. When Sergeant Major Canning of A Squadron found his tank in the middle of a number of slit-trenches into which his guns could not depress to fire, he jumped down to the ground, ordering his Gunner to cover him, and proceeded to shoot at the occupants of two or three trenches with his revolver. When that weapon jammed owing to an empty case slipping into the ejector, he produced his penknife and calmly dug out the case, reloaded and carried on. Another tank commander got out of his useless vehicle and set about him with a heavy crowbar, with devastating effect on the slit-trench occupants.

In early summer, as members of the bloodstock industry know well, this section of Northern France can be almost as attractive as England. Although less than twenty-five years ago it had been a devastated battlefield, it was now green and pleasant. Roscoe says, 'I had a very nice Corporal and, when we found ourselves in a little farm, with some delightful asparagus beds and rabbit hutches, I asked him if he knew how to skin a rabbit. As a good countryman, he knew well and we enjoyed a superb rabbit and asparagus stew. In another farmyard, my Gunner went into ecstasies when he saw a large litter of sucking-pigs. He wanted to pick them up there and then, but I told him that, as he might have noticed, we were otherwise engaged! Nevertheless, when we leaguered for the night, he walked back two miles and killed eight of them. As we had nowhere else to put them, we hung them round the tank!'

That nasty battle, at a place with the unlikely name of Huppy, saw the last of Second Lieutenant Kim Muir. Roscoe says, 'Colin and I were probably the last people to see Kim alive.' During the evening after the battle Roscoe and Colin in a scout car went out as near as they could to the enemy positions to try to locate some of their missing men. After crawling along the roadside ditch to within 250 yards of the enemy positions, they located Kim, who was lying unhurt in a patch of young wheat. With him was his Troop Sergeant, Sergeant Locker, who was badly wounded and whom Kim would not leave. 'It seemed unlikely we could get to them,' says Roscoe, 'because the ground for about seventy yards was bare and in view of the enemy, as we soon found out. We called out to Kim and about forty yards out into the field he answered, but as soon as he raised his head, there was a burst of machine-gun fire. The rat-tat-tat we were used to, but the frightening Spandau is like tearing calico. Unlike Colin, I had not been in the trenches in the First War and so I thought that I ought to try and get them. I just got about ten yards into the field when *brrrrrr* . . . and I did a couple of back somersaults into the ditch. We decided to try again later on when darkness had fallen, but of course the enemy had anticipated this manoeuvre and we couldn't find anybody. Two days later, when the 51st Highland Division had driven the enemy back towards the Somme, we were able to return to continue the search. We found Kim's body not far from where we had last seen him. He had been riddled by a burst of machine-gun fire.'

A series of messy engagements followed as the French, in complete disorder, ran away or capitulated on all sides. On June 8, away to the north, the last of the Allied troops were being evacuated from the beaches of Dunkirk. June 14 found the Regiment temporarily at Le Mans, contemplating a possible re-fit, when they heard that General Weygand had declared Paris an open city and that German columns were moving westwards behind them towards Cherbourg. By June 18, the anniversary of the day when, 125 years earlier, Wellington had defeated Napoleon and his French Army at the Battle of Waterloo, it was all over. Meanwhile, the 2nd Armoured Brigade had been making its way through the lovely countryside of Brittany, basking in a beautiful summer, to Brest.

Roscoe says, 'After we got to Amiens, we were supposed to be joining with the British Expeditionary Force, but on our wireless we heard that the BEF was embarking at Dunkirk. As one of our Troop Sergeants said, "This is the biggest fuck-up since Mons!" – not that he had been anywhere near Mons! We had little trouble getting back to Brest although we had no more than ten tanks left.

'Our Brigadier, Dick McCreery, later to command the Rhine Army as General Sir Richard McCreery, said he had a very important letter – from the Prime Minister – which said that we were to keep fighting in order to keep the French in the war. So I made a rather obvious remark – "It sounds rather like the Ten Little Nigger Boys to me!" Dick was horrified. "You must not say things like that, Roscoe!"'

As the Regiment passed through the lovely countryside

of Brittany, the people gave them a great reception. This was the more surprising in view of the impending collapse of the French government and the fact that a British division withdrawing could hardly be an encouraging sight.

During the night of June 15 the Regiment harboured in a wood near Dirinon. The men with all small arms and equipped with ammunition and personal kit were packed as tightly as possible into the minimum number of vehicles for the short journey to Brest, while a small rear party stayed behind to destroy the remaining lorries and equipment, later to re-join on the dockside.

On June 16 officers and men embarked on the *Manx Maid*, once the pride of the Isle of Man holiday season. At daybreak German planes flew over and dropped mines, which appeared to block the channel, and the naval authorities would not allow the ship to sail until it had been swept. No minesweepers were available! However, the British skipper of a rusty old cargo vessel, anchored offshore, said he had taken bearings on the fall of the mines and declared that he could give the *Manx Maid* a lead out to the open sea with a fair chance of missing them.

This offer was accepted and so, with a skeleton crew consisting of himself, two in the engine-room, a quartermaster and one deck hand, the brave skipper set off and the 10th Hussars followed somewhat anxiously. However, their faith in this splendid seaman proved justified. As they reached the open sea he drew upsides and exchanged signals. They left him with a cheer, increasing speed, and finally at 8.30 am on June 17 the *Manx Maid* docked at Plymouth.

The Regiment had had its baptism of fire and, in spite of a heavy reverse at Huppy and the loss of all its equipment, had emerged with comparatively light personnel casualties. Many were missing at Louviers, but the majority became prisoners-of-war and endured five long years before their release.

Chapter Eleven

Taurus Pursuant

Few events in history have shaken the British people so profoundly as the German Campaign of 1940 in France and the Low Countries. The qualities of the German Army, the Wehrmacht, as it came to be known, had indeed been demonstrated the previous summer in Poland, but Poland was a long way off and hardly a great power and, although it was hoped that she might hold out for longer, one month did not seem a frighteningly short time for her subjugation.

When however the enemy with his first big attack cracked the French defences; when he dispersed the great armies of France and drove before him our own little Expeditionary Force exactly as he pleased – until the desperate evacuation from Dunkirk saved most of it from his clutches; when Paris fell and France fell and England was threatened with invasion all in the space of three weeks, then the eyes of the British people were open to the full panorama of Nazi power and efficiency.

We are all familiar with the effects upon the British mind and spirit of this awe-inspiring performance and the highly perilous situation which it brought about. It was the German speed and mobility that shattered the thinking Briton. To men who only twenty-one years

154

before had returned from an almost static war fought in horrible conditions in trenches, the speed of the German campaign was unbelievable. Men like my father, who had been invalided out badly wounded towards the end of the First World War, and now rejoined the Army – a foolhardy move that was to overstrain an extra-gallant heart – were completely stupefied. They just could not believe that this new type of warfare had come to stay.

Of course, the Wehrmacht's success was based on two weapons – aircraft and tanks.

During the months that followed Dunkirk the words Panzer Division assumed a near mystical significance. Such a force was the magic sword, the Excalibur of the modern commander. Without Armoured Divisions no army could hope to win. So then, having miraculously escaped the threatened invasion, it was clear that we must have these Divisions; first, so that if the Germans were rash enough to invade us, we could counter-attack and throw them into the sea as they had thrown us out so unceremoniously; and, second, so that, when the time came, we could once more land on the continent, liberate France and even invade Germany herself. Those days might be far off, but the necessary Armoured Divisions had to be commissioned right away, and although we could not yet give them much equipment, they must have priority in men, for they were to be the elite of the new Army wherewith Britain might retrieve her desperate position and take the field once more with confidence against her enemies.

Out of these high resolves the 11th Armoured Division was born. The embryo began to develop in December 1940 when most of the Regiments were formed, including the 23rd Hussars, which comprised officers and men from the 10th Hussars and from the 15th/19th Hussars, under the command of Roscoe, newly promoted to Lieutenant-Colonel. The Divisional sign of the charging black bull on a yellow background, 'Taurus Pursuant', became famous. Later the Division was to be led by the two finest Armoured commanders in history, General 'Pip' Roberts and his great friend Roscoe. In any other country these men would have been idolised and hero-worshipped. Sometimes the British habit of understatement can be a fault.

Roscoe says, 'There were a number of old racing friends in my Regiment. We had lots of chaps arriving from Civvy Street in cloth caps and bowler hats, chauffeurs, miners and so on. Trying to get them really fit was tough. To this end and to keep the chaps amused, there had to be a lot of sport. At one time we were stationed up at Penkridge in Staffordshire and in that area lived some fairly famous footballers. Each of the three Regiments in the Brigade thought that they had a very good football team. We had a chap in the 23rd Hussars called Joey Beresford. Now, I knew nothing about soccer and had no idea that he was any good until I went down to watch a match as Commanding Officer and saw him playing well. After the game I asked who he had played for in Civvy Street, expecting him to say he had represented Puddleditch United. He replied "Preston North End and England, sir!" Needless to say, he was in our team and I had a nice bet with Mike Aird in the big match. Beresford scored three goals!'

About the beginning of June 1941 news that the 1st Armoured Division had been selected for the Middle East became fairly public. This announcement was received with great excitement and joy in the 10th Hussars, who were only too eager to avenge the setback in France. Preparation for mobilisation for overseas service and training in desert warfare then began in earnest.

A few weeks before the Regiment finally embarked, the Commanding Officer, Lieutenant-Colonel Derek Hignett, was medically declared unfit for service in the Middle East owing to a previous illness he had contracted in Egypt in 1930. Later, he was to be given command of the GHQ Liaison Regiment, better known as Phantom, and commanded elements of that unit in the famous Dieppe raid of 1942.

Luckily for all, that splendid 10th Hussar, General Willoughby Norrie, was commanding 1st Armoured Division and was able to reclaim Roscoe.

Roscoe received the news of his new appointment from General Hobart. He says, 'Hobart was sacking every commanding officer. I shall never forget. I was about thirty miles away and he sent an order saying "I want to see you at once" via his senior staff officer "Mac" Mackeson of the brewing family and the only member of the Scots Greys at that stage to have been to the Staff College. Mac said pompously, "I can't possibly tell you what he wants with you." I said, "Why the bloody hell can't you tell me?" I thought I was for the high jump.

'So I arrived at Hobart's headquarters in Yorkshire and he asked me to come upstairs where he told me I was going to command my own Regiment. I must have looked pretty sick because he asked me if I was feeling well and if I wanted anything.

'"The strongest whisky ever," I told him.

'"What do you mean?" he asked. "Don't you like the news?"

'"Of course I do," I replied. "It's a fulfilment of the greatest ambition of my life to command my own Regiment, the 10th Hussars, but Christ, General, you've been sacking so many Colonels, I thought you were going to sack me!"

'He laughed and told me that I was to be replaced in

157

the 23rd Hussars by my old friends and fellow jockeys Lieutenant-Colonel Perry Harding and Major "Monkey" Blacker from the 'Skins.

'A few years later, on the Second Front, I met Hobart again in France. He was a great man, but very, very tough. He congratulated me and said that I had done marvellously. I replied, "Well, they're always saying any fool can ride a horse as long as it is properly schooled and trained!" General Hobart said, "Do you know, that's one of the nicest things that anyone has ever said to me."'

Roscoe rejoined the 10th Hussars at Ogbourne St George, where Martin Hartigan trained, on the edge of the Marlborough Downs. A few weeks later in October 1941 the 1st Armoured Division sailed to join the Army in the Middle East. The Regiment, together with certain other elements of the Division, embarked at Greenock on a ship called *City of Paris,* and the whole convoy formed up off the north-east coast of Ireland. As one who, eighteen months earlier, had done the same voyage on the ill-fated liner *Empress of Britain,* I can vouch for the novelty and excitement. The 12,000-mile voyage was a hazardous trip in mid-Atlantic and round the Cape of Good Hope with chances of enemy air, U-boat and surface attack at many points. But, in fact, the journey was this time uneventful from that point of view. Thanks to the Royal Navy, sailing in this great convoy of Atlantic liners, merchantmen and naval escorts was a wonderful sight and the zig-zag tactics of a convoy at sea in wartime were of great interest to many of those who had never had the chance to find their sea legs. Sadly Colin Davy had to be left behind. He had, after all, been in the First War and was now considered too old for active service in the Middle East.

At the beginning of the voyage it seemed as though

the ship had been overloaded. Nevertheless, after a few days of grumbles and complaints everyone sorted themselves out and settled down. Although there was naturally a lot of recreation and games like housey-housey, or bingo as it is now known, several hours every day were devoted to such training as could be done on board ship. For example, Bobby Archer-Shee gave expert instruction in the use of the sun-compass, which was to prove a boon to many in the months ahead.

In order to avoid the enemy's shore-based aircraft which could now, of course, use the whole of the west of France for operational bases, and keeping clear as far as possible from Dakar, the potential enemy U-boat base that was now in Vichy hands, they eventually put into Freetown, the hot and humid West African coaling station, to re-fuel. Here, as the ship stood close in, the native young men came out to greet her, each standing on the flat part of a sort of punt called a 'bum-boat'. In accordance with time-honoured tradition, they would dive acrobatically to retrieve pennies thrown over the side by the soldiers. They never seemed to tire of this happy game and, periodically of course, had to relieve nature which they did naturally, peeing over the side of their little boats into the sea. They were all stark naked and some of them appeared to be particularly well equipped. Roscoe remembers being most amused when he was summoned to the rail by one of his officers who was pointing at a young black man in the action of relieving himself. 'Look, Colonel,' he said. 'He's using two hands!' – and so he was!

From there on until arriving on the same latitude on the other side of Africa, the dangers from enemy inter-ference lessened, although there was always a chance of a surface raider in the Southern Atlantic. But the con-voy continued without interruptions and, after rounding the Cape, it split into two portions, part putting into Capetown and the rest, including the 10th Hussars, going on to Durban. So, after a few more days at sea, the *City of Paris* sailed into that highly civilised, somewhat American-looking port. The officers and men of the 10th Hussars then experienced for five days the hospitality which I, as a nineteen-year-old sub-altern, had enjoyed unforgettably in Capetown. South Africans, men and particularly women, were kindness personified, generous in the extreme. I have never been lucky enough to return to South Africa, but my gratitude to its people for the wonderful welcome that they gave to all the troops in convoys heading for the war up north will remain forever. All those young men who passed through Capetown or Durban on their way to possible death owed a tremendous debt of gratitude for the hospitality that they received from the South Africans.

Roscoe says, 'When we docked in Durban the British authorities there did not want us to have any fun at all. A little snooty Captain or Major, who obviously had no intention of ever seeing a shot fired in anger, came on board to give us our instructions. I said to him, "I will tell you what my instructions are. I want to stay at the best hotel in Durban and remain there for the time the troops stay here and I shall visit them once during the morning and I will leave one Major on board each day."

'He said that this sort of behaviour was totally out of the question. "I've come on board to tell you the procedure. Every man on this boat has to be back on board by twelve o'clock and every officer by one o'clock."

'I didn't think this was at all a good idea, particularly as Simon Elwes, the famous artist who was a Captain in the 10th, was laying on some superb parties for us. He got to Durban before I did, I had not met him because

160

he had joined the Regiment while I was away with the 23rd, but as soon as we arrived he introduced himself. "I'm giving a dinner party for you," he said. "I've got all the best-looking girls in Durban waiting to meet you." And he had too! Simon not only gave good parties. He also fought well during the war.

'Anyway, the first night I did condescend to come back on board – at three in the morning. Toby Milbanke, who was now a Major, arrived back even later, escorted, or perhaps one should say supported, on either side by two very friendly black South African military policemen!

'The following morning four old soldiers who had been in the Regiment before the war were brought up before me charged with not getting back on the boat until 1.30 am.

'I said, "Do you know what time you were supposed to be back on the boat last night?"

'They said, "Yes, sir."

'"What time?"

'"Twelve o'clock, sir."

'"What time did you get back?"

'"Well, Colonel, you see, we met all these people and they were very kind and they took us to their houses and gave us a lovely dinner and then they wanted us to go on to a dance with them . . ."

'"What time did you get back?"

'"A little after one, sir."

'"Do you know what time I got back?"

'"No, Colonel."

'"Do you know what time I was supposed to get back?"

'"No, Colonel."

'"I was supposed to get back at one o'clock and I got back at three o'clock in the morning. As far as I am concerned the case is dismissed. But I want you to tell

161

all your friends that they must get back on board by one o'clock. If you can't do what you want to do as a 10th Hussar by one o'clock in the morning, you're no bloody good!"'

Roscoe stuck to his original plan. 'As far as the officers were concerned, we got back on board at any time. Why should I exchange those lovely sheets in Durban's best hotel for my cabin on the boat until I had to? We had a lot of fun – about five days there. An awful lot of the fellows who were with us got killed in the desert, but they had five bloody good days. I saw to it. On the last night the Regiment put on a super cabaret show in the Star Dust Club. I remember we had a wonderful pianist and a yodeller and all the rest of it. At midnight a military policeman came up to Jack Archer-Shee and said, "Why aren't you back on your ship? You were supposed to be back on board at midnight. The ship is sailing early in the morning."

'Well, Jack knew that I had found out from the Captain of the *City of Paris* that the boat was sailing at nine o'clock the next morning. So Jack said, "I don't know. You'd better go and ask my Colonel."

'"Where is he?"

'"He's over there."

'"Well, go and get him."

'"Go and get him! He's with a very nice lady. I wouldn't think of disturbing him."'

All good things have to come to an end and sure enough at nine o'clock in the morning the convoy moved on, arriving at Aden on November 3. Here the convoy anchored while individual ships were sent singly up the Red Sea to Port Tewfik (Suez) to avoid congestion at that port, which was subject to frequent air attacks.

While the Regiment was delayed at Aden, they were challenged to a polo match by the American Consul, who had some polo players on his staff and in the garrison. The 10th had been at sea for a very long time, and it was said by some that the American hospitality contributed to the defeat of the Regiment by 4 goals to 1! Roscoe's explanation is different: 'We had a bad team. Jack Archer-Shee was our only decent polo player apart, I suppose, from myself. Toby Milbanke and Arthur Grenfell composed the rest of the team. After the match we had to get back onto the boat. Our troopship was tethered outside somewhere. We went down to the quayside and asked a very nice Royal Navy Lieutenant if he could take us back to our boat. He said, "You'd better come to my ship first and I'll ask the Captain if I can take you."

'His ship was HMS *Cornwallis,* which was sunk with HMS *Repulse* off the coast of Malaya. As we drew near the warship in our launch, I said knowingly to my officers, "Don't forget we have to salute the quarter-deck when we get on board." As soon as we did, I was taken off to the Captain's quarters and the other officers were taken to the wardroom. We all had a hell of a lot of drink. They wouldn't let us go! Eventually we set off, well pissed by this time, in a small Naval boat. The coxswain was a good fellow. He said, "Have you any idea what your ship looks like?" It was getting dark and there were twenty-five ships in the harbour. We were really foxed. There was a big argument as to whether the *City of Paris* had one funnel or two – we'd been on the bloody thing all the way from England! – and nobody knew quite which. Eventually we got near and saw the name. "That's it!" we shouted. "*City of Paris!*" Then we had to go up a sort of ladder. We were so paralytic it's a wonder we didn't all fall in. Toby Milbanke, who had had a real skinful, did just that. We picked him out with a boat-hook and got him back again. We were met by the Captain of the *City of Paris,*

163

who was charming. He said, "There's nothing like having you back on board but I don't think much of you. I hear you lost the polo." After all, we were just waiting to go to war and it was damn difficult to find one ship out of twenty-five, to find the right one. We couldn't even have found it in daytime!'

Eventually it was the *City of Paris*'s turn to move up the Red Sea and the Regiment arrived at Port Tewfik (Suez) on the afternoon of November 27. They disembarked at once and were taken off by train to the Western Desert base-camp at Amariya, a dust-ridden spot on the western outskirts of Alexandria.

I can personally vouch for the fact that, despite the war and the threat of a possible, even probable, German invasion, 'Alex' and Cairo were very gay cities indeed – in the old-fashioned sense of the word – at that time.

The 10th were lucky indeed to have a Commanding Officer who had served in Egypt only twelve years earlier and knew every inch of the country by day – and by night!

Of course, even Roscoe had not been mechanised in Egypt, so for all the Regiment this life with tanks in that strange gravel-topped sandy terrain which comprised the desert was something new. The hot days and cool nights; the constant shortage of water; 'brewing-up', cooking meals over a fire made from petrol-soaked sand in half a petrol-can; rations, fuel and the eagerly awaited mail coming up in the Regimental lorries in the cover of darkness; the totally different dress of battered suede desert boots, pale khaki stockings, faded shorts and tropical shirt, equally faded cap (Roscoe hated berets); and the performance of natural functions by walking out into the desert with a shovel – all these had to become second nature.

Chapter Twelve

In The Desert

There was a barely concealed sense of urgency as the 10th unpacked its stores at Amariya and collected tanks from the vehicle ships. Although they did not know it at the time, history was to show that the 2nd Armoured Brigade of the 1st Armoured Division arrived in the theatre just in the nick of time. A few more weeks could well have been disastrous, not just for the Army in the Middle East, but for the entire Allied war effort. If they had not arrived in time and fought as they did, it seems almost certain that Rommel would have broken through to undefended Alexandria and Cairo, thus giving Hitler the Mediterranean and perhaps total victory.

'If we had had better tanks,' says Roscoe, 'we might possibly have defeated him then. Crusader and American Honey tanks against German Mk III and IV tanks was like putting a selling-plater against a Classic winner. It was not until many months later when the American Sherman tanks arrived that we had any chance. Very sad, but true.'

Until November 1941 there had been two offensive campaigns in the Western Desert. The first had begun in December 1940 under General Wavell, when the

Army of the Nile under General Sir Henry ('Jumbo') Maitland Wilson had followed up a brilliant victory at Sidi Barrani by driving the Italian army out of Egyptian territory, had pursued it through Bardia to Tobruk and had finally cut off many remnants south of Benghazi by a quick dash across the desert from Mekili to Beda Foum.

Then, in the spring, the Germans had joined the Italians on the African continent and their elite Afrika Corps under General Erwin von Rommel, later to be known as the 'Desert Fox' in German wartime mythology, arrived on the scene. He quickly retaliated, and the British forces, much weakened by calls from other theatres such as Greece and the Far East, were driven back to the Egyptian frontier. But, as they withdrew, they left a strong garrison in the fortress of Tobruk, which was to prove a thorn in the side of the enemy.

In mid-summer of 1941 the second British offensive was launched by the Western Desert Force in an attempt to relieve the hard-pressed garrison of Tobruk, which was by then becoming most expensive to maintain by sea without air superiority. The operation was not a success and British forces returned to the Egyptian frontier.

Now, at the end of November, just as the 1st Armoured Divison was arriving in Egypt, a third British offensive was being launched. This attack was made in considerably greater strength than had been possible in the last 'Operation Battleaxe'. There were now two Corps operating under the newly formed Eighth Army, commanded by General Sir Alan Cunningham. In the north along the coast road was Thirteen Corps consisting chiefly of infantry divisions, while further south was the new Thirty Armoured Corps under the command of General Willoughby

166

Norrie, containing the 7th Armoured Division and the 22nd Armoured Brigade, which, alone of the 1st Armoured Division's troops, had arrived in time for this offensive. The task of the Thirty Armoured Corps was to defeat the enemy's armour and relieve Tobruk. That of Thirteen Corps was to drive along the coast road and reduce the enemy forces before joining hands with the Thirty Corps at Tobruk. This was the general plan of the operations which were now in progress while the 1st Armoured Division, less the 2nd Armoured Brigade, was assembling at Amariya.

While the Regiment was still unpacking its kit, drawing ammunition and generally preparing its tanks and vehicles for active operations, news of the success of the battle now being fought away to the west came through to them.

At the same time they were joined by an experienced tank officer called David Bune, who subsequently transferred to the Regiment, and by some American instructors, who arrived to teach them about the engines and guns of the American Stuart or Honey light tanks, some of which had been issued in addition to the British Crusaders, as the latter were insufficient to complete their establishment. The Crusaders were particularly unreliable and the Honeys had the advantage that from a mechanical point of view they were sound. They were also fast and handy. But neither tank had any gun bigger than a 2-pounder.

During a short time a few months later when I was a prisoner of the Germans I saw Rommel himself travelling around in a captured Honey tank!

At the same time Tony Wingfield, who had been a Staff Officer on 1st Armoured Division now returned to take over B Squadron from Toby Milbanke.

Roscoe says, 'Winston Churchill knew Toby Milbanke's father, who had been awarded the VC in the first war. When somebody told him that Toby had been given the MC, he shrugged his shoulders and said rather meanly "Hm! That's not a VC!" Probably as a result of that remark Toby never stopped trying to win a VC for himself!'

Moreover, when General Willoughby Norrie was promoted to take over command of a corps, the former 12th Lancer, well known to the 10th, General Herbert Lumsden, was appointed to command the 1st Armoured Division.

Roscoe says, 'It was quite an eventful sixteen days at Amariya. We completed all our equipment, zeroed our guns (destroying one camel in the process!), had our first sand storm and set fire to a store tent with resounding explosions of tank ammunition. We had a few last-minute trips to the civilisation of Alexandria to stock ourselves up with such "goodies" as could conveniently be stored in the lockers of our tanks and then set off in pursuit of the Eighth Army, which, having relieved Tobruk, was now pursuing the enemy south-westwards.'

So the great moment had come at last for the 10th Hussars to start getting their revenge for the shambles in France. To many, it was going to be a baptism of fire and those officers and men experienced the same indescribable feeling of adventure, apprehension and excitement that you get when going out to ride your first race over fences.

On December 14 and 15 they moved their tanks first by the desert railway to Mersa Matruh, where their wheeled vehicles joined them by road. On the 16th the 2nd Armoured Brigade concentrated thrity-five miles to the south in preparation for their grand trek westwards which was to last for 400 miles before they entered the battle. Moving off, the Brigade formed up for the first time in desert formation with some 150 tanks deployed around Brigade Headquarters in the centre, with the Brigade Navigator flying a large blue flag from his vehicle. So they headed for the Egyptian border, which was marked by an enormous wire fence previously erected by Mussolini, presumably with the intention of preventing the Senussi from enjoying the fleshpots of Egypt. This wire fence stretched for hundreds of miles across the desert to the south, but was now broken in many places by gaps through which the opposing armies had passed. It was known as 'the wire'. They found the right gap in the wire, thanks to some good navigation, and were greeted as they went through by the familiar figure of the General Officer Commanding Thirty Corps, their own General Willoughby Norrie, who was waiting to watch his Regiment drive past. After a brief halt they drove on through the gap onwards for a further ten miles before reaching their leaguer area as darkness fell.

They were now in Cyrenaica, in occupation of enemy territory, which was a gratifying thought, and there they remained for some ten days, practising desert manoeuvres, while the whole of the 1st Armoured Division joined up to concentrate for the further move.

Trooper Roger Willetts was now with Roscoe, driving either his jeep in the forward positions or the staff car. 'He was my staff car driver right through the desert,' says Roscoe. 'We had a lot of fun. The desert was a wonderful place. Later on, everybody talked about Monty restoring the morale of the Eighth Army. It was a load of cock. The morale was tremendous long before he arrived. You felt so well in the desert. We spent that Christmas there just west of the wire and, although some people were lucky enough to receive a parcel and others may have kept sufficient of their "goodies" before leaving Alex, it was a fairly austere Christmas Day. The London papers reported that there were turkeys for the Eighth Army. Rubbish! The officers never even got their whisky ration! I had some nice friends in the Gunners and they had got their rum ration out. We'd been out for such a short while that we hadn't even received ours. So a splendid Gunner Colonel called Gregson shared his rum with us. It wasn't very good. Then they sent us up nuts instead. They told us they were very good for us, and better than Army biscuits.

'I got about a week's leave some time after that and went back to Cairo where I had been previously in 1928. I knew a chap who ran a clothing store. I think he was an Armenian Jew. He pretended he recognised me when I went in.

'He said, "What do you want? Do you want to buy some nice bush shirts?"

'"Bush shirts?" I said. "I want to buy some good scotch whisky."

'He told me he only had some Canadian stuff. He said, "Things are very difficult."

'I said, "I'm sure they are! How much?"

'"What do you want?"

'"I want Black and White or Haig. And I don't want the corks tampered with."

'We had been warned not to buy black-market stuff, but he quoted me about £3 a bottle, which was quite cheap, so I bought a couple of dozen. I had no reason to regret this, but when I was walking down the street I saw a wine store with some kummel, which I was rather keen on. So I went in and bought a couple of dozen bottles of that too.

'I was very popular when I got back. We were happily drinking the kummel when somebody said, "Look at the label. Have you seen what's on the bottle in very small writing? Made in Palestine!" Sure enough it was. You have to hand it to whoever set up a factory in Palestine to make kummel. It was as good as any produced anywhere else.

'We were supposed to get a bottle of whisky a week as officers, as long as it arrived, which it sometimes didn't. They sent up beer for the other ranks.

'Peter Farquhar was second-in-command of one of the Brigades. IIc was sent off to the NAAFI to get some stores and they told him that the booze had not arrived. Peter said, "Now I understand what your initials stand for. No ambition and fuck-all interest!"

'The water in the few wells was brackish and bad. When we had to edit all those letters that went home there was one from a fellow in the Regiment which said: "Dear Mum, Every time you pull the plug, you'll know my water ration has gone away for a week!" Quite untrue, but funny anyhow!

'Normally the water supply was well organised. Each tank had a crew of five. Part of its equipment was a five-gallon "jerry-can". So, when the water truck came up at night with the rations, all the jerry-cans were filled up and taken back to the tanks. A gallon a day for everything, washing, drinking, etcetera was not too bad. On the occasions when it got down to half a gallon or less, it was a shade uncomfortable. Naturally one had to shave every day – there were no electric razors in those days! – and anything less than half a gallon became distinctly uncomfortable.

'The troops learnt the unique feeling of the desert and something of the ways of desert warfare. They learnt how easy it was to get lost in that sandy emptiness, dotted with bits of scrub, without a compass, especially at night under a vast expanse of stars. I myself was terrified of getting lost. We grew accustomed to billowing clouds of sand behind each vehicle and the gritty feel of sand everywhere, in our clothes, our hair, our shoes, our food, as well as the

171

hordes of flies forever having to be brushed away from the face and eyes at each halt. There were no antibiotics in the first-aid kit and, if you cut or grazed yourself, the tiny wound was apt to fester and turn into what became known as a desert sore. Certainly it was cold at night, but this was a relief from the heat of the day and we had plenty of warm clothing to put on, so we never suffered from cold. Bathing, brushing your teeth and shaving in a mess-tin of water, brewing tea over a petrol fire at every opportunity, became a way of life and we enjoyed it.'

The war in the desert had many similarities to war at sea in that navigation and mobility were all-important and the side unable to move was inevitably out-manoeuvred and beaten. In this respect the Eighth Army suffered two major handicaps.

Their petrol-cans were weak, ineffective containers which leaked easily. Hence, in the bumpy desert conditions, the supply B Echelon lorries inevitably wasted great quantities from leaking cans. This was inclined to result in their movements being restricted through lack of petrol. The other disadvantage was that they were consistently out-gunned. The 50mm guns of the German Mark III tanks were effective against ours at 1000 yards. The 88mm gun, which was originally designed by the Germans as an anti-aircraft weapon, adapted to become the finest anti-tank gun of the war, was deadly at at least 1500 yards. As we have seen, Crusader tanks were mechanically unreliable and their 2-pounder guns were only effective at the most at 500 yards. So they always had to approach for 500 yards under fire to get within range.

Roscoe, the Desert's armoured hero as Colonel and Brigadier, takes great exception to Field Marshal Lord Carver's recent allegations that British armoured troops were badly trained.

He says, 'Field Marshal Carver was a Major at the time and I consider his remarks about the armour being untrained to be inaccurate and unfair.

'I would like to suggest that if, in the Desert, he had personally been in the position of fighting German Mark III and Mark IV tanks in Honeys and Crusaders, equipped with peashooter two-pounder guns, he would have realised that the fault lay not in the training but in totally inadequate tanks. The odds were at least 50 to 1 against us.

'And I think it's only fair to those who lost their lives against such odds that their training should not be blamed.'

I can do no better here than to quote Brigadier Tony Wingfield, later to be Racing Manager to the Queen, Roscoe's brother officer and great friend for no fewer than fifty-seven years. At this point, he had just been sent back from a Staff appointment to rejoin the 10th Hussars.

'We soon moved into the Western Desert and spent Christmas 1941 just west of the wire – the border between Egypt and Libya. We then set off westwards to relieve the 7th Armoured Division in the Agedabia area which they had exploited after the recapture of Tobruk.

'During this long journey we learnt the "desert lore" with the aid of David Bune, a delightful and excellent officer from the Royal Tanks, who was to join our Regiment. We now had the experience of making ourselves comfortable in an uncomfortable terrain, and with Roscoe's guidance, we studied the tactics for coping with the established fact that the German guns outranged and outgunned our miserable 2-pounders. During that period I think we all felt great confidence in our Colonel's logical sensibility and firm leadership.

'On one occasion during this period when Roscoe

took the whole Regiment out on an exercise, he manoeuvred us about in different directions of varying distances until switching off his wireless and telling us to
find our way back to our leaguer. Of course, none of us
Squadron Leaders had recorded our manoeuvreing on
maps and so had no idea where we were. The other two
Squadron Leaders were George Errington and Bobby
Archer-Shee. We argued for a few moments and then
went our separate ways. I got home first, but only by
the grace of God. I think Roscoe thoroughly enjoyed
his trick.

'No sooner had we in 1st Armoured Division relieved
7th Armoured Division in the middle of January 1942
than Rommel, who had been hiding round the corner at
El Agheila, building up his force, burst out of his lair
with a strong column of German and Italian tanks and
anti-tank guns. The battle of Saunnu then began on
January 23.

'Briefly, the 9th Lancers were the first to encounter
the enemy and the 10th Hussars were supposed to pass
south of this action which was to be broken off. My
squadron was in the lead. I asked the Colonel
permission to alter my direction a few degrees to the
right to avoid the enemy. This was agreed, but I still ran
into enemy anti-tank guns and then tanks. My communications were then shot away and I presumed
Roscoe would see the position and pass further to my
right. But I should have known better, for he threw in
the other two Squadrons on my left and the battle was
really on! Roscoe's own tank, as well as several others
at Regimental Headquarters, was hit and the Adjutant,
Captain Williams, who was acting as Roscoe's gunner,
was fatally wounded.

'In retrospect, although we had not conformed with
the Brigade's intention of breaking off the action, this
was not our own fault but that of the enemy, for, had

174

we not engaged and fought him as we had done, he would undoubtedly have embarrassed, if not destroyed, our Brigade and Divisional Headquarters.

'Undoubtedly we saved the Brigade and Divisional Headquarters from being overrun. By that evening all that was left of the Regiment was a few tanks and guns with Roscoe himself in one area and myself with the wounded and stragglers which I collected in another area not far away. During the subsequent withdrawal, the Regiment, which was only in fact a composite Squadron of seven tanks, was detailed as rearguard. And the following afternoon an enemy force of tanks and anti-tank guns in a mixed column appeared on our right flank and manoeuvred to cut us off from the main body of the Brigade. Roscoe now decided to rush this column and drive straight through it. The action, which was highly successful, completely surprised the enemy who were unable to use their own weapons effectively, owing to the damage they would have done to their own vehicles, while our own tanks, such as they were, including a troop of the Bays who had joined us, let fly with every weapon they had. This action closely resembled the flight from a mail-coach in an old Western film.

'I'm told that it was a splendid example of old-fashioned cavalry dash, typical of Roscoe, who was at his best and enjoying every minute of it. "Give 'em full belt!" he kept shouting. "Give 'em full belt!"'

Looking back on this action, Roscoe himself says, 'Bill Williams was a great loss. He was a good shot and as the German tanks came on I had said to him "Get him, Bill!" He shot five times and the little shells went *wheeeeee* and bounced off. Of course, finally they hit us and we had to move back. Bill's leg was half off and he got gangrene in it. We couldn't get him back quickly enough. When we made that charge young

175

Houghton-Brown, who was in my staff car, or as they were called utility car, was also killed.'

The Regiment had to break off this highly successful action as petrol supplies were low and arrangements had been made to replenish at a petrol point which it was known was shortly to be withdrawn.

Roscoe says, 'There was still tremendous spirit in the 10th Hussars, although we were all very green. I was frightened of getting lost. I'd heard stories of people dying of thirst in the desert – Foreign Legion and all that. We lost a great many tanks in that battle of Saunnu. It really was the most disastrous battle from that point of view. As night was falling, I had only two tanks left in the 10th Hussars and my friend Tom Draffen, who was commanding the Bays, had one. Our Brigadier at the time was Raymond Briggs, a fellow from the Tanks whom we called the "umbrella man" after the firm in Piccadilly. He came along and saw us both. He said, "We can't talk here. I must go. Follow on to Charuba!"

'So he scarpered off. Now Tom had a three-ton lorry full of petrol in addition to his one tank. I thought that might be very useful, because at least we could get to Cairo with it! As my tank driver was rather better than Tom's at night, we did a bit of map-reading which took us to a hollow in the ground where a number of our officers were. This was Charuba. I asked, "Where is the Brigadier?"

'They told me and I found the ACV, one of those big armoured boxes on wheels which formed a Command Headquarters with wirelesses and things inside them. It was like a great big sort of tin can, and you could sleep in it if you felt so minded. Anyway, I came up to this thing and banged on the door as hard as I could. A quavering voice came from inside. "Who's that? Who's that?"

176

'I shouted at the top of my voice: "Rommel!"'

'After a long pause our Brigadier's voice said, "I'm sure that's you, Roscoe!"'

'When he opened the door, I shook my finger at him. I said, "It bloody well might have been Rommel. You left two Commanding Officers without any supporting arms all on their own in the middle of the desert and buggered off! A great many of our tanks have broken down or been knocked out and we're reduced to three tanks between two Regiments."'

Despite the Regiment's heavy losses, it had been successful in saving the Brigade Headquarters and the Brigade of Guards from attack by a very strong armoured force at a critical time.

So the 2nd Armoured Brigade withdrew to Charuba, where the 10th Hussars retired to the rear area to re-fit. Here C Squadron was equipped with the second type of American tank to enter the war, the General Grant, which resembled a giant cottage loaf and carried for the first time in British tank history reasonable armour and, above all, a 75mm gun. This raised morale considerably. The defect, of course, was that the gun was in the hull, not in the turret, and so the tank had to be very exposed in order to fire it. Moreover, it had a very limited traverse, so you had to turn the tank rather than the gun in the direction of your target. Nevertheless, it was certainly an improvement on the 2-pounder.

Tony Wingfield says, 'During this defensive period in the spring of 1942, the regiments of the 2nd Armoured Brigade were withdrawn one at a time for re-fitting in an area south of Sollum. When the 10th Hussars were returning to Gazala on tank transporters, my tank on its transporter toppled over and fell several feet upside down going up the escarpment near El Duda. Luckily nobody was in the tank. The rain then poured down and Roscoe halted the column. As my bedding equipment was under the overturned tank, he kindly let me come into his car for the night. Otherwise I should probably have developed pneumonia!

'Again at a later stage, we were withdrawn when the 7th Armoured Division came forward again after re-fitment. Roscoe was able to take some leave and he had been told that I was to be posted to some job which would involve promotion. He did not know what or where this job would be, so he took me on leave with him to Alexandria before any posting order arrived! We spent a very noisy night in the Cecil Hotel and met in the hall, having been summoned from our rooms by some air-raid warden. We both agreed it was much quieter in the desert! We moved to Cairo the next day and I discovered my job was to be GSO1 at the new Tactical Training Centre being set up near Ghaza in Palestine. Thus I missed the battle of Knightsbridge for which Roscoe was awarded his first DSO.'

Chapter Thirteen

Courage and Endurance

I have deliberately built up to this first six months in Roscoe's forty-second year in the belief that the reader will share my conviction that this was what his life had been all about. The first half of 1942 was surely the culmination of all that had gone before. The hunting, steeple-chasing, pig-sticking, polo, during twenty-three years of military training; the nerves of steel, the quick, inspired decisions, the complete disregard of personal danger, the icy coolness at all times, the total intolerance of anythng but the highest standards in himself and those under his command; the sense of adventure coupled with a fierce determination to defeat the enemy whom he hated as much as he loved his own soldiers – all these factors combined to produce the man for this crucial moment, a small, wiry, bespectacled figure in long faded shorts, revelling in the conditions, commanding the Regiment he adored in its finest hours.

Some idea of the measure of the man under pressure can be gained from my own experience a few months later, when, as a young subaltern, Signals Officer to my Regiment, the Greys, who were under his command, I had to telephone the Brigadier, as he then was, in the middle of a very hairy battle. The reply was immediate. 'Hello. What do you want? £5,000 to £2,000? You must be daft. We're full right up on that one. I couldn't even let you have £600 to £400. Might let you have a little £50 to £40. Now, what can I do for you, boy?'

'Monkey' Blacker, now General Sir Cecil Blacker, who, as a Major, served under Roscoe in the Second Front, said, 'His humour and imperturbability should never be allowed to conceal the remarkable, tough, determined and inspiring character that lay behind them.'

Rommel again attacked on May 26 and the battle of Knightsbridge began. The plan was to trap Rommel's forces in a series of heavily defended box formations, cutting off his supplies. On the morning of May 27 the Brigade, 10th Hussars leading, went into action against the screen of approaching 88mm anti-tank guns, successfully driving them back without loss to themselves, by skilful use of the ground.

At dawn on May 28 the Brigade headed north with the 10th still leading. Contact was made with a force of anti-tank guns and C Squadron engaged, but, having to expose so much of their Grant tanks in order to fire, suffered some casualties. B Squadron then attacked in two waves with artillery support, successfully over-runing the enemy, capturing thirty-five prisoners and destroying six guns with few casualties.

The next attack was launched on a two-Regimental front with the 10th Hussars on the left and the 9th Lancers on the right. The setting sun blinded drivers and commanders. Roscoe says, 'We were advancing into the attack on a certain bearing, but the Brigadier (Raymond Briggs) suddenly changed the bearing and I was unable to inform Bobby Archer-Shee, who was commanding A Squadron and whose wireless had been shot away. So they went too wide and too deep into the midst of the

180

enemy anti-tank guns. The enemy were forced to withdraw, but not before inflicting casualties on the Squadron and capturing most of them, including Bobby.'

So Roscoe was left with two Squadrons, when, at 7 am, the 10th were engaged in a fierce battle with a force of 160 tanks.

George Errington says, 'This was some battle, never to be forgotten. We were fighting to defend the Knightsbridge box occupied by 201 Guards Brigade, commanded by John Marriot. On the third day we were ordered "stand and die" as we were being attacked by the 15th and 21st Panzer Regiments. We started fighting at 7 am and the Regiment stood its ground throughout the day, but all B Squadron tanks were destroyed and by 6 pm the Regiment had fought until they had no shells left to fire or tanks fit to fight.

'Colonel Roscoe's own tank was shot from under him and he walked about on his feet amidst all the shot and shell throughout the battle, saying, "Don't give one yard, please do not give one yard. Stay where you are and fight." Thanks to him alone, we held that position. John Marriot said that we and we alone saved the Guards Brigade. He said, "We have never seen anybody fight like you did. We thank you very, very much indeed."'

Roscoe was recommended for an immediate DSO. The citation, written by Brigadier Raymond Briggs, and supported by Major-General Herbert Lumsden, Commanding 1st Armoured Division, Lieutenant-General Willoughby Norrie, commanding 30 Corps, and General Auchinleck, Commander-in-Chief Middle East Forces, read: 'Almost continuously and without rest, Lieutenant-Colonel Harvey commanded and fought his Regiment and a Battery Group placed under his command from 27 to 29 May 1942. When his Regiment was reduced to three tanks I was compelled to withdraw him to re-fit. Throughout, his courage and endurance and energy has been an example to all who saw him. Throughout he has shown conspicuous skill in handling the combination of the three arms. In particular on 29 May 1942 his dispositions, orders and directions were responsible for the destruction of at least eleven enemy tanks and several anti-tank guns in the vicinity of Barrel 201. Confronted by superior numbers and under considerable anti-tank and heavier shell fire, his complete control, his absolute disregard of personal danger, his grasp of the situation, were largely responsible for the stemming of the Panzer advance from the Maabus Errigel feature. His handling of the evacuation of the wounded and of damaged tanks whilst he was still in action was an example of what courage, determination and direction can effect.'

Much later, when he finally escaped from an Italian prisoner-of-war camp, Bobby Archer-Shee said that he had been held at Rommel's headquarters for thirty-six hours, standing by at the German leader's command with a white flag at the ready. With his supply route cut, Rommel actually thought that he was within hours of defeat. However, he finally broke through, but not before the Eighth Army, thanks to the 10th Hussars' fantastic rearguard action, was able to retreat back to the Alamein Line.

George Errington says, 'We were allowed three days rest by the sea. Roscoe insisted that we have one parade a day just to ensure we had shaved that morning. It didn't matter that we had practically no clothes to wear, and some of us were starkers. We'd lost the lot! So we all turned up on parade with nothing on. This was typical of Roscoe!'

All this time Corporal Roger Willetts, as he was then, was with Roscoe. He is still with him today forty-five years on.

'I took over the Brigadier's car after the battle of Saunnu,' he says. 'He had a batman called Roberts and I drove the staff car and the Jeep. He had another driver for his tank. I was right up with the Brigadier at Knightsbridge. In some ways it was worse than being in the tanks because we were sitting in a thinner-skinned vehicle. Mind you, at Knightsbridge, when he was walking about telling them not to go back, he was a bit further forward than me!

'I then went off to the coast with him for four or five days where we had no clothes but there was one parade a day to see that we had shaved. We swam nearly all day long. The batman and I were more or less on our own. Eventually, the others were able to draw new clothes but we hadn't heard about this. The order came through from the Squadron that we had to fall in on parade. Of course they were all dressed and there I was with Roberts in swimming trunks!'

Roscoe chips in. 'In the desert when the Germans used to drop those splinter bombs, I said that everybody had to dig in at night, at least a shallow trench to sleep in so that the splinter bombs didn't get them. After a bit I found that nobody ever dug anything unless they saw Willetts digging me in. If they saw me being done, they all dug; but if Willetts didn't dig, they didn't!'

Willetts says, 'There was one night before Alamein round about Knightsbridge time when the RAF bombed us terribly. They were told there was a reported enemy convoy, but it was us. They tickled us up all night!'

Roscoe says, 'The next day I went to the chap in the RAF and said, "Thank you very much indeed. You gave us a lovely night." He didn't even know he had bombed us!'

Between them, Roscoe and Willetts went through several cars. Willetts says, 'The very next morning we got Stuka'ed, and I lost my car.'

These German dive-bombers, specially designed to frighten as well as inflict injury, were slow aeroplanes but particularly effective for the purpose for which they were designed – accurate dive-bombing. They dropped their bombs with a violent screaming sound. Like the 'Moaning Minnie' mortars, they were the first attempts at psychological warfare – and very successful they were too in inspiring fear in those on the receiving end.

Roscoe says, 'A little later, when I was commanding the 4th Light Armoured Brigade, I had a wonderful little Jeep driver, who used to follow me like a good retriever dog and drive his Jeep right up as far as he could under my armoured car. One day we found ourselves a bit too close to some German tanks, which started shooting – mainly at me. I was a bit vulnerable in my armoured car, so I said "Let's get out of this quick." We did just that with the Germans shooting at us as we went. Then I saw my little Jeep guy skidding off in front of me and disappearing. I thought that he'd got cold feet, or something, or gone mad. In fact he'd got a bullet through his radiator and gone to get it fixed. He had a radiator put in really quick, he said, "because the Brigadier wants me back as fast as possible". He was back in forty-five minutes! I said, "Where the hell have you been?" He said, "I got one through the radiator but I've got a new radiator now and I'm all right!" Well, that was splendid.

'He absolutely adored shooting German aeroplanes. This was his greatest kick in life. One day when I was with my second-in-command, Ronnie Joy, who was in the Royals, we suddenly saw these damned Stukas. My little Jeep fellow stood up holding a big machine-gun and, while Ronnie and I hurled ourselves onto the ground, there he was, never even crouching down, blasting away at the dive-bombers with his gun. He said, "Best shooting in my life. I hit that one. Can't you see that belching black smoke?" I said I couldn't because I had my head in the sand! But he didn't mind. Sure enough one of these aeroplanes did come down. Whether he hit it or not, I'll never know. But he was convinced he had and he said to me, "Could you wait for a moment?" I thought he wanted a pee. So he strutted off and came back and said, "No good. I thought there might have been some good German Airforce boots on the corpse!" Then he said: "Can I go down for some more ammunition off the Rifle Brigade? I've shot all my ammunition away, sir!" That's all he could think about, shooting down enemy aircraft. He was a splendid chap. He had no problems at all and had no use whatsoever for the Germans. I think he was in the Notts Yeomanry. I loved him and I would love to know what happened to him. By now he's probably in some frightful racket. Perhaps he's murdered a few people by now. He was one hell of a little guy, as brave as a lion.'

In July 1942 Roscoe was posted as second-in-command of the 2nd Armoured Brigade, and Jack Archer-Shee, who had received the Military Cross for his part in the battle, assumed command of the 10th. When Rommel was finally halted on the Alamein Line, changes in command throughout the Army were made. General Sir Harold Alexander had taken over from Auchinleck as Commander-in-Chief and General Montgomery had assumed command of the Eighth Army. It was the arrival of considerable reinforcements in the Middle East and the comparative ease of the administrative situation which assisted as much as other factors in enabling plans for further withdrawals to be destroyed and the final battle of Alam Halfa Ridge to be won, which finally secured the British position at Alamein. It was 'the beginning of the end' of the Axis forces, not only in Egypt but also in the whole of the North African continent.

The stage was now becoming set for the final act of

Alamein. At last, we were getting some decent tanks – notably the American Sherman which had reasonable armour, an accurate 75mm gun capable of firing high explosive as well as armour-piercing shells and was not only fast but tough and reliable. Roscoe says, 'I have always maintained that it was not Montgomery but the Sherman tank which won the battle of Alamein.'

Now that he had left the Regiment, Roscoe too was doing a little personal reorganisation.

Tony Wingfield says, 'One night I met Roscoe in the Hotel Cecil with Paddy Leatham. George Errington was there too. He arranged for us to go to a party with the Peels, wealthy cotton merchants, who had a lovely villa in Alex. There were lots of girls at the party. Roscoe and I competed for one of these girls and we nearly all went into the swimming pool in the struggle.

'When things got better at Alamein, I was sent back to the Middle East Training Centre in Palestine and Roscoe came up to lecture to the armoured wing of the school, of which I was the boss. I gave him the best Palestinian wine I could get hold of and a ride on one of the stable horses I had set up there. The students were spellbound by his account of the desert battles, and his lecture was a total success.'

Roscoe undoubtedly has a charmed life. On one of these visits from the desert to Cairo in order to go up to Palestine, he himself was driving, with Willetts in the front passenger seat and Roberts in the back. Willetts had just had the staff car overhauled and done up. 'It was a real treat, beautiful,' he says. 'We were going down towards Cairo and there was an Indian convoy moving up towards us. The Brig said airily, "Don't the pyramids show up splendidly?" And bang! We hit this 50-cwt truck with a tremendous crash. One Indian went yards in the air and we went over on our side. My lovely car was a write-off.

'I took all the skin off my arm because I had it out over the side. I'll never do that again in a hurry. We skidded along on our side. Roberts had all the bedding behind him and a great big ammunition box containing the rations. There was also a folding table in front of him. With the crash, the ammunition box fell over and hit Roberts on the back so that he had his throat jammed on this table. He was choking, but the Brigadier said, "Come on, Roberts. Jump out. Don't sit there shamming."'

Spasmodically the front-line troops received English newspapers and, at periods like this, they sometimes found time to read one. Roscoe says, 'I managed to get hold of the *Sporting Life* every now and again and, of course, would read it from cover to cover. One day I saw that Sir Humphrey de Trafford had been made a Steward of the Jockey Club. Now, I knew Humphrey quite well. So I wrote to him saying that when the war was over I wanted to be a Steward's Secretary, a stipendiary steward.

'Apparently he was absolutely delighted and rushed into White's, brandishing my letter, saying "All is not lost! Here's a senior officer in the Middle East who not only thinks that racing will start up again, but also wants to be part of it!"'

'It was good to get news from home and it was always particularly encouraging to know that our Colonel in Chief of the 10th Hussars, Prince Henry, Duke of Gloucester, was following our progress with interest. When I was commanding the Regiment before Knightsbridge, he had visited us and stayed the night with us. We made it a proper night too. George Errington was particularly good with the bawdy songs. Prince Henry was delighted and kept saying, "I want to hear that Deddington again!"'

'A great deal of the Regiment's success with the

Sherman tanks and their new 75mm guns was due to Major Henri Le Grand, a splendid Belgian officer who was attached to the Regiment at this time and who at one stage in his military career had been a 75mm-artillery officer. Henri was a very brave man whose great aim in life was killing Germans. He won the DSO during the battle of Alamein but was later killed in Normandy in 1944 while leading a tank patrol of the 23rd Hussars. His Squadron was commanded by Major Chris Seymour, and formed part of my 29th Armoured Brigade. So Major Le Grand was associated with the Regiment which he had always adopted as his own to the end. Among his many accomplishments was the art of sketching and some of the watercolours are a lasting memorial to this gallant officer's actions with the 10th.

'One of the only troubles with the American tanks was that, when they arrived at base in the Middle East, each one had to be overhauled by the base workshops before being sent up the line to us. When they arrived we were at first delighted to find a very nice map-case in each tank. It was only later that we discovered what we had been missing. The map-case was just the one remaining article that the base workshop chaps didn't want. The Yanks had filled every tank with goodies, hundreds of cigarettes, candy and cans of beer, for the fighting soldiers. We never got any of them. They were all pilfered at base by certain chaps who made damn' sure that they never saw a shot fired in anger.'

Cairo was a very active city at this time. There was so much going on and so many officers coming and going on leave. I have always liked the story of the evening at a night club when Roscoe persuaded the glamorous, seductive, topless belly-dancer to come and sit at his table and then to dance with General Sir Richard McCreery. Now General Dick, who was later to command the Rhine Army, was not only a brilliant soldier and a very fine horseman, but he was also a particularly upright, holy man. Nevertheless, he was nothing if not a gentleman. So, when he found himself dancing in full view of everyone with this embarrassingly naked young Egyptian lady, he felt that it was his bounden duty to make polite conversation. As an opening gambit he tried, 'Er, do you know Tidworth?'

Those of us who took part will never forget the battle of Alamein. Roscoe was in the thick of it, first as second-in-command to Pip Roberts in the 22nd Armoured Brigade and then as commander of the 4th Light Armoured Brigade, with my Regiment, the Royal Scots Greys, under command. As the pursuit of the fleeing Germans intensified, we were taken away and given to the New Zealanders as their armoured Regiment.

'I had eight or nine hens when I was commanding the 4th Light Armoured Brigade. They were a great treat because they laid any number of eggs when they were in the mood. Then one day we saw some gazelles and shot one and on another occasion Willetts and I saw one of these turkey bustards. I was very proud of that. I got my gun and hit the bird straight through the head. We had a Sergeant who was a great cook and we had roast bustard. It tasted lovely. I shall never forget that feat of marksmanship.'

For a brief period when Brigadier Fisher was sick, Roscoe took over the 2nd Armoured Brigade. 'We went round by Mersa Matruh. The weather was awful and we couldn't get any petrol. We saw the Germans streaming out of Mersa and if only we'd had some petrol we could have scuppered Rommel there and then.'

The advance continued with increased momentum. The Germans were making their best way back. As Signals Officer to the Greys, I was making my way back to the Regiment one evening when I was taken prisoner by the famous 90th Light, Rommel's crack troops, who had been cut off and were waiting in a hollow for a moment to beat a reluctant retreat. Horrified at the thought of having to spend the rest of the war in a prisoner-of-war camp, I knew I must escape quickly and, after a few days, under cover of darkness, slipped away. I made my way north to the coast road, and when daylight came, was very lucky not to be shot up by the armoured cars of the Royals who were the leading unit of Roscoe's Brigade. I think my Colonel was more annoyed at the loss of my Jeep than relieved at the recovery of a junior officer!

When we captured Tripoli we found that the Italians had organised quite a civilised little seaside town and port. Although he was, of course, a noted religious Puritan, Montgomery, to his eternal credit, appreciating that his troops had been a long time fighting in the desert and, furthermore, obviously wanting to prevent the spread of venereal disease, re-opened the organised brothels – one for officers, one for NCOs and one for other ranks. This was fine and the gesture of a good soldier, however much he may have disliked it. Before long, however, unhappily word inevitably got through to the bigoted churchmen in England, whose protestations managed to have the brothels closed.

As for Roscoe, his 4th Light Armoured Brigade by-passed Tripoli. When they halted, they found some Arab riding-ponies, and since the local police had some ponies too, the Brigadier decided to have a race-meeting.

'I invited these Arabs to race and made a circular track. When they saw it they held their hands up in horror and said they couldn't possibly go round corners, so we made a straight course. We picked the police ponies out of a hat and the one I was riding was known to be the best horse. I was a roaring hot favourite. I made an announcement that the only reason I was riding this horse was that it had been picked out of a hat. But this made no difference. We had quite a few ex-bookmakers and made a Tote. We made the mistake of having half-a-crown windows. We ought to have had all £1 or £5 windows, as they were betting like crazy men. Pay-day was the day before and they were betting like drunken sailors. In the event, John Persse, (son of the famous Atty Persse of The Tetrarch fame), won the race. Poor John, he was killed in Italy on the very last day of the war with his Battalion of the Rifle Brigade. The Arabs rode in beautifully decorated saddles that must have weighed about 2 stone. I suppose the Arab jockeys were riding at about 14 stone! The whole thing was a lot of fun.'

With the British First Army and the Americans advancing, albeit somewhat haltingly, from the west, the time was ripe for the final destruction of the Axis forces in Africa. Roscoe took over command of the 8th Armoured Brigade, which in turn was placed under the command of the New Zealand Corps commanded by that great hero, General Bernard 'Tiny' Freyberg, who had won the VC at Gallipoli during the First War. As their armour during the run up from Alamein, we in my Regiment had got to know the New Zealanders very well. In fact that magnificent great bear of a man, Tiny Freyberg, spent the advance travelling in my Colonel's tank, a topless Honey.

As the most recently mechanised Regiment, we had been given some particularly ropey tanks. When you start off with new tanks, they are usually given rather grandiose names. For example, B Squadron tanks all carried the beautifully printed names of packs of hounds beginning with the letter B, like Belvoir, Beaufort or Blankney. After a while in battle, the occupants of the tank were apt to have other ideas. One of our Shermans had 'THE BURGOO' painted in huge white letters

191

along the side – the Scottish name for porridge. This tank became quite famous, but not as much as the other clapped-out Sherman which bore the name in similarly large letters: 'THE FIGHTING HAGGIS'! If you asked the New Zealanders on the line of march whether they had seen the Greys, the reply invariably was 'Well, the Fighting Haggis came by ten minutes ago, so the Regiment's probably about half an hour ahead!'

Roscoe remembers one particular tank under his command which carried the most artistic seductive picture of a naked woman with arms and legs outstretched, and the caption underneath: 'UNCONDITIONAL SURRENDER'! This caused quite a stir in the towns and villages of Northern Europe a little later.

Roscoe and Tiny Freyberg, two fearless men with one shared aim, to defeat the enemy, hit it off from the very beginning. They could have been made for each other. Roscoe says, 'Freyberg was like an old fox.' Well, I reckon that by now the description could well have fitted the Brigadier commanding 8th Armoured Brigade!

When Montgomery visited Roscoe's Brigade area, he asked to meet his staff. 'I introduced him to my Brigade Major, Laurence Biddle, from the Sherwood Rangers, and to my DAQMG Matthew Arthur, later to be Lord Glenarthur, of the Greys.

'Monty asked, "When did you go to the Staff College, Major Biddle?"

'"I didn't go to the Staff College, General."

'"What! Brigade Major and never been to the Staff College? Why?"

'"Well, I only joined up for the war and I never had the chance."

'Then shaking his head, the General turned to Matthew. "When did you go?" Matthew replied exactly the same.

'Exasperated, Monty, saying that this was appalling,

192

turned to me and asked when I went. I told him I was in exactly the same position as my staff; I had never had the opportunity.

'"That's not true," he said. "I know you are a regular soldier." However, he smiled a slow smile and said, "It's quite a change to have a Brigade with a Brigadier and both his Staff Officers none of whom have been to the Staff College!"

'I got on quite well with Monty, even though I was a Cavalry Officer and he never really liked us. But he sacked poor old Herbert Lumsden, the Major-General who was such a good desert soldier and a great friend. Herbert had wanted to do one huge sweep round, taking a risk, quickly to cut off Rommel's supplies early. It might have ended the war in Africa very speedily. But Monty was not prepared to take the chance. Herbert also refused to go back from the front line to see Monty, whose headquarters were well behind at this time. He got the sack, but not before he had won the argument by saying that Monty had taught him at the Staff College never to get officers back from the front!'

One particularly sad incident at this time was the death of Roscoe's second-in-command, Colonel 'Flash' Kellet, an ultra-smart, extremely popular hunting officer from the Sherwood Rangers (Notts Yeomanry). 'We found that, when we were halted, we could put our two tanks together and sit down with reasonable safety. One morning when my Brigade Headquarters was not very far from the enemy, Flash said that he must have a shave. I said "Don't be so bloody stupid. Let's wait till lunchtime and the Germans are sure to stop shelling at one o'clock as they'll be wanting to eat" – which was what normally happened. However, he insisted that he couldn't face the day without shaving. Of course he was always frightfully smart. So I said, "In that case for God's sake get shaved in your tank. Get right down inside your tank. Don't make a target of yourself."

'However, he did just that. Flash sat on top of his tank with his shaving mirror, obviously attracting the early morning sun. Crack! A shell blew his head off.

'It was very sad for me as I loved Flash. He and Donny Player and I used to sit in the evening talking about anything but the war. All our hunting in Leicestershire and so on. Donny was killed a fortnight later.

'As the war went on and people were getting killed whom you'd only known for a very short while, it wasn't too bad. But when grand old friends like these got killed, it really upset me.'

As the Armoured Brigade Commander, Roscoe, of course, had to visit the New Zealanders' Headquarters at least once every day. 'I loved them all,' he says. 'General Freyberg may not have been the greatest soldier, but, rather like an old dog fox, he always knew what was going to happen. I was told that the New Zealanders were not the saluting kind. Freyberg said to me one day early on, "If they like you they will wave at you." And that's exactly what happened. When I drove up to Headquarters three or four weeks later I arrived roaring with laughter. The General asked me why. I said, "I must be getting on well. Everybody waves at me." He was delighted.

'Old Tiny was very attached to our Brigade. When we were advancing, I would either be in a tank or an armoured car. He used to come up in an open car, bang on the back of my vehicle and say, "You've got to get on, Roscoe." I would say, "We are getting on." My tank driver, who was a Sergeant, used to say, "Here's the old man coming!" Sure enough, he'd roar up again, "You've got to get on, Roscoe!" He was a very brave man.'

Various old cavalry 'sweats' were about at this time, including 'Chatty' Hilton-Green, the famous amateur huntsman-MFH, who had been in the Royals and was now back on the Reserve. Roscoe says, 'I had a sign in

194

the shape of a fox's mask made for the transport to follow in the desert, to show them the way up to the tanks. The 8th Armoured Brigade were always known as "the boys of the fox's mask". We were coming back one day and I went past a military policeman in a Jeep with a driver who was lying back with his feet up and paying no attention whatsoever. He never jumped to salute the Brigadier. So I went to see who he was. It was none other than old Chatty Hilton-Green who said, "I knew that if I followed the fox's mask I'd find the right fellow at the end of it. That's why I've come here."

'I said rather dryly, "I don't think much of your driver. He pays no attention at all to the Brigadier."

'Chatty said, "You remember him, of course. He used to be First Whipper-in to the Cottesmore at one time. I'll take you out to meet him." Do you know, even then the fellow didn't salute. He didn't even get up. He just took his army hat off like a huntsman!'

Chapter Fourteen

Skill and Coolness

By March 1943, when spring was breaking in England, the sands of the desert were running decidedly cold for Rommel and the Afrika Corps.

In November the British First Army and the Americans under General George Patton had landed in North Africa, and now the stage was set for the final assault on Tunis.

In February the Prime Minister, Winston Churchill, had visited the Eighth Army in Tripoli after the Casablanca Conference and had reviewed many of the troops. As he stood at the saluting base with the tears rolling down his cheeks, many thought that this Africa campaign was his particular baby and that they were tears of gratitude. We later discovered that he was suffering a severe attack of dysentery, or 'gippy tummy' as we used to call it!

During this visit, he delivered a speech in his best form on the subject closest to his liking, a victorious campaign. His peroration was: 'In days to come, when asked by those at home what part you played in this war, it will be with pride in your hearts that you can reply "I marched with the Eighth Army."'

Montgomery had decided to make use of that interval

in Tripoli to check up on the Army's battle technique and he considered that this would prove an admirable opportunity for passing on the Eighth Army's experience to others. He therefore arranged for a series of lectures, demonstrations and discussions. Among the Generals who attended was the legendary George Patton, the tough American leader.

The story is told of his reply when asked what he thought of Montgomery's address on 'how to make war'. His reply came slowly with a lovely Southern accent: 'I may be old, I may be slow, I may be stoopid and I know I'm deaf, but it just don't mean a thing to me!'

After the landings in North Africa, his troops had met with some fairly humiliating reverses which had given the enemy new heart. Roscoe says, 'When Patton returned to the United States on leave, he was asked at a press conference "How did our boys do? How did they fight? Were they good?"

'The old war horse thought and then said, "They were like a bunch of bananas. Some were green, some were yellow and others were just plain rotten!"'

So, in March, the Allied Forces were closing in on Tunis from both sides. Rommel's last formidable defence was the Mareth Line. Then came the celebrated 'left hook' by the New Zealand Division and the 8th Armoured Brigade round the enemy's southern flank. This envelopment, which would come in on the enemy's flank and draw off his reserves, would take place immediately if an attack in the north failed to breach the Mareth Line. The plan was for the New Zealanders, led by Roscoe and his Brigade, to go right round the south in a big sweep before turning north to capture vital objectives and then, having won those objectives, to hold them for the 1st Armoured Division, led by the 10th Hussars, to pass through after a night march with the aid of the moon. The attack was, for the first time in

197

Roscoe's experience, to be accompanied by close co-operation from the RAF.

He says, 'All the Brigadiers were called together and Tiny Freyberg said, "I just want to tell you that we are the big boys in this next push. Monty will never get through the Mareth Line in the north. I have arranged with General Oliver Leese that, when he fails to get through and I say when, not if – he is to send me the code word "Benghazi". And we'll make our way to El Hamma and then the coast behind the Mareth Line."

'Sure enough the code word came through and off we went all the way round for the start of this big battle. I had my three armoured regiments with a battalion of New Zealanders behind each. The great thing was that we had to get through at all costs. We had a link with the Air Force, and they knew what they had to do. They had to keep bombing and strafing in front of us. The problem was that they got too close for comfort and were apt to drop the bombs on us! Of course this sort of joint operation had never been done before.

'I told my commanders, "I'm going to have my tank on the track and everybody has got to keep level with me." I must admit it was the only time I was ever really frightened in the war. It worked like a dream. We got through all right. There were Germans on the higher ground and I was sure I was going to be shot, but nobody seemed to fire at me. As we went down the road, if I saw anybody falling behind I would get on the wireless and say, "Come on you're dropping behind on the left there." I should think they hated me! Then, when we had gained our objectives, Monty switched to the 1st Armoured Division and they all came through, led by the 10th Hussars. I sat on my tank, waving my cap to my old Regiment shouting "View Holloa! Tally Ho! Forrard On!"

'The 2nd Armoured Brigade then went on through

until dusk, when they halted some fifteen miles from El Hamma to wait for the moon to rise at a quarter to midnight, when the advance continued. Very soon the two leading Regiments began shooting up enemy transport with their machine-guns. At about every half mile could be seen a burning enemy vehicle on one or other side of the road. Furthermore, enemy staff cars came tearing into the rear of the 10th Hussars, so that it soon became apparent that we had broken right through the enemy who had very little idea of their situation. Confusion was perhaps at its height when a battery of the deadly 88mm guns surrendered to the Padre of the 9th Lancers, who approached them to enquire if they were by any chance the B Echelon of his Regiment! Perhaps the worthy cleric was equally confused on receiving the answer, "Nein. 256 Flak Battery, 21st Panzer Division."'

Roscoe continues: 'We battled on through to a place called Enfidaville, where we received orders that we, the New Zealand Division, were to lead a final assault which appeared absolutely suicidal.

'Freyberg called all his Brigadiers together. He said, "We've got to go through this place Enfidaville and we've got to lead the attack again. Those are Monty's orders." We all looked rather glum and the great man appreciated it. He knew that the plan was an appalling one from our point of view and he also knew that the 56th Division of the First Army was coming up on the other side at Tunis. So he said, "Gentlemen, it reminds me of the story about a Sultan who had a donkey of which he was so fond that he offered a very large reward to anybody who could make his favourite animal talk. The trouble was that the penalty for failure was death. Several men tried and all were executed. Eventually one man volunteered, arrived and announced himself. The Sultan said, 'You must be a very brave man because you

199

know what will happen to you if you don't make this donkey talk.' The young man said, 'Yes, it is a very difficult task and will take a very long time. But I'll take the money and the job.' When asked by a friend why he had been so foolhardy as to take on this seemingly impossible task, he replied, 'Yes, it will take me a very long time to accomplish the feat. So long, in fact, that both the donkey and the Sultan may be dead!"'

'We waited for about six hours and then came the signal from Freyberg: "The donkey's dead!" So we didn't have to do it.'

Roscoe says, 'Then we went up to Cap Bon with the New Zealanders. There were thousands of German and Italian prisoners who couldn't get out. Minnow Prior-Palmer, uncle of that fine horsewoman Lucinda, took over the 8th Armoured Brigade from me. Old Freyberg, who wasn't really under Monty, could do what he liked with the New Zealand troops. So he said to me, "I'm very sorry. I've got to leave you behind. I'm off to Cairo. Monty can't stop me doing that and I want to take my boys back there to have a bloody good time. I told Monty I would take you with me for three or four months of the war, but he said he couldn't spare you." So I was kept up there for a long time doing nothing.

'I joined the 10th for the Victory celebrations at Azzizia and on the 21st of June King George VI, disguised for security reasons as General Lyon, arrived to inspect the Eighth Army. He had several complimentary words to say and recalled his last visit to the Regiment just before we left England in the Autumn of 1941.

'Any vehicles that were any good had been taken away, but we were told we could go to Cairo if we could get there. After a few of our old vehicles had been tinkered with, I managed to get back to Cairo where I was met by Tony Wingfield.'

Tony says, 'I did not see Roscoe again until the North

African campaign was over and I had been sent to GHQ Middle East in Cairo as GSO1 of the Armoured Corps Directorate – a job I simply loathed. It was here that I saw Roscoe and told him that he was to be posted to command the 29th Armoured Brigade, part of the 11th Armoured Division in England. This was part of Monty's request for interchange of experienced leaders with those who had not been in action before the Second Front. I was surprised that Roscoe did not seem too pleased at the posting, but I told him that I would have sold my soul to get home for a while. However, I soon found out that it was his loyalty to the 8th Armoured Brigade which was the trouble and that he wanted me to send the whole Brigade home. This was beyond my power. Oddly the Brigade did get home in the end and I commanded it for a few days in Normandy – but that's beside the point.'

Roscoe was now awarded another DSO in addition to his previous one, and two Mentions in Dispatches. This one was recommended by General Sir Bernard Freyberg, commanding 2 NZEF, strongly recommended by General Horrocks and endorsed by Generals Alexander and Montgomery. It read: 'Brig R Harvey commanded 8 Armoured Brigade Group during the time that formation was under command 2 NZ Div, from 10 March 43 to 16 May 43. During that period he carried out several difficult operations with skill and coolness. In the outflanking movement and subsequent battle for Hamma Gap, he led his Brigade with outstanding courage and determination and his personal example was an inspiration to all ranks. In subsequent pursuit he led his Brigade with the greatest skill and his thrusts greatly assisted the Force to drive the enemy back onto his final position on the Enfidaville Line. Every task given to Brig Harvey was cheerfully and expeditiously carried out and at all times he showed the greatest devotion to duty.'

'Wonderful man, Freyberg,' says Roscoe. 'He was no

stranger to medals. In addition to his Victoria Cross, he had so many others that the New Zealanders called him "The Collector" – the collector of medals!

'Tony told me, "You're for England. You're to be flown back. You've got to go and get yourself a suit of civilian clothes as you have to be non-military to pass through Portugal."

'So I bought a suit from some awful Egyptian tailor. When I got on this aeroplane, I found that the Archbishop of York was a fellow traveller. I thought that we would be all right with him. God above wouldn't let him be shot down! He was a dear man.

'We arrived in Lisbon and had to wait for about twenty-four hours. When we got out of the plane, we saw Germans on the other side of the airport doing exactly the same as we were!

'Anyway, that evening we went out to some bar and I expected to meet up with a gorgeous blonde sort of Mata Hari spy who would come up and say "What do you know?" But nothing happened at all, except that a whore came up to me and asked, "Are you doing anything this evening?" I said, "Thank you very much, I'm off!" Then we got onto the plane next day and there was no more trouble. I came back to Bridlington in Yorkshire to take over the 29th Armoured Brigade.'

Roscoe found an England changed out of all recognition from the one he had left. Unlike other countries, including Germany, where the rich still lived in style, Britain was now in the grip of total war, affecting every member of the community. Austerity was a way of life. Rationing of many commodoties, including food, clothing and petrol, had produced a new camaraderie. The whole country was now pulling together and all the old values were being called into question. Roscoe says, 'I found that everyone was very short of everything. Petrol, food, whisky, you name it. They had suffered and were still suffering quite a lot. But the successes in North Africa and now beginning in the "underbelly of Europe" were having an effect. It was the first fillip that England had had. We were, somewhat dubiously perhaps at the moment, back on the winning trail.'

The Americans were now in the war and there was a vast influx of uniformed Yanks. For example, my wife, with her family, had to be evacuated from their South Devon farm because the Americans were using that part of the coast to practise landings. She says, 'Tea in the evening would be saved for another cup in the morning. Every cigarette end would be saved so that the tobacco could be rolled up to make more cigarettes. It was as bad as that!'

Soldiers like ours who had been abroad for any length of time, away from their wives and girlfriends, were, needless to say, worried about the American "invasion". The saying that GIs were "overpaid, over-sexed and over here" did nothing to alleviate the worry of those troopers whose letters we had to censor. It was not a happy situation.

Roscoe took a month's leave at the house in Derbyshire which his wife had bought. He discovered that he and Biddy had drifted apart. 'It was nobody's fault really,' he says. 'I think that with their husbands constantly away, fighting the actual war, thinking of the next battle, or picking up the bits from the last, wives at home coping with the daily round of wartime England, bringing up their children in a changing world, inevitably became more independent. Many of them got to the stage where they didn't need their husbands. We had been working on different wavelengths for too long.

'The children, now, were something different. Jeremy and Jenny were both hunting with the Meynell. Jeremy was hunting this lovely little 15.3 hands chesnut, Aquilo. Just before the war, when we were at Tidworth we had gone over to Collingbourne Ducis to see Alec Kilpatrick, who had a couple of horses for us to look at. I told the children that they could buy one horse. It was up to them. There was an oldish grey brood mare and a two-year-old chesnut that Alec had bought in Ireland. "We can't quite make up our minds, Daddy," they said. "We like that grey horse, but will you help us?"

'I said, "No, you'll have to make your own minds up. I'm not going to teach you. You've got to do this all on your own." So after getting their little heads together, they said "Then, we like the chesnut."

'Alec ran Aquilo in fairly competitive races – of course all racing in the war was specially competitive because it was zoned – he finished third and fourth in three-year-old races on the flat. Then Jeremy hunted the horse through the war.'

The decision not to send the 11th Armoured Division to North Africa is said to have been made at the Casablanca Conference. For, as we have seen, in the days immediately preceding that meeting, the military situation in Tunisia had altered in such a way that not armour but infantry were now required and the military command in that theatre accordingly made representations that an infantry formation should be sent. Cancellation orders were at once flashed back and the Division never sailed; but it was too late to stop many of the preliminaries. Vast orders had been issued and digested. A considerable number of vehicles had actually been loaded onto the ships in the various western ports. These had to be unloaded and driven back, reappearing at their units much to the surprise of the men who had expected their next contact with them to be on the Mediterranean coast. Only the first-line reinforcements that had already gone were absorbed into units already in the North African theatre and were never seen again by the 11th Armoured.

So, when Roscoe took over the 29th Armoured Brigade in Bridlington during the winter of 1943, a considerable amount of training had been done. But the Division was now to play a major role in the forthcoming invasion of Northern Europe, and Montgomery, cunning as ever, brought the experienced veterans to take over the key positions of command. No sooner had Roscoe been appointed to command the Brigade than the Division was taken over by Major-General Pip Roberts, who had served throughout the campaigns of the Western Desert and Tunisia in a variety of ranks and appointments and had commanded two Armoured Brigades with great distinction. All wars produce their crop of distinguished officers who climb the military ladder faster than their fellows, simply by virtue of outstanding achievement in each successive grade. General Pip probably held the record for World War II. When Germany invaded Poland he was a mere Captain in the Royal Tank Regiment, Adjutant of its 6th Battalion. Now, practically on his thirty-seventh birthday, he had been appointed to his first Division. Roscoe describes him simply as 'the greatest General I ever knew' and the two became firm friends. 'If anything had happened to Monty,' says Roscoe, 'Pip would surely have commanded the Army. As it was, if he had not left the Army so soon, I am convinced that he and not Carver would have been the big chief overall.'

So 'the terrible twins' of British Armour, who were to wreak havoc amongst the Germans and perhaps do more towards winning the war in north-west Europe than anyone else, came together.

The new Brigadier quickly made his presence felt in no uncertain fashion. 'The first day in my office I was surprised that nobody came to see me, and I told my Brigade Major so,' says Roscoe. 'He said, "Well, sir, the red light was on outside your door." I asked him what the hell he meant by a red light. He told me that when the light was on, it meant that the Brigadier did not want to be disturbed. So I said, "You will now smash that red light. Anybody who wants to visit me can always do so. If for some reason I don't want to see them I'll tell them to f . . . off!"'

He discovered that all other ranks on the Brigade staff had been orderd to wear black berets and the Armoured Corps badge of a clenched fist instead of their own Regimental badges. 'To their great relief, I said that all those clenched fists should be thrown away and they could go back to badges of the 10th Hussars, Royal Scots Greys or whatever Regiment they belonged to.'

Montgomery came up to visit the Division. When his special train arrived at Bridlington, Roscoe was invited to dine with him. 'I got there early and was given a drink by one of his staff officers,' says Roscoe. 'When the General arrived he said, "Would you like a drink?" Knowing his views on alcohol, I said immediately, "Yes please, General. I'd love another one!" He seemed quite surprised. "Oh, you mean you've had one already?" I got on well with him, although he never really liked Cavalry officers. He said, "I suppose you had a pack of foxhounds?" "No, General," I said. "Really?" said Monty, "I thought all Cavalry officers had packs of foxhounds." "Well, General," I said, "if the war hadn't come I certainly would have had one. There's nothing I'd have liked better. And I'll tell you something. Being a Master of Hounds is a damn' sight more difficult than being a General!"'

Roscoe says, 'As we were training ready for the invasion in Normandy, waterproofing our vehicles and so on, General Eisenhower visited us. He stood up on a Jeep and made a very good speech to the 11th Armoured Divison. Then he came round and shook hands with all the senior officers. His expression was "I'll see you!" I thought he was a very nice man indeed.'

Roscoe was so right. General Ike Eisenhower was something special in the way of a man and a commander. Small wonder he became one of the most popular Presidents that the United States has ever known.

Many words have been written about the build-up to D-Day, to the invasion of Europe which, after long months of planning, was at last to take place in June 1944. Everything was poised for 'Off' for the final momentous battles which would free the world from the yoke of Hitler and his Nazi tyrants. The tides in the Channel were right and everything was in readiness on June 3. The senior commanders assembled at the country house which Eisenhower used as a Headquarters in southern England. Yes, the tides were right and they would not be right again for a fortnight, but the weather was wrong. Twenty-four hours passed while the senior officers of all the Services debated whether it would be too much of a risk, involving the lives of over a million men, to land on the continent.

Finally on the evening of June 4 Eisenhower said, 'Gentlemen, this is a decision that I must take alone. After all, that is what I'm here for.' The meeting waited. Then the Commander-in-Chief said, 'We will sail tomorrow.'

Chapter Fifteen

Retribution

The 11th Armoured Division was never intended to be part of the initial assault, but of the 'follow-up' troops.

For some weeks they stayed at Aldershot, which was, of course, pleasantly close to London, and then just before embarkation moved down to the Portsmouth area.

Roscoe says, 'We went into one of those camps where – not that I was ever starved – we had the most appalling filthy stew which we just couldn't eat. I said that there should be a notice placed up on the door "Abandon Hope All Ye Who Enter Here" and I told my Brigade Major that I had no intention of stopping in the camp. He told me that they would not allow me out. I said, "They bloody well will."

'We were very close to Bosham where there was a very nice little restaurant, rather like a club, run by a fellow who used to be in my Regiment. The Officer of the Gate asked me where I was going and I said, "Don't worry, I'll be back!" I went out and had a bloody good dinner and came back again. The next day we embarked for France.'

General Pip Roberts, Roscoe and his 11th Armoured Division landed on French soil on June 13 and 14, 1944. The exact spot was the Normandy coast between Bernieres and Courseuilles, just north of a little village called Beny-sur-Mer. In the dusty Norman villages behind the lines nearly a fortnight passed before the Division was called upon to undertake active operations. Once past the beaches, the countryside seemed peaceful and relatively undamaged. The welcome we found was guarded, as though half the inhabitants still believed the Germans' parting threat that they would return. We soon learnt that every church tower in the little villages was apt to contain a German artillery observation officer and that as we approached he would immediately launch a barrage onto us. As a result every church tower had to be treated with an armour-piercing shell followed by explosives from the leading troop. Sometimes we would see the offending German officer falling to his death from the church tower like a rag doll.

'It was either him or us,' says Roscoe. 'He could bring down a hell of a barrage of concentrated accurate fire on our chaps if he was allowed to stay up there.'

Roscoe was now the most experienced Armoured Brigadier in the Army. He was hard, tough, fair, a true professional, who came out of his corner fighting, but still had time to enjoy the lighter side.

'We didn't have any real problems until Caen,' Roscoe says. 'The only trouble was that we were always being given Normandy's speciality, Camembert cheese and Calvados, that fiery spirit that they love so much. A Norman farmer told me how to drink it. You eat sugar, crunch it up in your mouth then pour in the Calvados.

'I had a very good tank driver who sold cattle-food in civilian life in England before he joined up. One day we set off and went round a corner only for him to crash straight into a little cottage on the side of the road. The roof came crashing down on us. I said to him, "What the hell do you think you're doing?" He said, "The steering wheel jammed!"

209

'I said "You bloody liar! It's the Calvados that's got to you. For Christ's sake look what you're doing!" He was as pissed as a newt. I don't think there was anybody in the house but we didn't wait to see. People still drink that stuff, but I had some the other day and it burnt my guts.'

It is easy to believe that old soldiers never die when you have a session with General Pip Roberts and Roscoe. Although he is eighty years old now, General Pip is still the same neat, slim, alert, natural leader, with a rare grasp of the essentials and a memory as good as Roscoe's – and that's saying something! The friendship which began in Yorkshire way back in 1944 remains as solid as ever today, based as it is on mututal respect and admiration. Both are agreed that the battles in Normandy for Caen and the crossings of the river Orne were the worst that the 11th Armoured Division had to encounter.

The battleground was so different from the desert in which both soldiers had been fighting. Now so well known to those of us in the racing and breeding world, we can look back to our first impressions in that summer of 1944 – a lovely summer when the Camembert was ripe, the Calvados flowed, washed down by cider, and the bloated bodies of dead Germans lay unheeded, rotting in the ripening corn.

The Bocage, as that country is called, stretches southwards from Bayeux. Richly wooded and always undulating, its many little rivers and steams irrigate the region and make it so green and lush for cattle and bloodstock. Between thick hedges, the roads wind and rise and fall, broken every hundred yards or so by a corner or a crest. The farms are small and white and the towns are small and grey.

The area was never intended to be a battlefield. Despite the ghostly arguments of William the

210

Conqueror and his chivalrous Norman knights of old, the whole character of the region is ill-suited to the arts of war. There are few wide expanses for tactical deployment and no scope for manoeuvre or reconnaissance. The country is difficult for infantry and vastly unpromising for tanks, and to launch an offensive through it might in other circumstances have appeared most imprudent.

Nevertheless, to the Allied Armies come for retribution, the country showed itself a friend. The benevolence was not at first apparent. Many hundreds of Britons and Americans died in the leafy lanes and many cruel and costly and destructive battles were fought for those little towns and villages before the issue became clear. It was here however that the first irreversible victories were won; here that our troops first advanced without the prospect of subsequent withdrawal. In the Bocage, decisively and irrevocably, Germany lost the war in the west.

This defeat of the enemy was quite different in character from his previous reverses. Stalingrad was the arrest of a hitherto triumphant drive, achieved by desperate defence and counter-attack, involving very heavy losses, the most serious of which was the loss of initiative. Alamein was a pitched battle in the grand style in which the enemy finally broke after ten days of heavy fighting. The landscape of Normandy is quite unlike the desert or the Steppes and the situation was peculiar to an Army in a bridgehead. Victory was won by a series of thrusts at the enemy positions, tentative in inception yet strong enough to exploit the situation should they chance to hit a weak spot. Some of these thrusts achieved only limited advances and were seemingly unsuccessful, but they inflicted on the enemy continual losses in battle until he became incapable in the area. At last too, allied aircraft enjoyed the supremacy in the air and made seriously disabling attacks upon enemy supplies and communications.

The Germans were compelled to yield and the Americans surged westwards and southwards to St Lo. Then, as the enemy frantically endeavoured to rush divisions across to stop the gap, he was assaulted also at other points where his new situation rendered him most vulnerable, his defences were pierced, his roads were cut and his whole position was disrupted.

General Pip used his armour, commanded by Roscoe, and his infantry Brigade, commanded by solid, steady Brigadier Jack Churcher, with incredible skill.

I saw a lot of this fighting at first hand, as I had of the desert battles, because my Regiment, the Greys, were upsides at the time of the battles for Caen. I can vouch for the fact that it was a most uncomfortable few weeks, from the middle of July to the beginning of August, even though it was preceded by the biggest aerial bombardment from our own aircraft that any of us had ever known. As Roscoe says, 'It did a lot to raise our morale, but that was about all. It may have shaken some of the enemy a bit, but it did quite a lot of damage to our own troops as well.'

It was in this battle around Caen that we had quite a few casualties, including my Squadron Leader, Peter Paget, potentially the finest Master of Foxhounds in the world.

Roscoe says, 'In my Brigade we lost no fewer than 140 tanks going up the hill out of Caen. A Panzer Group was at the top of the hill and picked us off like rabbits. Luckily we didn't lose many crews, got some more tanks and had a fairly easy passage afterwards.'

General Pip says, 'Yes, one of the worst battles we had was that one on Perrier Ridge. Winning this particular battle was a great triumph and a very significant move.'

General Pip and Roscoe who combined so brilliantly, unlike many commanders, take very little credit for themselves. On the evening after the battle, one of the officers at Divisional Headquarters congratulated General Pip on the day's performance, saying 'Why, sir, two men and a boy could have held you up there.'

'Yes Joe,' replied the General, 'but they didn't have the boy!'

Even Roscoe could make his mistakes, as he admits: 'I made a pretty good balls-up siting my Brigade Headquarters one day. East of the river Orne there was a large ridge and a little railway which had a fairly substantial embankment. I thought this would be an ideal place to park my Headquarters. I soon found out differently.'

General Pip takes up the story: 'There was this big ridge and this little railway with a large embankment. So Roscoe comes down with his Headquarters and sticks it on the side of the embankment so that it looks straight into the villages on the north side of the hill. Then he was rather surprised when they suddenly shot at him! He'd been there a little while and the German artillery was getting pretty accurate.

'We had a new idea for controlling the airforce. An armoured car was fitted up by the RAF and attached to Roscoe's Headquarters so that he could guide them where they should drop their bombs and fire their guns in support of our attacks and so on. So the Commander Royal Artillery, Brigadier Frizz Fowler, and I said that we'd better go and have a word with Roscoe. We stopped our vehicles about two or three hundred yards away and walked over to Roscoe, who had, luckily, taken the precaution of digging a big trench. Nevertheless we discovered that Roscoe's own artillery commander, Bob Daniels, a very good chap in the Royal Horse Artillery, had protested strongly against Roscoe putting the Headquarters right up against the embankment. Roscoe had asked why not and was told: "They can range on you here. They've got this embankment to range on." "Well," Roscoe said, "they must have some shells that'll miss, some that will hit the embankment and some that'll go to the other side – and they won't hit us."

'So the Artillery Commander told him that was very stupid. And to this day Roscoe admits that he was wrong and the gunner was dead right. We'd only been there for two or three minutes when the German 88s opened up and we shot under the tank or into the trench.'

Roscoe says, 'We all scrambled underneath the tank. Tony Kershaw, my Brigade Major, the present Member of Parliament, had his bum sticking out and crack! got a bit of shrapnel in it. He was sent back to England, like all casualites in those days, had a bit of sticking plaster put on it and was back with us within forty-eight hours!'

Now that the break-through had been achieved, the chase was on and Roscoe was even more in his element. Hounds were running!

'We got to within thirty miles of Amiens,' he says 'when General Horrocks came along at tea-time and suggested to Pip that we should go for a night drive. He said it would be a moonlight night. In fact it wasn't. It poured with rain. But nevertheless the enemy was in complete disarray. We drove through the night through columns and columns of Germans who didn't fight. I think most of the time they thought we were their own troops. David Silvertop, who was commanding the 3rd Royal Tanks, my leading Regiment, came through on the radio and asked what he should do when he got to Amiens. I said, "You'd better knock and see whether they say come in!" So at five o'clock in the morning the leading tanks entered the outskirts of Amiens, half an hour later they were over the first railway bridge and by six o'clock the centre of the city was reached.'

One of the many prisoners taken was General Everback, who had recently taken over command of the German Seventh Army and had selected that very morning for personal reconnaissance, hoping presumably to discover some method of defending the line of the Somme. He might have saved both his time and himself. At eight o'clock a staff car from his Headquarters was captured by Perry Harding's 23rd Hussars. Its main occupant, a colonel, fled and when the car was searched it was found to contain a large map showing the entire enemy dispositions in the west. A quarter of an hour later, the General himself with various members of his staff fell into the hands of the Division. He was by far the most valuable prisoner so far captured by the Allied Forces, but there was no time to wait. However important the General may have been, he just had to be evacuated by the normal channels and the advance had to proceed.

They had now cleared the Germans out of the area of the Somme. Roscoe and General Pip agreed that it was a funny feeling driving through those places with famous, notorious names from the First World War.

'There we were,' says Pip, 'just rattling along through places with names like Amiens, Somme, Ypres and so on, which had become horrifying legends only twenty-five years earlier; where hundreds of thousands of men, millions even, on both sides slogging it out in muddy trench warfare, had perished. All that ghastly business of going over the top, the barbed wire, the machine-gunfire, and yet here we were just driving through those places.'

Of course the advance was not simply a question of motoring. Frequently on the way some of the advancing troops had to be detached to deal with pockets of German resistance, but the advance continued apace.

Now was the time of liberation. No longer were the

local inhabitants of France and Belgium worried about the Germans' return. Out came the girls and the flowers and the wine and the thanks and the cheers. These were the heady days of liberation.

As they crossed the Belgian frontier Roscoe felt particularly sad that Major Henri Legrand, the Belgian artillery officer who had won a particularly good DSO with the 10th Hussars in the desert, was not with them. Sadly in the battles round Caen this extremely gallant and popular officer had been killed. Roscoe had so hoped that he would have been able to re-join his much-loved family.

Chapter Sixteen

The Black Bulls Again

If there is any one exploit for which the 11th Armoured Division is to be remembered and worshipped for evermore, it will probably be the pursuit to Antwerp and capture of that city. The importance of Antwerp as opposed to Brussels was in retrospect obvious. Roscoe says, 'We wanted to go to Brussels, but unfortunately the Guards Brigade were following up and they got the privilege of going into the capital city. However, I suppose Antwerp was more important.'

Of course it was. It was to become for so long the main supply base for our Armies. When Roscoe says that the American Sherman tanks played a vital, essential and possibly decisive part in winning the war, it is worth recalling here that in this memorable Cavalry charge for which it seems Roscoe's life had been designed, the tanks of his Brigade had covered all the way from Caumont some 580 miles – and for that matter all the way from the beaches of Normandy – on their own tracks. Never once had they been lifted by transporters. By the time they reached Antwerp many of the tanks had done considerably more than the mileage prescribed for them. A few fell by the wayside, but on the whole the Shermans stood up splendidly to this severe test of their mechanical reliability.

In passing, too, it is worth remarking on the amazingly efficient organisation of the supply columns. They had to travel backwards and forwards to get the food and the ammunition and the all-important petrol and pull up again to deliver it. Don't forget, these tank aero-engines were using high-octane aeroplane petrol and were lucky if they did as much as one mile to the gallon. During the pursuit the supply men covered prodigious distances, and when the objective was obtained nobody needed a rest more than they. For most of them had enjoyed only one night's sleep in a week – and a short one at that.

The Belgians, and particularly the people of Antwerp, had no doubt and never had had any doubt about the identity of their liberator. Their local paper headlined 'THE LIBERATION OF ANTWERP BY THE "BULLS" UNDER COMMAND OF BRIGADIER C.B. HARVEY DSO.'

Pip Roberts knew his man. He gave him his head. Now we saw the Roscoe who went like a scalded cat when hounds were running down over the Berkeley Marsh; the legendary 'On! On!' of the Kadir Cup; the dashing top-class polo number 1; the brilliant amateur rider who was so nearly killed at Cheltenham. This was the Roscoe who would flout the orthodox methods; the Roscoe who, at the suggestion of that old brigand General Tiny Freyberg in the desert, would indent for ten more tanks than he actually required in order to get the number he needed; the same Roscoe who, when a certain very senior General demanded the court-martial of a junior officer who was only doing what Freyberg and Roscoe wished of him, threw all the papers relating to the case in the wastepaper basket until there was no more need and the whole business was called off.

Serving under him must have been inspiring, but hardly a bed of roses. Roscoe says, 'I always left in the morning half an hour before anybody else. This sometimes made it a little difficult for them to find us, but then, after all, we were in full cry!'

He was so right. Just as when you are hunting a fox, it is an old principle of war that, when you have got the enemy on the run, you must never lose contact.

I can do no better than quote General Sir Cecil ('Monkey') Blacker, now Deputy Senior Steward of the Jockey Club: 'In 1944-5 I was a Squadron Leader and later second-in-command of the 23rd Hussars, commanded by Perry Harding. This Brigade was extremely lucky to find itself commanded by Roscoe just prior to D-Day. The Division was extremely lucky to find itself under command of Major-General 'Pip' Roberts. We were thus commanded not only by the most experienced Armoured Brigade commander in the Army but also the best Armoured Divisional Commander.

'Despite this and despite the fact that the Brigade and Division were extremely well trained, during the following eleven months each Armoured Regiment sustained casualties equal to its total strength of some 450. The Infantry Battalions sustained three or four times their strength. This gives some idea of the intensity of the fighting.

'Pip Roberts was several years younger than Roscoe and also Churcher, the Commander of his other Brigade, 159 Infantry Brigade. Both Roscoe and Churcher were not only formidable characters, but did not by any means see eye to eye. It was a remarkable feat of leadership by the young Divisional Commander that he controlled them throughout with such harmony and humour. He was wise enough to surmise that when the Brigadiers had to mix, it would be better to leave the 23rd Hussars under Roscoe. Perry Harding and Jack Churcher would NOT have combined well and in fact Roscoe was probably the only Brigadier in the Army capable of controlling Perry. So we fought all our battles under Roscoe's command.

219

'Once the battle was joined the first thing we realised was that any failure to push ahead, even in the hairiest situation, would generate an even hairier situation back at Brigade Headquarters. An important element in a Commander is the ability to make his troops feel less inclined to incur his displeasure than to face the enemy. The sight of Roscoe's Sherman tank following close behind, with his red hat poking out of the turret (he always refused to wear a tin hat, though we had to), was a considerable deterrent to any desire to linger.

'I remember meeting him when I was proceeding away from the enemy (on legitimate business, I hasten to add) and he was clearly not in a good mood. He stopped his tank, motioned me to a halt and directing at me a gimlet stare over his glasses, asked, "And where are you goin'?" I was extremely glad my conscience was clear, otherwise I had a feeling that any number of Panzers would have been preferable.

'He must have made an enormous, unrivalled contribution at his level to winning the war. He fought in France in 1940, commanded a Regiment and Brigade in the desert and a Brigade from Normandy to the Baltic. His humour and imperturbability should never be allowed to conceal the remarkably tough, determined – and inspiring – character that lay behind them. He fully deserved his three DSOs.'

The GSO1 of a Division was what an Adjutant is to a Regiment or a Brigade-Major to a Brigade. He is the right-hand man of the Divisional Commander, the man who can see the whole thing through his master's and his own eyes. Lieutenant-Colonel Robin Hastings, now President of the British Bloodstock Agency, was another of the great heroes of the Second World War – even though he was a foot soldier! Robin commanded a batallion in action at the age of twenty-one and earned himself three DSOs and three MCs. As he rode well as an amateur over fences later on and has been so involved with racing and breeding all his life, particularly as the guiding light of the world's biggest and best bloodstock agency, he is well-qualified to speak about Roscoe at this time.

He says, 'Roscoe commanded the Armoured Brigade in 11th Armoured Division when I was GSO1. He was definitely a Cavalry officer turned tank commander and had an irresistible desire to press on. He was always at a prominent position himself and, though he did not adopt the front-line tactics of some of his misguided contemporaries, he was always stationed where he could see what was going on. As one Squadron Leader said, "You liked to know that if you wanted him, you only had to look over your shoulder to see the Brigadier!"

'The Infantry Brigade was commanded by an excellent infantry officer whose methods were the opposite of Roscoe's. He liked to make the most thorough preparations and move as little as possible.

'Their aims and talents were exactly opposed. General Pip Roberts, a brilliant soldier, a good tactician and experienced in tank warfare, was not keen on getting himself involved in the minor squabbles between these two. It was for the GSO1 to sort out the differences between the Brigade Commanders. General Pip often used to sit in the corner of the armoured command vehicle and laugh at my efforts to appease both.

'When we were approaching the Elbe, I think it was, the Armoured Brigade reached the river and held one end of the bridge. They urgently needed infantry support, the task which Brigadier Churcher's Brigade was expected to perform. But his Brigade was very slow in coming up to scratch. Roscoe protested to me and then said on the wireless, "Tell Churcher we need him. And to encourage him to go faster tell him we've captured a wine store near the bridge and if he gets here

221

by tonight, I'll give him a case of 'ock – a whole case of 'ock – the lucky chap." The ploy worked!'

Just recently I asked Robin why, in my many enquiries, I had found that a number of younger officers who served under the Brig during the war were critical of him. Robin replied, 'Roscoe was a true, brave, fearless Cavalryman of the old school and so great was his Cavalry spirit that these young officers under him were frightened that he was going to get them killed.'

Then Robin wrote to confirm our conversation. 'You asked me why there were certain reservations on the part of tank officers about Roscoe Harvey. The answer is that he belonged to the Cavalry tradition of Prince Rupert and the Charge of the Light Brigade and he most certainly believed in getting on with it without, perhaps, the tactical cunning to support himself. That is why Pip Roberts, perfectly balanced and composed, was so good at reining in Roscoe and pushing on Churcher.'

The capture of Antwerp could well be compared to a tremendous Cavalry charge. Roscoe says, 'When we arrived in Antwerp we were, I suppose, very lucky, because a Belgian Resistance Lieutenant came roaring out on his motorbike and offered to show us the way to the only bridge which had not been blown up – a long wooden one. I told David Silvertop to go like hell for the docks. After an hour and a half I was sitting with my Brigade Major, Tony Kershaw, waiting to hear, when the radio came on and David said he'd done everything I'd asked. I said, "What are you doing now?" He said that he was "sitting outside probably the smartest club in Antwerp drinking Heidsieck 1928 – and it's iced!" I said that I would have to go and see the poor troops! He told me to follow the tramlines to find them. And there they were, waiter, white napkin and all, sitting drinking this glorious champagne!'

There is in Antwerp today a British tank surmounted

by a Union Jack and carrying the yellow-backed black bull on its near fore, symbolising for evermore the liberation of the city by the 29th Armoured Brigade and the 11th Armoured Division, for which the people of Antwerp expressed their gratitude in many ways.

An article in the local newspaper *Het Handelsblad*, dated September 14, 1944, and signed Morris, translates as follows: 'Never will Antwerp be able to express in full its gratitude to the heroes of the 11th British Armoured Division (we can now name this division as the BBC has already announced it to the whole world, both friend and foe alike). Through their unmatched courage and the speed of their heavy tanks they overcame every difficulty and broke down all resistance.

'People of Antwerp! It was a noise like thunder that these long, unending columns of steel monsters roared their way from Normandy to the north. For Antwerp was their goal – that city which by virtue of its situation on the east bank of the river Schelde had become a point of great strategic importance – Antwerp, which by reason of its tunnel had become the sole way of escape for the German troops in north-west France and Flanders.

'This escape route had to be cut, and cut it was by the unexpected speed and outstanding daring of the advance by night as well as by day – *700 kilometres in nine days*.

'Who could have expected it, when under conditions of utmost secrecy and great danger we listened to the BBC and learnt that the British had crossed the Seine and reached Beauvais by way of Gisors?

'The slow advance in Normandy had not prepared us for the lightning thrusts which were to follow. The first surprise came with the announcement of the capture of Amiens by the BBC correspondent who gave the following breath-taking account of the operation:

'"At Beauvais it was decided, as the supply of petrol

223

was just sufficient, to push on to Amiens. Night was already falling and the troops tired after a day's fighting; through unknown country and over roads rendered even more difficult to see by driving rain, the tanks roared their way through the night with a noise like thunder. Such were the conditions which gave rise to the following incident – at a road junction several vehicles joined the column, the darkness making their identification impossible. This was how they were un-masked. A soldier seated on the back of a truck noticed a man trying to make out the sign on the British vehicle and recognised him as a German. A shovel was seized and the German finished off with a blow on the head. At once a short but brisk fight with grenades and machine-guns broke out. It finished with the destruction of several German vehicles. This incident did not stop the advance, and at daybreak it was noticed that several other German vehicles had slipped into the column by mistake. Just before Amiens was reached the main bridge over the Somme was blown, but the soldiers of the FFI (Resistance movement) had succeeded in capturing three other bridges and the advance was not halted. No time was lost in Amiens and after a brief rest the advance went on. On, always on! During the night of Saturday/Sunday the Belgian frontier was crossed. Towns which might have resisted were by-passed and left to the formation following up behind."

'I remember how, when on the Sunday I was watching the Germans escaping through the tunnel, I was thought mad to suggest that this very day would see Brussels free, and the city of Antwerp would be liberated on the following day. Even I myself hesitated to express this opinion, though I knew it was only a matter of a few days.

'But even while we stood here, already in the distance the columns of the irresistible British Armoured

Division were approaching. When I was told on Monday morning "They are in Malines and Boom", I could hardly believe my ears and yet it was true!

'The broad river Rupel was crossed without any obstacle, thanks to the outstanding courage of a civilian, whose name has been given to me. This man extinguished the burning fuse and the bridge was saved. By eleven o'clock the tanks were already in front of the defences of Antwerp. The remainder of the story is already known.

'The shouts of joy, the scenes of wild enthusiasm – these will never be forgotten and served as first proof of our gratitude to the heroes of the 11th Armoured Division who, covered with dust and half dead with fatigue, brought us the liberation which had been so long awaited, and was yet entirely unexpected.

'It is hoped that very shortly a great monument will commemorate this feat of arms by the 11th Armoured Divison, who by the lightning speed of their advance saved our beloved town and renowned harbour from certain and total destruction.

'With all our heart we hope the Commander of these picked troops aged but 37 years, his Brigadier of 30 years, (he was actually 44 of course!), the even younger chief of staff, and the charming and handsome officers and men will be able to be present in large numbers at a dinner offered them by the grateful citizens of Antwerp.'

I have translated another article, which appeared in the Antwerp newspaper *Le Matin,* signed by Paul Ransant, under the heading 'THE LIBERATION OF ANTWERP BY THE "BULLS" UNDER COMMAND OF BRIGADIER C.B. HARVEY, DSO.' 'The people of Antwerp,' it read, 'will never forget September 4, the wonderful day of their liberation. *Le Matin* has already described the smashing advance of the British Army on Antwerp. In a very interesting article published on Monday September 18, MG de Chaffoy revealed details of the brilliant action that secured the prize of our great port captured intact, from the moment when Lieutenant Vekemans performed his splendid and courageous action until he met the first British tanks; the entry of the British into Boom, the battle in the Avenue van Rijswijck, and the race to the tunnel and the port.

'We ourselves, in an article dedicated to the men of the Resistance Movement published on the same day, told of the big part played by Commandant Pilaet and his Lieutenants Rummens and Calluy, of the first clashes at the Chateau de Damman, at the Hofter Beck, at Paermeke's garage, and then the triumphal entry of the British tanks into the city, through the Avenue Reine Elisabeth and Avenue de Belgique, acclaimed by great crowds of people, all quite delirious with joy.

'Other articles have told of the fighting which took place in the town itself, at the Park and at the Place de Meir, also of the elimination of scattered pockets of resistance which the Germans had organised in various parts of the city.

'Also, in *Le Matin* of September 7, one was able to read of the banquet given by members of the "Console" and the "Philotax" to Brigadier C.B. Harvey, DSO and his officers, a banquet during which our director M. Paul de Canwer, said to our liberators: "You have come so quickly that even the BBC could not follow you."

'For security reasons we have not until now been able to tell our readers who our liberators were. Antwerp was liberated by the 29th Armoured Brigade, by the "Bulls" or "taureaux noirs" as we should normally say.

'Now, these "Bulls", who had passed successfully through an intense period of training, had never been in action until they landed in Normandy on the famous D-Day, but they had been joined by some hand-picked elements from the Desert Rats, and with these troops

226

the "Bulls" became as famous as the famous Guards Brigades. Though their crowning achievement, the lightning advance from Vernon through Arras to Antwerp, they are now definitely classed among the aces of modern warfare.

'We would point out that since their entry into Antwerp, they have been seen everywhere, and always in the front line.

'When in December, Rundstedt's offensive took the Allied Armies momentarily by surprise, the "Bulls" were immediately sent to the Ardennes, where they very soon changed the fortunes of the Boche. The 29th Armoured Brigade commanded by Brigadier C.B. Harvey (Roscoe to his friends), was supported by Lieutenant-Colonels Antony Hunter, David Silvertop and Perry Harding. It was Colonel Silvertop, later killed in action in Holland, who in his tank was the first to enter Antwerp.

'Among the other officers of the Brigade we also name Major James Gammell, the man who assumed the heavy responsibility for the supply of petrol and who nearly went crazy when he realised the terrific advance of the 29th Armoured Brigade's tanks; Captain Nick Rolt, son of the Dean of Johannesburg, an aesthete, who on a recent leave realised his dreams by marrying his beloved Lavinia; the charming Captain Basil Gibson and Captain Thompson, a wonderful dancer, who broke many hearts among the Antwerp girls.

'The "Bulls" were delighted by the reception given them by the people of Antwerp, where they did not stay for long as they were sent to Holland to the Ardennes and then to Germany.

'But they promised to come back to us, and we await them impatiently. Then only they will be able to realise how Antwerp receives those whom she loves.'

It is not difficult to see why the citizens of Antwerp

were so concerned when an American who commanded the anti-aircraft unit there was given the freedom of the City of Antwerp and Roscoe was not. 'POURQUOI PAS HARVEY?' was the headline in a local paper.

'It wouldn't have done them any harm to give us both the Freedom of the City,' Roscoe says.

Roscoe made his Headquarters in a glorious château just outside Antwerp, but only temporarily. There was no time to waste. The battle must be won, and the Nazis must be defeated once and for all. So it was again a case of 'On! On!'

On out of Belgium which had been the scene of so many comings and goings by occupying forces in the last thirty years. On into Holland. With Roscoe and the 29th Armoured Brigade in the lead, the 11th Armoured Division forced their way on. Then came nearly the great disaster of Roscoe's life. 'The only time I was wounded at all was when I nearly had my balls shot off,' he says. Roscoe had gone forward with his Brigade Major to St Anthonis to clarify conflicting reports of the position of the leading troops, and he had arranged to meet the Colonels of his two leading units, the 3rd Royal Tanks and the 3rd Monmouthshires, at a crossroads in the village.

Says Roscoe, 'I went up to see what was happening. Perhaps I had some idea that there was danger about because I told my Jeep driver, "Get this thing off the road and stick it in the hedge."

'So my Jeep was out of the way. We were talking about what we were going to do next and could hear a gun going off, getting closer. There were two roads coming the other way and I remember saying to David Silvertop, "We've got a troop attachment on that other road, haven't we?" and he said, "Yes, of course we have."

'I said, "But I don't think that was one of ours. It

sounded a bit like a German machine-gun." David said "Yes, it did a bit."

'Damn me but round the corner came this six-wheeled German half-track with machine-guns blazing. It got poor old David Silvertop and killed him stone dead and it got Hubert Orr who died in hospital immediately afterwards. My Brigade Major said, "I've been hit!" So I told him, "Christ! Lie down for God's sake!" He was all right, as it happens. Thank God he didn't die, but it wasn't a bad do for the Germans to get two Commanding Officers and a Brigade Major in one go!'

I asked Roscoe, 'What about you?'

'Well, I got the bugger, didn't I? Got him and his driver with my pistol!'

'But what about you? Weren't you wounded at all? You must have been.'

'Well, yes. It was the only time I was ever wounded in the war and I nearly lost my balls. He got me with a bullet just about an eighth of an inch below on the inside of my thigh. It was nothing, just a little graze, but, believe me, it was a bit too close for comfort!

'It only needed a tiny little bit of plaster, but it was very lucky that it wasn't a few millimetres higher. The telegrams that I got the next day! The signals from senior officers who should have known better were amazing. A staff officer in Corps HQ sent me a cable saying, "I always knew you'd rather lose your Brigade than your balls!" and the general tone of the other signals was expressed in that one lucid message from Colonel Geoff Phipps Hornby which said "Lucky it was a cold day!"' I nearly made that the title of this book!

The Germans were putting up some very tough resistance now. It was a matter of life or death for them. Winter was drawing on and the weather was not particularly clever. It was in October that Roscoe earned his third DSO.

229

The citation reads: 'During the advance of this Division to the Venrai area between 16–19 October 1944 Brigadier Harvey's Brigade was severely held up by boggy ground in addition to receiving heavy casualties from shelling and mortaring. Brigadier Harvey, who was determined to get forward, succeeded by his own personal leadership in overcoming these difficulties and pressed on with such effect that in 48 hours his Brigade took 700 determined enemy prisoners and inflicted casualties on many others. This action had a decisive result on the whole operation and was undoubtedly due to this officer's fine leadership, military skill and offensive spirit which permeated to all ranks.'

This was an immediate second Bar to his DSO recommended by General Pip Roberts, seconded by Lieutenant-General O'Connor commanding 8 Corps and backed by Miles Dempsey, Lieutenant-General commanding Second Army and endorsed by B.L. Montgomery, Commander-in-Chief 21 Army Group.

Although the 11th Armoured Division were being equipped with their new tank, the Comet, which was the first comparatively decent English tank, Roscoe had to get his old Sherman tanks out of pawn temporarily to help cope with the last German offensive, which was to be their final burst – the attack in the Ardennes. His Brigade was ordered to hold the Meuse bridges at Dinant Givet and this did much to save the situation in the Ardennes.

The Comets were low-slung and fast, like the Cromwells which they closely resembled. They carried a 77mm gun, which proved extremely accurate in trials. Although it had not quite the hitting power of the 17-pounder, its performance with high-explosive shells was superior, which turned out to be important because now most of the German attacks came from infantrymen armed with bazookas.

But the refitting had not been without a hiccup. The Brigade had gone back to an area north of Brussels to re-equip and learn how to handle these new tanks. Roscoe had a very nice Headquarters and had discovered some first-class woodcock shooting. Christmas was only three or four days away when suddenly in the middle of the night he was woken up by a staff officer asking him to talk to Brigadier Belchem, one of Monty's right-hand men, on the telephone. Belchem said, 'You personally have got to come up here to Brussels. You've got to move your whole Brigade at once back into Brussels, pick up your old tanks and get onto the Meuse.'

Roscoe says, 'I answered, "Well, to start off with, I'm not going to go straight away. I've been woken up and there's a thick fog here and I've no intention of trying to get to Brussels in thick fog. I'll be with you in the morning. I will meet you at Army HQ in Brussels." I knew that would really annoy Army HQ as everyone would arrive in dirty battledress. However, all the troops got themselves together really well. When I arrived they told me, "You've got to take over the three bridges on the Meuse because the Germans have launched a big push and are coming through the Ardennes." I said "OK." It was not a difficult military manoeuvre, as I had three armoured Regiments. I put one on each bridge, which was easy, but we were rather short of infantry, not unnaturally. I thought that unless the Germans were making a tremendous push we would probably stop their armour, but would be unable to stop a lot of their troops. Anyway, we got down to the Meuse and I saw old Horrocks. I told him "We're very thin on the ground." So he said, "You'll be all right. There are a lot of Americans down there at a sort of rest camp. You can get hold of some of them to act as your infantry."

'Fine. So I got down there and went to see the

American General, but was met by his Chief of Staff, who looked a very stony-faced sort of chap. I said, "Now we've got here, I'm not going to blow the bridges, but I am worried about not having more soldiers on the ground. You have that rest camp down there. Can I have someone I can liaise with to get hold of these chaps?"

'He turned to me with a very frosty face and said in his pronounced American accent, "Before we go any further, Brigadier, I want to know whether I'm under you or whether I'm under General Montgomery, because I don't care a damn."

'"Jolly marvellous," I said. "You wouldn't care to put that in writing, would you?" The Chief of Staff looked dismayed. "Why?" he asked. "Well," I said, "at the end of the war it would be a frightfully nice thing to have framed and hung up in my gentlemen's lavatory at home. A senior officer like you to say that you don't mind a damn if you're under me or General Montgomery. After all, I'm only a small-time Brigadier, whereas Monty is the big guy!"

'The American laughed. "I get the point," he said. "What do you want?"

'It was OK then and I got the soldiers. We only knocked out a few German tanks, but we needn't have worried because old "Blood 'n Guts" George Patton was coming up from the south.'

So von Runstedt's offensive was repulsed and now the end was nigh. This did not mean that the Germans were going to surrender easily. They were not. Roscoe says, 'We never really had any more serious battles. However, we did have some rather annoying minor ones. I remember in one small town I was told to watch out for the "Werewolves", who were a sort of Nazi underground organisation. I had my tank Headquarters. One of our tank commanders was shot in the back by some bloody fellow – I suppose it was a Werewolf! Anyway, I

232

had a very tough young man in the third tank and I said, "You know what you've got to do." He said, "What's that?"

'I told him, "Go back to the village and burn down three houses straight away and tell them it is because they shot one of our fellows in the back." He did just that and we had no more trouble until a little later on we met with Hitler Youth. This was one of the saddest things I've ever seen. The Hitler Youth behaved very badly and had also shot some of our chaps in the back. We captured about sixty of them and brought them down. Believe me, they were only between the ages of fourteen and sixteen. They came down over the hill and it could have been our own children coming down. They fought like bloody demons. They were tough boys.

'We captured a German Chief of Staff to whom I took an instant dislike. I went to see him with my Belgian liaison officer. He was lying in the back of his car and I said, "Tell him to bloody well stand up when he's speaking to me!" The man got sullenly to his feet and stood to attention. "Ask him why he fights with children." He replied, "Children fight very well." I will never ever forget that.'

The war in Europe was now coming rapidly to an end, but there were still a few unpleasant surprises in store, such as Belsen, which was on the Division's line of march. We had, of course, all heard about concentration camps, but hearing is not seeing. For my part, I wish that I had not done so, for the experience will haunt me for the rest of my life. I think perhaps that, in addition to all the poor, suffering, emaciated inmates and the skeletal corpses, I was horrified by the rows of killer dogs, mostly Dobermans and Alsatians, or shepherd dogs, penned in little hutches alongside each other, slavering whenever they saw a human being because they genuinely wanted to kill. Of course they were all shot.

233

Roscoe says, 'We were the first lot into Belsen. There was typhus in the camp and so we wanted to have a truce in order not to return. But Pip and I did go back. We had to put on protective clothing and powder ourselves with disinfectant powder.'

Pip says, 'Belsen was really unbelievable! We had no idea what it was until then. There was quite a large village on the other side of Belsen and we went through it. I said to the Burgomaster, "I want you to get together every man, woman and child here at five o'clock this evening." We had just got the pictures of all the awful things from Belsen. I said that we would pin them up on the wall of the barn and they must all come and look at them. I got the four most important people at first to look at them and they said, "You can't show those to the children." I told them, "Well, you've done it." They all protested that they didn't know what was happening. They knew that there was a camp up there, but that was all. They said they were not allowed anywhere near there. So I said, "Well you can all come along tomorrow" and laid on a number of three-ton lorries. But no-one turned up!'

Roscoe says, 'We saw Commandant Kramer and his notorious mistress, Irma Grese. I always wondered why the hell those two didn't get into their Mercedes and bugger off. Kramer's excuse was that he had no petrol. Pip and I had to go in, in case the whole thing was forgotten after the war and nobody believed that such things had taken place. The woman was tried and hanged. My liaison officer went to her trial.

'For some reason they had about a hundred SS guards at the camp. The bodies were lying about outside and there were these Germans carrying the bodies and putting them into these huge graves. They would pick up the corpses and carry them over their shoulders one at a time. I don't know how anyone could do that sort of thing to other human beings. I saw an English soldier – not one of mine – suddenly lose his cool, pick up his rifle and hit this German with all his might across his face, shouting "One for one, you fucking bastard!"

'Later I had a German officer working for me who had been at the Russian front and I showed him these awful pictures of the concentration camps. He had never seen them before and he looked horrified. He said, "You know what I think? I don't think that it is just British propoganda, but you must believe me that I never knew these things had been happening. The only time I thought there was something going on was two weeks ago when I saw two lorry-loads of people coming back from somewhere. I didn't know what they were doing or where they were going."

'One of my officers said, "I think he's telling the truth, Brigadier." So did I. He was a decent sort of fellow.

'An extraordinary thing happened in Belsen at that time. Dick Taylor in the Northumberland Hussars was a great friend of mine and of Noel Murless. A splendid chap, a keen, knowledgeable racing man who loved a good bet. Sadly, Dick has just died. After we had gone on, Dick was told to guard Belsen. A French woman prisoner suddenly came up to him, saying, "Mr Dick. Mr Dick!" She had been his first wife's lady's maid and had been captured!'

Pip says, 'We went to a lot of prisoner-of-war camps and even "liberated" one of those Nazi breeding-farms containing three or four blond stallion men!'

April was drawing to an end and apart from sporadic pockets of resistance, the enemy was defeated. The prisoners were coming in in embarrassing numbers. 'Then,' Roscoe says, 'Pip Roberts came up on the blower and said, "I want you to go like hell to Lubeck. You must get there before our friends." I thought he was talking about another Division on the Rhine, so I said,

"Christ, we'll get there before them. What friends are you talking about?" 'Pip said, "You know, the big boys. The bloody Russians!"

'I had these new fast tanks which we put on the autobahns and we went flat out at thirty-five miles an hour. We got to Lubeck on the Baltic coast just before the Russians.'

It was not long before Hitler was dead and Admiral Donitz was Führer. Most of the Germans who gave themselves up to the 11th Armoured Division stated that the new leader had given orders to the armed forces not to resist the British and Americans but only the Russians. Roscoe says, 'That final gallop was a close-run thing. I remember asking my driver, "How fast are we going?" He replied, "Over thirty, sir, and still on the bridle!"'

The war was over. The 11th Armoured Division had hoped and in fact expected to be sent to Denmark. It was not to be. They were given the area of Schleswig-Holstein up to the Danish border. Pip Roberts went home on leave and Roscoe took over as Divisional Commander with his Headquarters in a magnificent schloss by a lake.

Every morning for nearly six years the British people and the Services had been taunted on the radio by the tormenting voice and insidious propoganda of a man called William Joyce, who became known as Lord Haw-Haw. To Roscoe's great surprise he received a message one day that two of his officers had captured Lord Haw-Haw trying to escape over the border. 'These two young officers were gathering some firewood and saw this chap who said, "It is very cold here." How often had they heard that horrible, slimy voice: "Germany calling. Germany calling . . ." The man's voice was very suspect, and they asked to see his papers, and thinking he was reaching for his gun, they shot him in the backside. So he was taken off to the hospital and I had to interview him. I had half a mind to finish him off myself, but it was not to be. I went into the hospital where he was and it was lucky for him, I suppose, that there was an English matron in the room – I imagine she didn't want to miss the fun! So I couldn't tell him what I really thought of him. I asked, "What nationality are you?"

'"I might be an Englishman. I might be a German. Or I might be an Irishman," was his reply.

'"You know what you are, don't you?" I said.

'"No."

'"You are a filthy bastard and a bloody traitor!"

'"I am no coward," he said.

'I couldn't tell him in front of the matron what I really thought of him. Actually he was an Irishman. He had a wife who was said to be a glamour-girl. She was sent down to my country Headquarters on the lake. When I got there I found a car drawn up with a British officer and this bird. A number of my soldiers were sitting around wondering what the Brigadier was going to do. Anyway, I went up to her and I said, "I hear you're Mrs Joyce."

'"Yes."

'"What nationality are you?"

'She said, "I think a wife takes her nationality from her husband. I understand that there is considerable doubt what nationality my husband is."

'She had it properly taped. She wasn't very glamorous anyway. I had a very good lawyer on my HQ who said he thought that they would have a hell of a job to hang Joyce. But they did. They strung him up all right. Mind, I think they did bend the rules a bit!'

Joyce was not the only one. 'We also had Himmler. All these Nazis were coming down from Norway through Flensburg, trying to escape. They had to be vetted as they came through. Himmler came in a car with a bodyguard and our people realised quickly who he was. So they summoned a doctor and took him to a place where they could interview him. They told him to take off all his clothes. The doctor, rightly suspicious, said, "Open your mouth." Himler had been carrying something in his mouth all the time and bit on it. Even though they turned him upside down and shook him, he was dead within thirty seconds. It was rather sad that they didn't get him before he could bite the pill. They didn't find anything on him of any use. The doctor did everything to revive him. All these chaps fled towards the border and then they had to come down our way. We had to vet them all. But Himmler was the biggest Gestapo sod and bastard of the lot. They would have strung him up very quickly.'

One of Roscoe's most prized possessions is the charming private letter of congratulation sent to him by the Army Commander, an old friend, General Sir Miles Dempsey. 'Headquarters, Second Army. December 12th. Dear Roscoe, My very sincere congratulations to you on your Bar to the DSO. No one has ever deserved it more than you have. Yours ever, M Dempsey.'

The trouble was that the overall Commander-in-Chief was still Monty and there were certain things, including racing, of which the great man strongly disapproved.

Roscoe says, 'There was wonderful news for me in Lubeck. Perry Harding came up on the wireless and said, "I have found exactly what you want." I knew at once what he meant and replied, "How many?" His answer was, "About 150 and they all look good."'

'Major von Bulow had marched these horses from Berlin to Schleswig-Holstein, a remarkable feat as there were colts and fillies. His staff were all Poles. He had all the pedigrees and some were by Pharis and Bubbles, stolen from the French. What fun we and the troops were going to have. Alas it was not to be. Monty said no racing.

'I could never understand him over this. The troops had

little enough fun or amusement, and to make it more galling, we heard that our old friends in the Eighth Army were having plenty of racing in Italy.'

Monkey Blacker says, 'The end of the fighting found us on the Danish border, and on the way the Brigadier had ear-marked a large stable of flat-race horses which appeared to him badly to need an owner. Roscoe lost no time in arranging for their collection. They included the German Guineas winner, the St Leger winner, and many others only slightly less distinguished. Some had been looted by the Germans from Marcel Boussac's French stables and we now re-looted them.

'Resisting the temptation to keep the best for himself, Roscoe dished them out between the 23rd Hussars and 8th Rifle Brigade. He organised race-meetings on a local aerodrome, ignoring Monty's strict order that no racing in Germany was to take place.'

Roscoe says, 'I had these thoroughbred horses. Perry Harding, who was commanding the 23rd Hussars and who was probably the finest amateur (or "shamateur") of all time, his second-in-command, Monkey Blacker, and John Straker, who was with the 8th Rifle Brigade, and I rode out every morning. One day, a German lorry failed to slow down and drove on too fast past the string. Perry, riding a thoroughbred, calmly pulled out his revolver and shot the lorry through the radiator.

'So we started to have our little race-meetings on the aerodrome. The Corps Commander, General "Bubbles" Barker, telephoned and asked me about these meetings. I thought I'd better be a bit careful, but he knew we'd been having them and so I told him that we were staging some horse trials. He asked to come and ride. "Delighted," I said. So I hatched a little plot. I decided to put the Corps Commander on a good front-runner in one race. I told Perry, Monkey, John and a couple of others that under no circumstances must he discover that we were not trying to beat him. At the finish we all came at him, challenging hard, apparently riding for our lives, our whips going, and he won a length. He was absolutely delighted. He was a very good chap and he came to every meeting we had after that. Monty never knew.'

One of our pet abominations in Germany at this time were the Military Government officers who were really only civil servants in England, most of whom had never seen a shot fired in anger. They were the typical breed you find in every over-staffed town hall throughout Britain. Now they were given Army uniform and sent out to occupied Germany. Inevitably there was a lot of dissatisfaction among both Germans and the Army with these people.

For some time 'fraternisation' with the Germans was strictly forbidden. Roscoe received one typical complaint. He says, 'A German was ushered into me who said, "I want to make a complaint. A Military Government officer has put a German woman into my lovely home and I have been removed from it. The officer comes regularly most nights."

'This seemed to me a very fair complaint, so I told my chaps to get on with it. They decided to raid the house and found the Military Government officer's car in the drive. They surrounded the place and an attractive woman put her head out of the window, asking what they wanted.

'"We want an interview with the British officer who is in this house," they said.

'"I am sorry there is no British officer in this house."

'"We are sorry too, but there is. There's his car."

'"He always leaves his car there."

'"We must come in and search the house."

'They searched everywhere except one room in which apparently the lady's two little children were asleep who

240

would have been very frightened if they had seen the soldiers. They searched downstairs, then upstairs and finally they insisted on seeing that room. They searched it thoroughly but could only find the children and their nanny. Then they had an idea. They pulled the sheets and blankets off her to reveal the Military Government officer at the bottom of the bed below her feet. The fraternisation rules had been relaxed, but they were jolly well going to get him for something. The matter was reported to General "Bubbles" Barker, whose answer was so delightful. "What the hell has fraternisation got to do with it? He's been using Military Government petrol for adultery."'

Chapter Seventeen

A Job of Real National Importance

With the war in Europe over, Roscoe was trying hard to
get back to civilian life, but, until he did, he was going to
have his creature comforts. 'I had a marvellous Belgian
liaison officer,' he says. 'I told him I wanted shoes for my
horses, which he got, and I wanted the head chef from
the Adlon Hotel. He didn't exactly manage that, but he
found the head chef from the Bremen Line. He was a
bloody marvellous chef. About one night a month we
would have a band and Wrens and girls from the
Malcolm Club, Kiel, came over. It went like a dream. A
couple of years later in Germany a new Brigade was
taking over and the Brigadier was told that "it was a very
nice dancing place". He said pompously, "I don't think
that's the sort of place I want!"

An agreeable diversion at about this time was the
Allied Steeplechase in Paris. Roscoe says, 'The French
steeplechase authorities proposed holding a race at Auteuil for officers of the Allied Forces. Each country
should enter a team of three. I was asked to select and
manage our team. So I picked five from which the team
of three would be chosen. I selected Lieutenant-Colonel
Monkey Blacker, Captains Tom Hanbury, George
Archibald, Jack Bissill and Major Peter Herbert. On

reaching Paris Guy Pastré, the trainer, was most kind and let us ride work.

'The only cloud in the sky was the status of Archibald and Bissill, who were, after all, both top professional jockeys before joining the Inniskilling Dragoon Guards. I therefore wrote to the organisers of the race and asked them for the qualifications for the riders. Their reply was anyone who has held an officer's commission for over six months. So we were in the clear.

'Bissill and Archibald were off to England to get demobilised and I told them not to do so until after the race. I suggested they went to Paris before the race to ride work and get a ride if they could at the meeting to get to know the course. This they did and of course had to ride as professionals. This caused much excitement and disapproval in the French racing press when they heard that they might be riding in the British team. Apparently French professional jockeys did not become officers and fight for their country.

'Unfortunately, the race was not a success. Although the stake was good, £2,500, the owners were chary of letting unknown riders ride their horses. The Russians did not turn up and on the day two British, Archibald and Bissill, two French, one American and one Belgian (the winner on his own horse) took part. Archibald was third.

The frustrations caused by Field-Marshal Lord Montgomery to his victorious Army were extraordinary at times. Roscoe has always liked and driven good fast cars. He says 'There were some excellent cars in Germany. I found one superb Porsche coupé, but the owner had taken the wheels off to make sure that it wasn't commandeered. We got some wheels and put them on and it went like a bird. It was a joy to drive. Then Monty issued instructions that nobody was to drive around in German cars and that they all had to be

243

handed in. What really annoyed me was that about a fortnight later I saw a Military Government captain driving around in my sports car. So I lost that one. At the same time I had a lovely Mercedes-Benz which had been painted khaki. Of course, as Brigadier commanding the Division, I had to hand that one in too. So I told my excellent Belgian liaison officer, who had a very nice house near Antwerp, "If you think you can get that car back to Antwerp, you can have it. If you're caught, mind, I don't know anything about it." He said, "All right, not to worry."

'About six months after the war he sent me a case of champagne and wrote: "If you ever come out here, I have a very nice Mercedes-Benz painted sky blue which I would like you to use at any time you wish to come over." I never did – but it was a lovely story.

'I was having dinner one night shortly after this in Divisional Headquarters with Perry Harding and Len Livingstone-Learmonth, when a young Welsh Guards officer, who was one of the junior staff officers at Army Headquarters, was sent up by the Field-Marshal. I asked, "What do you want, my boy?" He said, "I was sent up by the Field-Marshal to see if you are all happy up here and if you have everything you want, sir." I said, "Right. I think I had better start. I am not at all happy." And I told him the story about my cars and handing them all in. "Do you want me to drive around in a bloody rattletrap? Perry, now it's your turn."

'Perry said, "I've got about 120 horses up here. The soldiers are bored. We would like to have some race-meetings to amuse ourselves, but we're not allowed to. The Field-Marshal says we're not allowed to have racing and we're very upset about that." I said to Len, "Now then, it's your turn." Len said, "Well you can tell the Field-Marshal from me that I fought all the way through the desert with him, the whole bloody way up from

Arromanches to here, and I have lost all confidence in him." This poor young chap, who later became a Member of Parliament and now lives near me, was an old man by the time he went away to Army Headquarters. I said to the others, "I wonder if he'll repeat any of that. If so we'll get a signal telling us all to report to Army Headquarters at once."

'Not long after that Dick McCreery came up from Italy and took over command of the Army of the Rhine. Then of course there was a lot of racing in Germany.'

Roscoe was now determined to get out of the Army at the earliest opportunity. He had had twenty-seven years' service and it was high time that he got back to racing in England, to the job which he had actually applied for in the middle of the desert.

'I was told that I would be very lucky indeed to jump the queue and get out of the Army. So I took a month's leave, came back to England and went to the War Office to see Brigadier Brown, who was assistant to the Military Secretary. I asked him: "What are you going to do for me?" He said, "We'll find you a job."

'I said, "Not that sort of a job. I am the senior Armoured Brigade Commander of the British Army." The Brigadier said, "I don't think you're that at all."

'I said, "Well, I am. Even if you don't know it, I commanded three different Armoured Brigades and never got the sack!"

'"Well," he said, "what do you want?"

'"I'll tell you exactly what I want. I want seventy-six days' allowances (which I knew I would not get!) and I want immediate release."

'He said, "Of course you can't have immediate release. You will only get that if you are going to a job of real national importance."

'I said, "I am going to a job of real national importance."

245

'"What's that?"

'"As Stewards' Secretary to the Jockey Club."

'"Racing? You call that a job of national importance?"

'"Winston Churchill allowed racing to go on, so it must be a job of national importance!"

'I knew I wasn't going to get very far there, so I went to the top man, General Menzies, and told him, "I want to get out. I've got to get out, as I want to get this job." It's always better if you go to the top. He was a very decent chap. He said, "All right. If you can get someone from the Jockey Club to write a really strong letter saying that it's essential that you get out of the Army and into this job, we might be able to square it."

'So I got on to "Gugs" Weatherby (later Sir Francis Weatherby) and told him the form. I told him, "Get that letter off and lay it on the line that racing might stop if I don't get this job."

'Gugs said, "I can't say things like that."

'Anyway, he did write a letter which must have been pretty strong because I got out in 1946. I met a senior staff officer friend who said, "You don't know how lucky you are to be out. I told Monty the other day that he ought to give you the senior Regular Armoured Brigade in Germany, but he thought that you'd been in armour much too long and had decided to give you an infantry Brigade."

'"Oh Christ," I said, "I thought you might say that! But anyway, I'm out!"'

He was out of the Army at last. At the age of forty-six, he was finally finished as a regular soldier. Later he was to become Colonel of the 10th Hussars, an honour which he greatly prized, despite his constant regret that there are virtually no genuine horsemen among the Cavalry officers of today.

There was some talk that Roscoe would be given the

Légion d'Honneur. 'I wanted that,' he says, 'but I didn't get it because I suppose I didn't have enough to do with the French. I shall always remember just after the start of the war Colin Davy, who had been in the First War, said "If there's one thing we want to get, Roscoe, it's the Légion d'Honneur. It's the best thing in the world. You wear a little red thing in your buttonhole and when you go to France you get through customs and they say, 'Bravo!' and kiss you on both cheeks and pass you through without looking at your bags."

'As soon as I saw that Pip Roberts had been awarded this honour I telephoned him. "Congratulations, General," I said. "I'd love one if another comes up again."

'Pip asked me, "Why are you so keen on it?" I told him what Colin had said. "It's very handy you know. You're an absolute hero if you have one." But the great honour never came Roscoe's way.

On his last leave the tragedy occurred which was to change Roscoe's entire life. It involved the little chesnut horse, Aquilo.

Michael Williams, who writes up the point-to-points so excellently for the *Sporting Life* told me this year: "Aquilo was quite outstanding as a point-to-pointer. When the late Ted Lyon asked me if I'd do a piece for the 1956 edition of *The Horseman's Year* which he was editing on the best point-to-pointers of the last decade, Roscoe Harvey's Aquilo was one of four horses I made my final selection from – the others were Prince Brownie, Teal (later the Grand National winner) and the late Frank Gee's Signet Ring (not to be confused with Major Rushton's horse of the same name.) In the end I plumped for Signet Ring as *the* best with Prince Brownie as runner-up, but it was a decade which also saw such horses as Halloween, Marques and the Gold Cup Winners, Four Ten and Limber Hill, running in point-to-points. I was, of course, picking strictly from

247

point-to-point performances and so I discarded the first three on the grounds that they had only had a single season in points and Limber Hill because he finished point-to-pointing before losing his greenness.

'Aquilo, who lost his maiden certificate in the Maiden Race at the South Staffs in 1946 (the same season as Jeremy's fall) ran in twenty point-to-points during a career which stretched from 1946 to 1951 and his twelve wins, all with Roscoe Harvey up, included a dead heat in the Open Nomination Race of the North Staffs with Sir Isumbras, the Dudley Cup winner of that year. He won the Osmaston Cup for the Open Nomination Race at the Meynell three years running between 1948 and 1950 and went through the 1948 season unbeaten. In his twenty-two appearances he was out of the first three only three times. As Roscoe Harvey says, he was not permitted as a Jockey Club official to ride his horse under National Hunt Rules, but there is no doubt in my mind that Aquilo would have been fully capable of winning hunter "chases".

Roscoe says, 'Aquilo is the only horse ever to have won that Meynell Open Race three years running. And we'd have won it the fourth time if I hadn't slipped up on the flat, breaking my stupid neck.'

That was in 1951, Roscoe says, 'When I broke my neck I was in plaster for three months. Plastered right up all round. I didn't realise that a beard was growing underneath it. Most uncomfortable thing ever. Whenever I see a fellow with a broken neck since then, I always tell him, "Whatever you do, get somebody to come in and shave you between your plaster and your chin." I had to get someone when it was quite raw. He was a local chap from Ashbourne and he used to come and shave me. God, it hurt!'

Sadly, Aquilo was involved in a much worse accident when Roscoe was on leave. He went up to Derbyshire to join Biddy and his children. Jeremy had been hunting Aquilo, and getting on particularly well with him. They were ideally suited. 'My son had good hands and I think he would have made a jockey all right,' says Roscoe. 'He was going to be a regular officer in the 10th Hussars, but he had only recently joined up for training at Catterick and was not yet commissioned. He came over on his motorbike to ride in his first point-to-point at the High Peak meeting. I was riding in the last on something else. It was the first time he'd ever ridden in a point-to-point and, as events were to prove, he would surely have won, but it was a filthy wet day and I blame myself. I forgot to tell him to put on string gloves. With his hands slipping on the reins, he couldn't control the horse properly and it came down with him, giving him a nasty fall. He must have been a bit concussed because he set off back to Catterick on his motorbike and was killed. I didn't know what had happened for some time because I too had a fall in the last and broke my collarbone.'

George Errington says, 'The only time in my life that I have seen Roscoe deflated in any way was at Jeremy's funeral.'

Roscoe soon settled down to his new responsibilities. A famous jockey, acting on the instructions of an even more famous trainer, had been at the rear of the field in a race, not trying very hard. Afterwards he was approached by a small, smartly turned out, bespectacled figure, who sauntered up and, looking the other way, and talking typically out of the corner of his mouth, said quietly, 'Be careful, Bill. If you must pull a horse, which I don't recommend, you must also keep your elbows moving to make it look as though you're trying.'

The knowledgeable commentator was none other than the new Stewards' Secretary to the Jockey Club. The reprimand was enough to show that Roscoe had not been taken in, and it put the fear of God into the jockey, who would think twice about doing the same again.

Lieutenant-Colonel Douglas Gray, who had just beaten Roscoe in the final of the Kadir Cup all those years ago in India, says, 'As a Stipendiary Steward, Roscoe was highly respected by the jockeys because they felt that he had been a skilled race-rider who had authority, but who also knew all the "tricks".'

His contribution to racing was so much more than that, however. Roscoe ran the discipline of the Turf in the same way he had run his Troop, his Squadron, his Regiment and his Brigade, with courage, understanding, leadership, scrupulous honesty, and a profound sense of fair play. He had total dedication to the sport he loved so well.

Major David Swannell, who has recently retired as Senior Jockey Club Handicapper and now organises his own brainchild, the National Racing Museum at Newmarket, served with the Brigadier for many years as a racing official. David says, 'I could never handicap any racing official within light years of him. Roscoe's retirement leaves a totally irreparable gap. The number of people whom he kept out of trouble is legion. That was his method. He alone had the authority to do it. He would speak once and no more was needed. Instead of punishing crime, Roscoe's method was to prevent crime, to prevent stupidity. He went out of his way at all times to keep people out of trouble. He was quite unique.'

Back home at Shirley Hill in Derbyshire, Roscoe's forty-year-old marriage to Biddy was virtually at an end. Even if there had been any chance before, after Jeremy's death the gap between them was unbridgeable. 'My wife of course was terribly upset about Jeremy,' says Roscoe.

Roscoe now threw himself with renewed vigour into his hunting, point-to-pointing, National Hunt racing and his job on the Flat. He still had his daughter Jenny, to whom he was devoted, and in 1947 he was rejoined by Willetts, who had nearly gone off to Australia with

Willoughby Norrie, but was now thrilled to be back with his Brigadier. 'I looked after Aquilo for him, amongst others,' says Willetts.

Roscoe chuckles, 'He was a big trainer!' Willetts adds, 'We had some good horses. The Brig rode one or two and then we had one or two young jockeys from the Regiment. The best we had afterwards, and by far the finest chap for a young horse, was Colonel Piers Bengough.' Roscoe agrees. 'Piers was very good,' he says. 'My horse won the Beaufort Open one year ridden by Piers. I remember his wife, Bridget, being frightened to death and I told her, "That horse is a good jumper. He won't fall, but I don't think he'll win." Anyway he absolutely trotted up at 25–1.'

The job of a Stewards' Secretary or Stipendiary Steward is basically to assist the local Stewards at race-meetings and help them to interpret the Rules of Racing. Of course, there is much more to it than that, but that is the general idea. Roscoe says, 'When I joined in 1946 there was Algy Howard, the Honourable Algernon Howard, Penn Curzon-Howe and myself. I was forty-six but I was the "young man". Gugs Weatherby wanted me to do National Hunt racing as well, but I told him that I wouldn't do that because I'd been riding not all that long ago with most of the jumping boys. So there were three of us. Now there are ten.

'I had an offer to go into Tattersalls. I think that if my son had been alive I would probably have taken the job. I remember talking to Ken Watt and he told me that I would have to put in a little money to come in as a partner. I asked him how much and he said £10,000 or something like that. They told me that I would get a very handsome dividend back. I told them I wanted to think about it. Then I said that I'd just taken on the Stewards' Secretary job so that I could go racing all the time and see my friends. I said, "I think I must turn it down."

251

'I know that perhaps I was a bloody fool, but then I have enjoyed myself as a Stipendiary Steward. I had enough money to buy myself some gin and that sort of thing. If I had gone into Tattersalls and stayed there, I'd have been as rich as an Arab by now!

'The other thing was that you had to pore through the Stud Book and go round looking at these various studs. I wouldn't have minded standing up, saying, "Is that your bid?" Old John Coventry got the job that was offered to me.'

The job as a Stipe had its lighter moments. 'One day at the Doncaster St Leger meeting, my daughter and I went into the Stewards Room for lunch with Hugh Sefton, who was one of the best Stewards I've ever known. The waiter greeted us, "Good morning, m'lord."

'"Good morning, Ewling. What have we got for lunch today?"

'"Chickens, lobsters, salmon, my lord."

'Sefton asked, "No grouse?"

'"Sorry, my lord, the grouse have all gone up to the Royal Box."

'"Royal Box! Who the hell's up there?"

'"The Duke of Norfolk, my lord."

'"Good God, the Duke of Norfolk? That's the sort of thing that breeds Communism!"

'Before the war, when Stewards' Secretaries were first introduced, the trainers were very suspicious of them. The first case I was involved in as a Stipe was when a horse trained by Cecil Ray was given a dope test. The Stewards' Secretary at that time had to be there to see the saliva taken. So down I went to the stables with Ray, who was furious and creating about it. I just said I was doing my job. They found the horse was hopped up and Ray was warned off for life.'

Roscoe's second season was 1947 when Gordon Richards rode the hot favourite Guineas winner, Tudor

Minstrel, in the Derby, and had to fight him all the way to get him round Tattenham Corner. Roscoe says, 'Gordon always used to sleep downstairs in his house, and his wife upstairs. Margery had the telephone so that if it rang, either she answered it or they left it unanswered. Anyway, in the evening after the Derby somebody telephoned and demanded again and again to speak to Gordon Richards. Margery said, "You can't, he's asleep." In the end Gordon picked up the telephone and said, "What do you want?"

'"Is that Gordon Richards?"

'"Yes, what the hell do you want to wake me up for?"

'"We thought you would like to know. We were walking round Tattenham Corner and found a horse's head and a bridle there. We thought you'd like to know that!"

'Gordon was hopping mad and rang up the police, who traced the call to a pub in Reading. They went there and asked who had made the call and were pointed towards a group in the pub. I don't know what action the police took, but they certainly frightened the life out of them!'

Roscoe thinks back to those days forty years ago. 'Do you remember the old Aga Khan, grandfather of the present Aga? Nobody would speak to him because he'd skipped off to Switzerland during the war and they hadn't thought much of that. He sold all those wonderful horses to America. Every single one – even Bahram.

'Then there was that extraordinary eccentric Dorothy Paget. I had nothing to do with her really, but I do know she used to eat masses of food and after the race she'd start having enormous feasts in the racecourse restaurant. She would summon her trainer, who wanted to get back with his horses. She had a right do with Fred Darling. When she summoned him, he told her, "I'm not coming. I'm looking after your horses."

253

'One day at Newmarket Percy Whitaker told me that he had just finished his dinner and she invited him to have dinner with her. He said, "All right" and they arranged for dinner at 10.30 pm. She lived not too far away. The butler was there and offered him a drink. Time went by, and she didn't appear for some time. The butler apologised for her being delayed. Percy asked him, "It must be very awkward for you being on all the time like this?" The butler said, "No, I only come on at 8 pm. and keep going until 8 am. Then the second butler comes on." She had two butlers and they worked like that. She lived by night.'

The pay of racing officials on whom so much money depends has for some time caused considerable controversy. Roscoe says, 'When I started as a Stipe, Gugs Weatherby said to me, "We're not going to pay you very much."

'Nowadays Stipes start at about £9,000 a year rising to about £18,000 with expenses, car etc. In 1946 I got £750 and £1,500 the next year. After serving faithfully for nearly twenty-five years I got a golden handshake of my salary – £3,200 in 1970. You had to have independent means, but I wanted to do it because I love horses and racing. I would never be a Handicapper myself. If I had the choice all over again I would either be a Judge, which is too bloody easy now with a camera, or a Starter. Perhaps Starter would be my first choice because you're nearer the horses for one thing. Stewards' Secretary would be third, and last of all a Handicapper. A Stewards' Secretary has to do a little bit of homework, but a Judge or a Starter has none once the day is over.

'In the early days the local Stewards and indeed some members of the Jockey Club, were very moderate.'

Like the time when the late Duke of Roxburghe developed a quite unfounded dislike and mistrust of a certain northern trainer. 'Bill Weatherby said to me one

254

day, "Do you know a fellow called A who trains up in the north?" I said, "Of course I do. I think he used to be with so-and-so. He's a very nice guy – not a big boy, but he's a bloody good horsemaster." Bill said, "Well, Bobo says he's a crook." "I don't know whether he's a crook" I said, "but he's a very nice chap." "Well," said Bill, "when you're up north next, see what's happening." So I arrived at Newcastle and Bobo Roxburghe said, "Ah, Roscoe, I want to talk to you. Do you know this fellow A? He's a bloody crook." I said, "I think he's a very nice chap." He said, "In that case you want to keep your ear a bit closer to the ground. He's no good." I said, "I don't agree with you." At that moment a certain trainer went by. I think it might have been B. As he walked past, Bobo said, "There he is. Bloody crook." I said, "That's not A." "Of course it is," he said, "you want to keep your ear a bit closer to the ground." I said, "I'm sorry, Bobo, that's not A." So anyway he summoned a fellow standing outside the weighing room. "Come here," he said, "who's that bugger?" "Mr B, your grace," he said. Bobo was absolutely deflated. "Oh," he said, "I've made a mistake." I said, "You certainly have." And that was that. Bobo was like that. But from that day on he was my best friend. We never had a cross word after that.'

Another Steward whom Roscoe quotes in this connection was the late Major Hugh Peel who, with his wife, had owned the dual Grand National winner of 1918 and 1919, Poethlyn. 'At Haydock one day,' says Roscoe, 'a young jockey burst his way through the field. I thought it was fairly obvious. He came in front of the Stewards and the Senior Steward, Hugh Peel, said "Well, my boy. I've got to tell you about your riding. You've got to ride to win. There's too much of this not trying. We've got to stamp it out." I whispered, "I think you've got the wrong enquiry, sir." I told the jockey to go out. The Senior

255

Steward said, "What's the matter." "Well," I said, "he tried to win, only he tried a bit too hard." So the jockey was brought back in again and the Senior Steward said, "You must certainly try to win, but you mustn't knock people about trying to do it." He got it the wrong way round and it was certainly very embarrassing.'

As Senior Stewards' Secretary for twenty years, Roscoe had to guide the Stewards. Many of the local Stewards had no idea at all. He says, 'Today the Stewards are 200% better than they were in the years after the war. Then they just thought it was a nice outing, an opportunity for a good lunch and a glass of port. Most of them knew nothing about racing. By far the best were Hugh Sefton, the Duke of Norfolk, Lord Derby and a little later Jakie Astor. They were first-class. Some of the others were very far from good.'

Roscoe was in charge all through the bad doping period of the 'fifties and 'sixties. With his own knowledge, strength and tact, he guided the Stewards, gradually improving racecourse discipline and control.

He says, 'At Sandown park one day a trainer was had in, and one of the Stewards said, "I can't sit on that enquiry." I couldn't think of any reason why he had any connection with the case and I asked him. He said "Because that chap has the best covert in the Belvoir country!"'

Like most racing people, Roscoe laughed when we spoke about Lester Piggott. 'I'm sorry he's retired. He was the last of the real characters. There are none today. Lester was riding at his best, or worst(!), all the time that I was an official. He did everything. One of the things which did not appear in any paper occurred just after he had been suspended for a month or so. It was at Worcester, and after he had passed the winning-post I saw him pick up his whip and hit another jockey four or five times over his back. I went back to the Stewards'

Room and said, "What are we going to do about Piggott?" They looked at me blankly and asked what I meant. They had seen nothing. I told them, and we discovered that the other fellow had weals all over his backside. So I told the Stewards that there were two things that we could do. Either we send him up to Portman Square – to the Jockey Club – or I would give him a bollocking myself. They quickly agreed that I should deal with him on the spot.

'So I said to him, "What the hell were you doing?" Piggott said, "Didn't you see him? He nearly put me over the rails on the top bend." I said, "I didn't see anything of the sort, but I don't care what he did to you. If you want to punch his nose in the weighing room afterwards, nobody knows anything about it. But you do not hit him in front of the whole racing crowd. You are very lucky. If you'd been sent off to Portman Square, you'd have been warned off for a year. As it is, you can take this from me, that you will never do it again."

'Then, believe it or not, his father Keith came to me and thanked me the next day for being so kind to his boy. He said, "When I drove him home I told him what I did to Jack Anthony when he tried to put me through the wings and how I hit him over the head with my whip." Talk about the way to bring up your boy! I told him he must be crazy.'

Roscoe adds with a smile, 'Mind you, Gordon wasn't always innocent. His will to win was so great. At Bath there is an elbow just below the distance and Gordon used to pull out as though he were riding a motor-bike, pull out and drive in. Woe betide anyone who was on his inside when he did this!'

As a matter of fact I myself know this to be only too true. When Gordon was riding for me I was delighted that he could use these tactics, but on one occasion, one of my apprentices, riding my own filly, tried to come up

257

on his inside and was chopped off. The filly came down and had to be destroyed. The boy broke his collar-bone badly.

Roscoe says, 'I got the Stewards at Bath to put a crow's nest on that bend and I've always said that Gordon never rode there again.'

Noel Murless told Roscoe the story of one day at Brighton where Lester was riding a horse belonging to the famous old owner-breeder, Jockey Club member Colonel Giles Loder. In the paddock beforehand, the Colonel said to his trainer: 'I must tell young Piggott how to ride this horse. I know this course well. I will make sure he does what I say.' So when Lester came in, the owner gave him explicit instructions on where he was to be in the race and how he was to ride the horse. Then he walked off back to the Stewards' Box to watch the race. Lester looked up at Noel and said, 'What did he say?' Noel said, 'He told you to ride your own race.' 'Oh,' said Lester, went off, rode his own race and won. Afterwards Loder came to Noel and said, 'You know, they think that Piggott is a bit of a moron. He's not really a ruddy fool. He did everything I told him!'

Among the many Piggott stories, Roscoe likes the one of the pouring wet day at the York Summer meeting when there was the usual miles-long traffic jam from the Great North Road to the course. Lester in his big Mercedes passed up the whole stream on the outside but was stopped near the gate to the racecourse by a big Yorkshire policeman, soaking wet in the rain. When Lester lowered the window slightly, the policeman shouted, 'Where do you think you're going?' Lester replied calmly, 'To the races, of course.' The policeman, water dripping off his nose and cape, trying to write in a sodden notebook, looked a bit closer and said, 'Ee. I know who you are. I know who you are indeed. You're a menace. You're a bloody idiot!' Lester lowered the window a little further. 'I suppose it depends what you mean by a bloody idiot,' he said. 'There you are soaked to the skin, cold and miserable. Here am I sitting in the nice warm car, comfortable and dry. Which of us is the bloody idiot?' The policeman waved him on. 'Oh, get on,' he shouted. 'Don't waste my time.'

Roscoe says, 'When it was my last day as Stewards' Secretary, they gave it out on the loudspeaker at Newmarket. I was walking up to the stands and Piggott said, "Sorry you're giving up. You and I have always got on so well together." Piggott just wanted to win, that's all. Winning and money were all he wanted. He said, "What are you going to do now?" I answered, "I think I might become one of your punters!" Piggott said, "Oh, so you'll be allowed to bet now, will you?" "Oh yes," I said, "you may be sure of that."'

He adds 'There was a wonderful story about the time when Vincent O'Brien gave Pat Eddery the ride in the 1984 Derby on El Gran Senor in place of Lester. Pat was beaten a short head by Roche on Secreto. As Lester came out of the weighing room, he passed Vincent and said to him, "Are you missing me?" Vincent didn't know what to say.'

When Lester was about to retire, Roscoe said to him: 'So you're about to start as a trainer. Do you think you'll be any good? You and I know plenty of people who've tried and haven't made much of a hand of it.' Lester answered, 'I don't know about that, but it should take some of the wrinkles out of my face.'

'I thought that was quite a good reply,' says Roscoe.

'Piggott,' he comments, 'was one of the great jockeys of my time. It was said he had so many troubles early in his career mainly caused by his desire to win.' I am sure this is true.

Roscoe says, 'I always think if you want to have a nice quiet job racing, you want to be a Starter. You used to

259

have to use your brains but now the horses all go into stalls. In the old days, Major Kenny Robertson was a great Starter. Perhaps you'd have forty-five runners – and no balloting out – and he would shout out, "Non-triers in the second rank!" There never seemed to be any trouble or accidents. They used to say that another great Starter, Allison, waited for Gordon. There may be some truth in that. Allison would shout out, "Are you all right, Gordon?" "Right," would come the cry from Gordon and up went the tapes!

'I didn't run many people up to Portman Square. I might have been wrong, but, unless it was something very dastardly, I didn't think it was necessary. I'd tell the others, "You want to watch so-and-so," or "Watch such-and-such. He had very bad luck." This would go all round the Stewards' Secretaries by pigeon post and I had them all thinking alike. It was so much easier for them to make decisions which agreed with the others.

'But suppose, for example, that you had a jockey who cheated at the start. Say the best draw was number one and a chap who had drawn fourteen started at around about number three. You could have run him up in front of the Stewards, but I used to go to him afterwards and say, "Where were you drawn and where did you start?" He would pretend he didn't know. And I would say, "Well, I know. I'm not blind. You started about number three." He would protest that his horse was messing around and that he had to get in somewhere. I answered, "In that case, if you find him messing around next time, you go out to about number eighteen. It'll be quite quiet out there. And don't ever bloody well do that again!" And they never damn well did! I think they got the message. Much better than running the fellow up to be told by the Stewards "Never do that again" or receive an official caution or be fined. My way, they knew that I knew and so did all the other Secretaries, and it didn't half have an effect.

260

'I used to say things on the side to trainers too. You know, like: "That horse of yours didn't have a very hard race today, did he?" They got the message too, soon enough. Do you know, I have never met any trainer who was had up in front of the Stewards and when asked "Did you back that horse?" said that he had. They all answer: "I never bet." Maybe they don't, although when I first started in racing, the prize money was so low that I don't know how they kept going without betting, unless they had a lot of money of their own. And I certainly know one or two who used to bet. I think quite a lot of them used to keep one for themselves. Martin Hartigan told me that he used to keep one every year.'

Roscoe never tires of talking about Gordon Richards. He says, 'Gordon was a tremendous help to me. He was respected by all the other jockeys and he kept order in the changing-room. When I asked him to get the jockeys out quickly for the race because they'd been hanging about in the weighing room, you may be sure that for the next race they all came out very smartly. Of course Gordon belonged to the old school of jockeys who were riding before the war and, although a bit long in the tooth, rode for some few years afterwards. I don't think I'm being too nostalgic for the old days when I say that you can't compare the jockeys of today with people like Donoghue, Carslake, Childs, Beary, Gordon and so on. They were not just great horsemen and jockeys. They were great characters and true gentlemen. Gordon told me that when Carslake came into the changing-room, all the other jockeys would stand to their feet. Like the commanding officer.

'I'm afraid that the jockeys of today are pretty moderate. Even the Smiths were not regarded as great by the standards of those days. But now they'd be at the top of the tree. I remember poor little Ephie Smith, who's now dead. He was very deaf and if for some reason the

Stewards wanted to see him about anything, he would say "Wait a minute please" and he would put his hearing-aid in and connect it up. There was a story about when he went to Ascot and the Queen had a horse which arrived at the course having bumped its eye coming out of the box. The Queen was discussing this with him and Ephie said, "Well, the 'orse is 'alf blind and I'm 'alf deaf, ma'am!"

'When I was stiping Phil Bull wrote an article entitled "Why are Stewards' Secretaries recruited from the Army?" About two years later Bull came to me at Newmarket and said, "I've got a French jockey to ride for me. Would it be all right if he brought an interpreter into the ring with him? I don't speak French." I said, "Of course it's all right, Mr Bull. The Military are always prepared to help."'

Chapter Eighteen

The Hero

Roscoe was on the British Boxing Board of Control for three years. 'They knew I was interested in boxing,' he says, 'and they asked me to come along. It was a shame that I had to give it up, but I just had to tell them that I couldn't go on racing while they were having their meetings. Onslow ('Pop') Fane was a good chap. He was in charge when I was on the Board. It was quite interesting. Some of the promoters were terrible people trying to get around everything, and then there were the boxers themselves who made complaints. The Board would control who would fight whom and make sure that a very bad fighter from America wouldn't fight against one of our good lads and vice versa. Some of the promoters were sharks. I had free tickets for some of the big fights. I don't believe there was much fixing of the bigger fights, but I have seen quite a few boxers lay down pretty quick so as not to get any more beating. I went more recently with Geoff Lewis to see Bruno fight. It cost us £50 each and the fight lasted two minutes!

'Gordon was very keen on boxing and he used to have Henry Cooper and his brother down when he had those stable lads' boxing competitions in Marlborough.

'The photo-finish came in during my time. I

remember on one of the first occasions the camera was ever used in this country, at Birmingham I think, one of those trainers who was always too clever for his own good and had constantly complained in the past that the result was wrong because the Stewards and the Judge had had too much port for lunch, now came to me questioning the result. He wondered whether the camera was sited properly! Of course, it did make the job much easier for the Judge. Gordon in the old days always kept riding several strides past the post in a close finish to give the subconscious impression on the Judge's mind that he had been ahead. It must have worked many times and, although I was not concerned, when we were out in Cairo before the war there was a Judge who always gave a dead-heat when there was any doubt at all, which stopped people coming up and screaming at him. We debated the Aga Khan's idea of two lines and anything between those two lines being a dead-heat, but we decided against it because you would still have the problem of what was inside those two lines. Mind, they do get some tricky ones on the photo and of course it does make a tremendous difference to the value of the horse in a race like the Derby. It can make a difference of millions. Look at the time when The Minstrel just beat Hot Grove.

'Apart from going down to see the dope tests done in the early days, I was not involved very much in the doping incidents. But the fellow I always felt very sorry for – only because I liked him very much – was Charles Chapman. He was supported by the Duke of Richmond in the case he brought against the Jockey Club which he won. All the latter part of the war he had the anti-aircraft battery in my Brigade Headquarters. He was as brave as a lion and would do anything. He'd go out with his Bofors gun and capture Germans – a splendid chap. I never knew of this case until he told me all about it – I

264

was in India when it all happened before the war. He said, "I know my horse was doped but I never knew it was being done by my head lad, who was a fellow I'd got over from France. These days I would never have been warned off because the security boys would trace the whole thing back, but I was then – warned off for life." Sure enough he never got his licence back, although I tried to get it very hard, but they said "No". I thought that was a bit unfair, but on the whole I think that justice was done.

'As Stewards' Secretary you have to know each course backwards. You must know what is happening and the various reputations of all the jockeys. You would report on what had happened in the race to the Stewards and report on the racing record of the jockeys. Sometimes the Stewards asked your opinion and what you thought they should award in the way of punishment, but your advice was not always taken. They asked you what you saw in the race itself. Now they don't do that so much because they have the patrol camera. We used to situate ourselves in crow's nests at the various stages of the course. We had a crow's nest at Tattenham Corner, but now it's all done by the camera patrol. We used to have a very vital one at Ascot just as you turned into the straight. That's where the trouble always used to occur, just where you crossed the road below the five-furlong marker.

'The Jockey Club sent me off to America to study the camera patrol and I was out there for two or three weeks. When I left I asked for, and was given, about six films of various incidents. On my return Jim Joel gave the Jockey Club Stewards and me a very nice lunch at the Savoy and I thought, "I'm not going to be caught out over this. I will show these films and then ask their opinions on what they think is the answer." Rosebery was there and Sefton too among others. I put on the first

265

film. "Couldn't see a bloody thing wrong," said Rosebery. I said, "The answer here is that the champion jockey in America, Eddie Arcaro, got suspended for ten days for bumping. "Never heard such balls," said Rosebery. And so it went on. There were the most diabolical incidents but all the Stewards said "Balls" all the time. I really enjoyed it.'

Roscoe has strong views about the controversial Rule 153. 'I think, whatever the jockey does, the horse that is first past the post should be allowed to keep the race. The only time he should be disqualified is when the horse himself has somehow savaged or in any other way hampered or impeded the runner-up, preventing it from winning.

'One of the main troubles with the patrol film was that the Press didn't understand it and couldn't read the films. That was probably because most of them had never even ridden a donkey. Still, who can blame them if the Stewards of the Jockey club that day at the Savoy couldn't understand the films?

'When the Jockey Club sent me to America to study the camera patrol and the way they kept order on the racetrack out there, I asked them to give me a couple of hundred pounds for expenses. They gave me £350. I arrived out there and was met by a splendid fellow called Marshall Cassidy, who was head of the New York Jockey Club.

'I stayed the first night with him and he said, "We have a very nice place for you where you'll be looked after by a man and his wife." It was rather a long way from the bright lights, so I said, "Wouldn't it be much better for me to stay in New York and I'd be nearer at hand for the 8 o'clock start in the morning?" He said, "Well, if you would like that, of course." So he first telephoned the Waldorf Astoria and said, "Have you got a room for a fortnight for Brigadier Harvey who's come over from the Jockey Club?" Unfortunately they hadn't. Marshall came back and said, "Where would you like to stay?" He said he knew a good little hotel just down the road. All bills, he said, were to be sent to the New York Jockey Club. So I said, "I've got some money, you know." "No," he said, "you're our guest." "I'm not your guest. I was sent out here to learn about your patrol camera." "You are our guest," he insisted. I wasn't allowed to pay for a thing all the time I was there. I telephoned England and they asked me: "How are you doing?" "I'm doing very well indeed. I haven't spent any of your money and I'm going to spend it all on riotous living for the next ten days. They're paying everything for me!" So that's what I did. I held a great cocktail party and only spent about £150.

'We don't do anything like that over here. I thought it was pretty nice, all that public relations. I learnt a lot too. People over here talk a lot of rot about professional Stewards. You cannot have them, in my opinion, unless you have centralised racing. Those professional Stewards in America – two of them had never ridden at all and the other had been a jockey – were always officiating with the same horses, owners, trainers and jockeys. They did it six weeks at a time at Aqueduct, six weeks at Belmont, six weeks at Saratoga, with the same professionals in charge.

'The whole circus lives on the track. The horses are checked over before racing every day and naturally the Stewards' decisions on every subject conform from day to day. In this country it just would not work. You'd have to have three Stewards at Newbury, three at Ayr, three at Newmarket, three at Pontefract and so on, on the same day. However much people may bleat about it, it wouldn't work. It's bad enough with the judges and the magistrates. Look at the rows there've been recently over the conflicting sentences for rape! Moreover, while

267

I'm on the subject, don't let's hear any more about this idea of making professional flat-race jockeys into Stewards' Secretaries. Remember, the reason why I had refused to work as Stipe under National Hunt Rules was because I had been riding with and against a number of the jump boys who were still going round. It would be totally wrong for any professional flat-race jockey to act as a Steward's Secretary and try to discipline his former brethren.

'They're still much stricter in the States when they watch the films. If a horse jumps out of the stalls and veers the smallest bit from a straight line, the jockey's in trouble, whereas in England it would be regarded as just bad luck.'

There were very few real Turf scandals which hit the front pages during Roscoe's time. He was not actually in on the biggest of them, the Francasal ringer case at Bath. He says, 'In the early days, in fact until he died, I still saw a lot of Colin Davy. He was an unlucky guy – a good jockey who never really got the chance. He didn't have much money, you know, and maybe he was a little weak. He married much later in life – very nice people and I used to stay with them. Babe Moseley, Colin and I would stay together for the Ascot Meeting. He had no children, legitimate ones anyway!

'His books were bloody good. They were more fun than the Dick Francis books. Do you remember that business of Francasal at Bath? Colin Davy had at the time half written a book called "The Twister's Double" or something, with more or less the same plot as the criminals had used at Bath. The only thing he did which was much more sensible was that when the ringer won, Colin had in his book a great friend of the villain who was the huntsman of some pack of foxhounds. So when it won, the horse was sent off to the kennels and fed to the hounds. In his book it was never discovered. These people at Bath sent it to a livery stable near Newbury and of course it was found. They all seem to fall down, these people. The Francasal case was the best organised one that has ever been. They bought a bookmakers' business in Cardiff and had all the wires cut so that none of the money could get out from the course. Then they put up this jockey, who had been a very moderate one even in his prime and was now over the top, and they said "Whatever you do, jump off and don't go up the inside. Just go straight down the middle of the course." He did just that and duly won. Stupid fellows, instead of sending the horse back to France where it had come from in an aeroplane or sending it to the kennels, they sent it off to the livery stables and got caught.'

To his friends and colleagues, as to his brother officers during his Army career, Roscoe's loyalty is legendary. David Swannell very nearly resigned from his job when he had not long been a Handicapper. He says: 'It was up at Newcastle one day and I was in the Stewards' box. The Duke of Roxburghe made some particularly insulting remark, referring to me. I lost my temper, banged the door behind me, so that the pane of glass shattered, and came down to the bottom of the stairs where I met Roscoe. I said, "I'm finished. I'll be out of a job and the kids will starve." Roscoe, imperturbable as ever, said, "Don't think any more about it. Bobo's like that. He can't help saying unpleasant things. Don't let it worry you." I took his advice, didn't lose my job and will never forget Roscoe for it.'

Roscoe despairs of the present standard of jockeyship. 'Take away Cauthen, Eddery, Swinburn and possibly that other American, Asmussen, and what have you got? Nothing. They're not just moderate. By the standards we are talking about, with a few exceptions they are downright bad.'

The increasing dearth of good horsemen is one of the

only sad features in Roscoe's life. For example, he has always, as the reader knows, wanted to win the Grand Military Gold Cup, but first as rider and then as owner, helped of course also by the fact that he did so much service abroad, victory eluded him until his good strong 'chaser Burnt Oak finally obliged three seasons ago. 'But,' says Roscoe, 'even though the two best Cavalry Regiments in the Army, the 10th and 11th Hussars, have amalgamated into the Royal Hussars, I had to put a Gunner officer on my horse in the two years after Sandy Cramsie had won it for me.

'I always try to go to the Regimental Dinner and when I was proposing the toast of Piers Bengough, who was taking over as Colonel of the Regiment, I said: "Now I'm going to be a little personal. I would like to thank so many of you for writing and congratulating me on my horse winning at Sandown in the Grand Military Gold Cup; but it was with a little sorrow, as there was nobody in the Royal Hussars who could ride it. And I don't believe any of you could ride a donkey on Margate sands!" Well, nobody threw any buns at me!'

The Gunner officer is now Major Malcolm Wallace, who became Director General of the British Equestrian Federation. He was asked by David Nicholson to ride Burnt Oak while he was still commanding the King's Troop, Royal Horse Artillery. He was delighted and was asked to have dinner with Roscoe, who told him that although he was pleased to offer him the ride, "it grieves me to have to ask a Gunner, albeit a Horse Gunner, and I am extremely sad that I cannot get an officer to ride him."

'I was absolutely tickled pink,' Malcolm Wallace says, 'and totally understood what he meant.'

He rode for Roscoe for three seasons, regrettably without a win. Twice Burnt Oak finished second to the Queen Mother's Special Cargo. After every race,

Roscoe wrote to his jockey to thank him, but he did comment once that Wallace had somehow managed to win on the only other horse he had ridden out of Nicholson's yard, which happened to belong to a different owner. 'The Brig reckoned that this was a bit below the belt,' says Wallace.

'On one occasion,' he continues, 'when the front-running and hard-pulling Burnt Oak had hacked off with me for the first mile and a half, I was summoned by the valet, while I was wearing only a towel, to have an "audience" with the Brig. "Let him run a bit free, didn't you?" he suggested. "Yes, Brig, but I couldn't stop him," I replied. "I see," was his response. "Well, if it's any consolation, I couldn't have done better myself. There is a glass of champagne for you in the Cavalry Bar."'

When Roscoe broke his neck riding Aquilo, he had to give up point-to-pointing, but although he was not riding them himself, he continued to run his horses with considerable success in point-to-points, and Royal Magnet, First Away, Fairtheewell and Monarch's Thought were all good winners. The latter won the Meynell Open Race in 1962, ten years after Roscoe had returned to the county where he had spent the first years of his life, Gloucestershire, although this time it was in the Heythrop country near Stow-on-the-Wold that he settled with his daughter Jenny. 'My wife had left me,' he says. 'I didn't marry again for a long time. I didn't hop from one hot bed to another.

'I telephoned John Smith-Maxwell to see if there were any suitable houses. He said, "There's one coming up for sale which is right in the middle of the country and could make a decent house for someone. It wants a bit doing to it, but you should get it for about £5,000." It required another £5,000 to make it proper so it stood me about £10,000 or a bit more. I bought the cottage for

271

about £600 on a plot of land and I built onto the cottage, so it's now worth quite a lot. Then I managed to get fifty acres from my neighbour at about £500 an acre. I had no idea what it was worth. Very shortly it was going for £2000 to £2500 an acre. So now I've got a very nice house, a cottage and about fifty acres. When I want to change the field and put my horse in another field, my farmer friend changes over and puts his cows in a different field. It's very satisfactory.'

So Roscoe, Jenny, Mr and Mrs Willetts, the horses and dogs moved down to Oddington Top, about two miles out of Stow-on-the-Wold and equally handy for Moreton-in-Marsh, into a charming Regency house, one of the few in the Cotswolds with an old red brick facade, but with Cotswold stone all round the back and a charming courtyard with garage and loose boxes.

Roscoe was immediately among friends all round and was quickly enrolled as Clerk of the Course to the famous Heythrop Point-to-Point which was held on that magnificent course at Fox Farm and Swell Wold. Roscoe was now far more centrally situated for his job as Senior Stewards' Secretary and both he and Jenny enjoyed their hunting with the Gloucestershire packs.

Within six years, fair haired, attractive, vivacious Jenny, with all her father's twinkle, was married to Peter Matthey and Roscoe is now not only a grandfather but also a great-grandfather. Although he had given up point-to-pointing he went on hunting with all his old zest on good horses until he was seventy. He hunted with other packs, too, when he had the chance. Of course he had to go back to the Berkeley, but, sadly, the country is not what it was. He says: 'The only fellow who didn't get on well down there as Master hunting the hounds was Chatty Hilton-Green. God, they hated him. He was made for Leicestershire, of course. I remember I went up to the Cottesmore and met Chatty who said, "You must come down to the Berkeley Hunt Ball." At that time it was held in Berkeley Castle. I went into the Berkeley Arms and didn't see any of my old pals there. Maybe they were in the White Hart, which is the pub opposite. As a boy of seventeen that was where I used to go! I went over and there were two or three of them. I said, "Nice to see you. How are you?" and so on. "How's the huntsman going?" "Not very well," they said, "he's never with us when hounds are running properly." He wasn't at all popular. And they weren't particularly keen on his extra-marital affairs. Chatty had the hounds for a couple of years, but there was a very good chap who had them for seven or eight years about ten years ago, Brian Bell. He hunted here and there and mostly Warwickshire, but he's not hunting hounds now. Mind, I wasn't quite as brave as I was. I could still remember the country and we had quite a good hunt. When hounds started running I fairly shot along and when they came to crossing a lane, there I was. Brian Bell shouted, "God, Roscoe, how the bloody hell did you get here?" I said, "I bloody well know how to ride over this country." I don't think I jumped a fence, but as a kid I had got to know it very well indeed.'

Roscoe hunted with the Beaufort as well, but as we saw earlier, although they were almost exactly the same age, he never really got on with the Duke.

'One day, I jumped into a field and saw that the whole field, with the exception of the hunt servants and the Duchess of Beaufort, had gone round. As soon as I realised that it was a wheat field, I turned around immediately and galloped up the side where there was a huge congregation trying to get through the hunting gate at the top corner of the field. Trying to get the gate open was a bit difficult, so I just skittled along up the top and Master absolutely tore strips off me. At the end of the day when I went to say "Thank you, Master" he

273

wouldn't speak to me. Babe Moseley and I stopped on the way back to wait for the horse-box and we went into a house to have a drink and he was there. He turned his back and refused to speak to me. He couldn't have been ruder. I saw him a month later somewhere up in our own Heythrop country and he couldn't have been nicer. "How are you Roscoe, dear boy? Lovely to see you" and so on. I thought "My God!"'

Roscoe decided to give up hunting very suddenly. He explains why, and typically he never spares himself: 'Hounds started running and I found a little boy of twelve with me. I said, "Come along, my lucky lad, away we go." He galloped on and we went over a number of walls. I said, "Keep him going!" Then we came to what looked to me a decent sized post and rails. Actually I don't think it was more than about three feet high. My little friend went chug-chug and over he went. I didn't like the look of the fence and pulled up. I went out on the road, came back home and said to Willetts, "Do you know, Willetts, I'm not going to hunt any more."

'Willetts said, "Why not, didn't the horse go well?"

'"It went smashing. It's not the horse, it's me." I patted my chest. "It's in here. I've just been put to shame by a twelve-year-old boy on his pony. It's high time I gave up. I'm never going to hunt again." I had been frightened to death that day. The red light was shining bright.'

Roscoe does not think much of today's hunting. 'Certainly round here there are far too many people out, the plough is killing it, and they never seem to do a lot,' he says, 'and yet my grandchildren always seem to enjoy it. They come back and say, "I had a wonderful time today, granddad. I jumped eight fences." That was their wonderful day!'

Roscoe had been divorced for some time when he met his second wife, Betty, a delightful American who was

274

staying at Newmarket with Pat O'Callaghan, who had been in the 10th Hussars and, at one time after the war was on the security side of racing. Betty was related to Mrs O'Callaghan, who was also American. Roscoe says, 'She had been married twice before and had one son from her first husband and two from the second, whom I see quite a lot over here. One of them, Johnnie Horn, has a horse with David Nicholson. He told me he wanted to see his mother's colours running again. So he bought the horse for that reason.'

Betty had been born a Stoddard, that great Long Island hunting and polo family. Her father and brother were both magnificent international horsemen, inseparable from Pete and Brother Bostwick. They had horses in training in England with Aubrey Hastings and later with Ivor Anthony. Pete Bostwick, of course, was not only one of the finest amateur riders in the world, but also a superb international polo player. Bruce Hobbs tells how, when he had won the Grand National as a seventeen-year-old on Mrs du Pont Scott's Battleship, and he and his father, Reg, who had trained the horse, were feted in America, he was invited to ride for Louis Stoddard, one of their friends from Leicestershire, in a race which was called the Cedarhurst Grand National on Long Island. Says Bruce, 'My horse didn't just win, but won by half the track and so obviously he'd been readied up for the race and for me to ride. That was quite a thrill.'

So Roscoe brought Betty down to the lovely rolling Cotswold countryside to live at Oddington. 'She was a great girl, my second wife – an absolute topper,' he says.

'She had a horse with Geoffrey Brooke, Derrick Candy, to begin with and later with David Nicholson. Geoffrey's usual jockey, Doug Smith, had three rides at Newmarket and could not get down to ride Betty's horse, Royal Flirt, at Newbury. He rang up to say that he'd got Ron Hutchinson. I said, "You will be there, Geoffrey, won't you." He said, "I'm afraid I've got to be at Newmarket, I'm not coming to Newbury." "Well," I said "who the hell's going to give the jockey his instructions?" "You, of course," said Geoffrey. "Christ," I protested, "I'm a bloody Stipe." "Doesn't matter about that" Geoffrey said.

'So we arrived and I told Hutchinson: "I ought to tell you how to ride this" – I had my own ideas – "give the horse plenty of room and come on the outside." Anyway, he followed my instructions and he pissed up at 50–1! I was in the Stewards' Room afterwards when old Geoffrey Freer, the Senior Handicapper, came in and said in his rather loud voice, "one of the old sort, Roscoe." However all was well. There had been no coup. Obviously nobody had had a bet on the horse, except a friend of Betty's from America who had fifty quid on it.

'Hutchy wrote a very nice letter to my wife, saying how much he'd enjoyed his ride. I always liked him and I see him about now quite a bit. He's a very nice Australian.

'Then there was a fair sort of horse called No Defence, which didn't win on the Flat, so we brought him down here and gave him to David Nicholson. Roscoe was Clerk of the Course to the Heythrop point-to-point for twenty-five years. That splendid fellow Bing Lowe who farmed Fox Farm where the Heythrop point-to-point was held for forty years (God, didn't we have trouble with those bullocks of his!) had a lovely loose school. David Nicholson is not paticularly keen on them, but, like Reg Hobbs and Fred Rimell, to quote but two, I think they're magnificent for young horses. So we put this horse, whose stable name was Noddy, in the loose school and got him going properly. He was our only horse in training at that moment and his first race was at

276

Towcester. David was still riding as well as training at that time. No Defence had shown us enough while schooling over hurdles for us to think that he could win first time. As far as I can remember, the first race was at about 11 am. The fog was very thick indeed and my Missus did not want to go racing at that time of day and, in any case, she said that she wouldn't be able to see in the fog. So I told her, "You can give me the horse, then." She said, "I will give you the horse if I don't have to go." So off David and I went to Towcester and David duly won the race.

'I told the Press, "My wife is going to give me the horse," just to pull her leg. Of course it couldn't run in my name, but it won about twelve steeplechases. It was a super jumper. God, it could jump. Looked like a hurdler but jumped like a stag.

'I had been on my own for about eight or nine years when I married Betty. We had fifteen very happy years together, but latterly she was very ill for about six months. She couldn't get about much, only in the house, and couldn't go racing. She only saw No Defence run once. Betty died in 1980.'

Roscoe has had great fun with his excellent steeplechaser Burnt Oak, who this year won the Horse and Hound Grand Military Gold Cup at Sandown Park. This was the horse's second victory in the famous old race for serving servicemen and women, and this year the race attracted unusual attention, for among the fifteen runners were the Queen Mother's Special Cargo, winner of the last three runnings, and Princess Anne's Cnoc Na Cuille, which she herself rode very stylishly.

The Queen was present to watch her daughter ride and, if she had mixed loyalties, how about David Nicholson who saddled both Roscoe's horse, which was ridden by his son Philip, and the Princess's horse? There was also a French rider in the race, Guardsman J-P

Scomparin on Priansko, to add to the colour, and there was an owner even older than Roscoe – for the favourite, Maori Venture, ran in the celebrated colours of Mr H J Joel.

Philip Nicholson, a Lance Bombardier in the King's Troop, Royal Horse Artillery, was winning for the first time in only his eighth race. He may have been inspired by the fact that Burnt Oak's owner had ridden two winners at the Grand Military meeting getting on for forty years before he was born! The twenty-three-year-old six-footer led from start to finish, bringing his mount home at 4–1 by what looked an easy 10 lengths from Maori Venture, with Knock Hill third and Special Cargo fourth; Cnoc Na Cuille finished eighth. It was a good win because Burnt Oak, who carried joint top weight, had finished behind Special Cargo in two previous runnings of the race. Unfortunately the gallant horse died not long afterwards.

The Queen Mother, who is the same age as Roscoe, was no doubt delighted that her granddaughter had ridden a fine race and completed the course on a horse not expected to win, having started at 20–1, and I daresay that if she could not have won the race herself for a record fourth consecutive time, there was no one she was happier to hand the cup to after the race than to Roscoe – for a second time of course.

Everybody, almost without exception, when they hear that I am writing the Brigadier's book, has said, 'What about the day he went down the motorway the wrong way?' Well, it all happened with Babe Moseley, whose name has occurred several times in this book.

'As for that motorway business,' Roscoe says, 'Babe and I were going out of London in the afternoon, and at about four o'clock we went to turn off the M4. Babe said, "We turn off here." I said, "Don't be daft, it's the next turning." Babe said, "I know it's bloody here. I

278

know you're bloody wrong." When we turned off and got to the top at the junction, I knew for certain he was wrong and he knew it too. "All right," he said, "I'm wrong, let's get back on the motorway." Now it was not one of those roundabouts that you just go round and you are back on the motorway. We had to go quite a long way round, about half a mile. We turned straight down one of those roads which we thought should have taken us back onto the motorway. As it turned out, it was lucky we met no vehicles coming up. It was just a fluke. Because we'd gone down on the wrong side of the motorway, still going the way we wanted to, but on the wrong side. We were in the fast lane. Babe said, "Oh, we're sitting in the fast lane. God, what a ruddy thing. What are we going to do?"

'I knew it was the next one we should have gone on to, about five miles on, so I said to Babe, "There's only one thing to do. I shall turn our headlights on and go like hell. So they won't know whether we're cops or robbers." So that's exactly what we did. There weren't many people in the fast lane – not like the middle, and we didn't meet anybody for a couple of miles. The first one swerved away, so that was all right. The next one held his ground. Babe said, "Look at the bloody fool." I thought "Oh, my God!" Luckily we didn't hit anything. When we got there we skidded across. We were lucky there was a gap in the crash barrier and went straight across the middle lane and the slow lane.

'Of course there were a couple of earnest citizens who reported us. A fortnight later I got a notice from the police and I was had up. I had to go to Maidenhead to be tried and my young barrister asked me, "Do you think it's a good thing to have Colonel Moseley with us?" I asked him why not and he said, "Well, I hear the Colonel has been dining out on this story, and when asked what he thought of the business, he's been saying it was his biggest thrill since he rode in the National." Anyhow, I said we'd got to have him in any case.

'When we were in court, the Prosecutor asked Babe Moseley: "Were you very frightened at this incident? I expected him to say, "It was the biggest thrill I've had since I rode in the National", but thank God he didn't. It took a long, long time for the magistrates to decide the case as I commented to my barrister. "That's a very lucky thing," he said. "They've got something to talk about."

'I think the only reason we got away with it – and we were dead right to get away with it – is that we had a lot of pictures taken of the roads at the junction. It was very badly signposted. Anyway, they came back and we stood up as though we were on parade and the Senior Magistrate said, "We find you Not Guilty"!

'I suppose we were bloody lucky we weren't killed!'

We are all very lucky that Roscoe has not been killed many times in his wonderful life. It is always said that the subject of a biography should be a hero to his biographer. In this case there has never been any difficulty. Roscoe has always been a hero, not only to me, but to everybody who has ever known him.

As a true Christian soldier, he has marched steadfastly onward through perils and vicissitudes, never shirking his duty, always maintaining the highest standards set for him by God and his faith.

They don't make them like that any more.